Lean Six Sigma

FOR

DUMMIES

A Wiley Brand

3rd Edition

by John Morgan
and Martin Brenig-Jones

Lean Six Sigma For Dummies®, 3rd Edition

Published by: **John Wiley & Sons, Ltd.,** The Atrium, Southern Gate, Chichester, www.wiley.com

This edition first published 2016

© 2016 John Wiley & Sons, Ltd, Chichester, West Sussex.

Registered office
John Wiley & Sons Ltd, The Atrium, Southern Gate, Chichester, West Sussex, PO19 8SQ, United Kingdom

For details of our global editorial offices, for customer services and for information about how to apply for permission to reuse the copyright material in this book please see our website at www.wiley.com.

The right of the author to be identified as the author of this work has been asserted in accordance with the Copyright, Designs and Patents Act 1988

Wiley publishes in a variety of print and electronic formats and by print-on-demand. Some material included with standard print versions of this book may not be included in e-books or in print-on-demand. If this book refers to media such as a CD or DVD that is not included in the version you purchased, you may download this material at http://booksupport.wiley.com. For more information about Wiley products, visit www.wiley.com.

Designations used by companies to distinguish their products are often claimed as trademarks. All brand names and product names used in this book are trade names, service marks, trademarks or registered trademarks of their respective owners. The publisher is not associated with any product or vendor mentioned in this book.

For general information on our other products and services, please contact our Customer Care Department within the U.S. at 877-762-2974, outside the U.S. at (001) 317-572-3993, or fax 317-572-4002. For technical support, please visit www.wiley.com/techsupport.

For technical support, please visit www.wiley.com/techsupport.

A catalogue record for this book is available from the British Library.

ISBN 978-1-119-06735-1 (hardback/paperback) ISBN 978-1-119-07380-2 (ebk)
ISBN 978-1-119-07381-9 (ebk)

Printed in Great Britain by TJ International, Padstow, Cornwall

10 9 8 7 6 5 4 3 2 1

Contents at a Glance

Introduction 1

Part I: Getting Started with Lean Six Sigma 5
Chapter 1: Defining Lean Six Sigma 7
Chapter 2: Understanding the Principles of Lean Six Sigma 23

Part II: Working with Lean Six Sigma 41
Chapter 3: Identifying Your Customers 43
Chapter 4: Understanding Your Customers' Needs 53
Chapter 5: Determining the Chain of Events 73

Part III: Assessing Performance 95
Chapter 6: Gathering Information 97
Chapter 7: Presenting Your Data 117
Chapter 8: Analysing What's Affecting Performance 139

Part IV: Improving the Processes 155
Chapter 9: Identifying Value-Adding Steps and Waste 157
Chapter 10: Discovering the Opportunity for Prevention 171
Chapter 11: Detecting and Tackling Bottlenecks 189
Chapter 12: Introducing Design for Six Sigma 199

Part V: Deploying Lean Six Sigma 221
Chapter 13: Leading the Deployment 223
Chapter 14: Selecting the Right Projects 233
Chapter 15: Running Rapid Improvement Events 245
Chapter 16: Putting It All Together 255
Chapter 17: Ensuring Everyday Operational Excellence 281
Chapter 18: Comprehending the People Issues 291

Part VI: The Part of Tens 305
Chapter 19: Ten Best Practices 307
Chapter 20: Ten Pitfalls to Avoid 017
Chapter 21: Ten (Plus One) Places to Go for Help 325

Index 333

Table of Contents

Introduction 1

   About This Book 2
   Foolish Assumptions 2
   Icons Used In This Book 3
   Beyond This Book 3
   Where to Go From Here 4

Part I: Getting Started with Lean Six Sigma 5

   Chapter 1: Defining Lean Six Sigma 7
      Introducing Lean Thinking 7
         Bringing on the basics of Lean 8
         Perusing the principles of Lean thinking 14
      Sussing Six Sigma 14
         Considering the core of Six Sigma 14
         Calculating process sigma values 17
         Clarifying the major points of Six Sigma 20

   Chapter 2: Understanding the Principles of Lean Six Sigma 23
      Considering the Key Principles of Lean Six Sigma 23
      Improving Existing Processes: Introducing DMAIC 25
         Defining your project 26
         Measuring how the work is done 32
         Analysing your process 32
         Improving your process 33
         Coming up with a control plan 33
      Reviewing Your DMAIC Phases 34
      Taking a Pragmatic Approach 37

Part II: Working with Lean Six Sigma 41

   Chapter 3: Identifying Your Customers 43
      Understanding the Process Basics 43
         Pinpointing the elements of a process 44
         Identifying internal and external customers 45

Getting a High-Level Picture...47
    Drawing a high-level process map.....................................48
    Segmenting customers...52

Chapter 4: Understanding Your Customers' Needs 53

Considering If You Can Kano 53
Obtaining the Voice of the Customer..55
    Taking an outside-in view...55
    Segmenting your customers...56
    Prioritising your customers..57
Researching the Requirements...58
    Interviewing your customers 60
    Focusing on focus groups 61
    Considering customer surveys 62
    Using observations 63
Avoiding Bias 64
Considering Critical To Quality Customer Requirements.................65
Establishing the Real CTQs 69
    Prioritising the requirements...70
    Measuring performance using customer-focused measures 71

Chapter 5: Determining the Chain of Events 73

Finding Out How the Work Gets Done 73
    Practising process stapling 74
    Drawing spaghetti diagrams 76
Painting a Picture of the Process...78
    Keeping things simple 79
    Developing a deployment flowchart...................................80
    Constructing a value stream map 84
    Identifying moments of truth 93

Part III: Assessing Performance...................... 95

Chapter 6: Gathering Information 97

Managing by Fact..97
    Realising the importance of good data 98
    Reviewing what you currently measure 98
    Deciding what to measure 99
Developing a Data Collection Plan 100
    Beginning with output measures 100
    Creating clear definitions...102
    Agreeing rules to ensure valid and consistent data......102
    Collecting the data..105
    Identifying ways to improve your approach 107

Introducing Sampling 108
    Process sampling 109
    Population sampling 110

Chapter 7: Presenting Your Data 117

Delving into Different Types of Variation 117
    Understanding natural variation 118
    Spotlighting special cause variation 119
    Distinguishing between variation types 119
    Avoiding tampering 119
    Displaying data differently 120
Recognising the Importance of Control Charts 121
    Creating a control chart 122
    Unearthing unusual features 123
    Choosing the right control chart 126
    Examining the state of your processes 127
    Considering the capability of your processes 129
    Additional ways to present and analyse your data 133
Testing Your Theories 136

Chapter 8: Analysing What's Affecting Performance 139

Unearthing the Usual Suspects 139
    Generating your list of suspects 140
    Investigating the suspects and getting the facts 142
Getting a Balance of Measures 143
    Connecting things up 144
    Proving your point 145
    Seeing the point 147
    Assessing your effectiveness 150

Part IV: Improving the Processes 155

Chapter 9: Identifying Value-Adding Steps and Waste 157

Interpreting Value-Added 157
    Providing a common definition 158
    Carrying out a value-added analysis 159
    Assessing opportunity 161
Looking at the Seven Wastes 161
    Owning up to overproduction 162
    Playing the waiting game 163
    Troubling over transportation 163
    Picking on processing 164
    Investigating inventory 164

Moving on motion...165
Coping with correction 166
Looking Beyond the Seven Wastes..166
Wasting people's potential 167
Going green...167
Considering customer perspectives.....................................168
Focusing on the Vital Few..169

Chapter 10: Discovering the Opportunity for Prevention **171**

Keeping Things Neat and Tidy..172
Introducing the Five Ss...172
Carrying out a red-tag exercise...173
Using visual management 174
Looking at Prevention Tools and Techniques 178
Introducing Jidoka...178
Reducing risk with Failure Mode Effects Analysis..................179
Error proofing your processes...181
Profiting from Preventive Maintenance......................................183
Avoiding Peaks and Troughs 184
Introducing Heijunka..184
Spreading the load..185
Carrying out work in a standard way..................................186

Chapter 11: Detecting and Tackling Bottlenecks. **189**

Applying the Theory of Constraints..189
Identifying the weakest link..189
Improving the process flow 190
Building a buffer 192
Managing the Production Cycle..193
Using pull rather than push production 193
Moving to single piece flow 194
Recognising the problem with batches 195
Looking at Your Layout 195
Identifying wasted movement 195
Using cell manufacturing techniques..................................196
Identifying product families 197

Chapter 12: Introducing Design for Six Sigma **199**

Introducing DfSS 199
Introducing DMADV 200
Defining What Needs Designing...201
Getting the measure of the design.......................................202
Analysing the design 202
Developing the design..204
Verifying that the design works...204
Choosing between DMAIC and DMADV 205

Considering Quality Function Deployment..............................206
    Clarifying what these houses and rooms are all about...............207
    Undertaking a QFD drill-down...............................217
Making Decisions..218

Part V: Deploying Lean Six Sigma.................................. 221

Chapter 13: Leading the Deployment 223

Looking at the Key Factors for Successful Deployment.........................223
Understanding Executive Sponsorship..................................224
Considering Size...226
Introducing the Deployment Programme Manager.......................227
Starting Your Lean Six Sigma Programme..............................229
Understanding What Project Champions Do..........................231

Chapter 14: Selecting the Right Projects......................233

Driving Strategy Deployment with Lean Six Sigma.......................233
Generating a List of Candidate Improvement Projects.....................234
Working Out Whether Lean Six Sigma Is the Right Approach...............237
    Prioritising projects..239
    Using a criteria selection matrix...............................240
    Deciding on which approach fits which project:
        Doing the work right......................................242
Setting Up a DMAIC Project..243

Chapter 15: Running Rapid Improvement Events 245

Seeing Rapid Improvement with Kaizen or Kai Sigma Events...............245
Understanding the Facilitator's Role.................................248
    Planning and preparation.....................................248
    Running the event..250
    Following up and action planning..............................252
Creating a Checklist for Running Successful Events.......................252

Chapter 16: Putting It All Together 255

Working Your Way through DMAIC...................................256
Defining Where You're Going..256
    Looking at the outputs from the Define phase......................257
    Being prepared: Typical questions the team needs to
        address in Define..258
    Considering typical questions the champion needs
        to ask in Define...260
Getting the Measure of Things.......................................260
    Checking the outputs from the Measure phase......................261
    Noting some typical questions the team needs to
        address in Measure.......................................262
    Recognising typical questions the champion needs to
        ask in Measure...263

Analysing the Data to Find the Root Cause..............................264
    Checking the outputs from the Analyse phase.............264
    Examining typical questions the team needs to
        address in Analyse...265
    Examining typical questions the champion needs to
        ask in Analyse..266
Quantifying the Opportunity...267
Applying Solutions in the Improve Phase............................267
    Checking the outputs from the Improve phase............269
    Eyeing typical questions the team needs to address
        in Improve..270
    Noting typical questions the champion needs to
        ask in Improve...272
Confirming the Customer and Business Benefits.....................273
Implementing, Standardising and Controlling the Solution..............275
    Checking the outputs from the Control phase............275
    Listing typical questions the team needs to address
        in Control..276
    Noting typical questions the champion needs to
        ask in Control..278
Conducting the Final Benefit Review................................279

Chapter 17: Ensuring Everyday Operational Excellence.........281
Making Everyday Operational Excellence a Reality....................281
Clarifying the Role of the Manager.................................283
    Working on the process...283
    Engaging the team..285
Getting Better Every Day in Every Way..............................287
    Using the right methodology....................................289
    Creating a culture of continuous improvement.............290

Chapter 18: Comprehending the People Issues.................291
Working Right, Right from the Start.................................291
    Gaining acceptance...292
    Managing change..292
    Overcoming resistance...294
Creating a Vision..295
Understanding Organisational Culture...............................297
Busting Assumptions..298
Seeing How People Cope with Change.................................299
    Comparing energy and attitude.................................300
    Using a forcefield diagram.....................................301
    Analysing your stakeholders....................................301
    Focusing on key elements of change............................303

Part VI: The Part of Tens .... _305_

Chapter 19: Ten Best Practices 307
   Lead and Manage the Programme...307
   Appreciate that Less is More 308
   Build in Prevention..309
   Challenge Your Processes..310
   Go to the Gemba 311
   Manage Your Processes with Lean Six Sigma.......................311
   Pick the Right Tools for the Job 312
   Tell the Whole Story..313
   Understand the Role of the Champion 314
      Looking at the Lean Six Sigma programme executive sponsor.....314
      Perusing the role of the project champion...................314
   Use Strategy to Drive Lean Six Sigma.................................315

Chapter 20: Ten Pitfalls to Avoid 317
   Jumping to Solutions...317
   Coming Down with Analysis Paralysis.................................318
   Falling into Common Project Traps 319
   Stifling the Programme before You've Started 320
   Ignoring the Soft Stuff...321
   Getting Complacent...321
   Thinking that You're Already Doing It 322
   Believing the Myths...322
   Doing the Wrong Things Right 323
   Overtraining 324

Chapter 21: Ten (Plus One) Places to Go for Help 325
   Your Colleagues..325
   Your Champion..326
   Other Organisations..326
   The Internet...326
   Social Media 327
   Networks and Associations...328
   Conferences...328
   Books...328
   Periodicals...330
   Software 330
      Statistical analysis 330
      Simulation 331
      Deployment management 331
      Mobile apps 332
   Training and Consultancy Companies.................................332

Index .... _333_

Introduction

・・・

Lean Six Sigma provides a rigorous and structured approach to help manage and improve quality and performance, and to solve potentially complex problems. It helps you use the right tools, in the right place and in the right way, not just in improvement but also in your day-to-day management of activities. Lean Six Sigma really is about getting key principles and concepts into the DNA and lifeblood of your organisation so that it becomes a natural part of how you do things.

This book seeks to help managers and team leaders better understand their role and improve organisational efficiency and effectiveness.

If you want to change outcomes, you need to realise that outcomes are the result of systems. Not the computer systems, but the way people work together and interact. And these systems are the product of how people think and behave. So, if you want to change outcomes, you have to change your systems, and to do that, you have to change your thinking. Albert Einstein summed up the need for different thinking very well:

> *The significant problems we face cannot be solved by the same level of thinking which caused them.*

Lean Six Sigma thinking is *not* about asset stripping and 'making do'. Instead, this approach focuses on doing the right things right, so that you really do add value for the customer and make your organisation effective and efficient.

The main focus of the book relates to DMAIC (Define, Measure, Analyse, Improve and Control). This is the Lean Six Sigma method for improving existing processes that form a part of the organisation's systems, and it provides an ideal way to help you in your quest for continuous improvement.

When you need to develop a new process, the Design for Six Sigma method comes into play. Known as DMADV (Define, Measure, Analyse, Design and Verify), we provide an introduction to this method in Chapter 12,

About This Book

This book makes Lean Six Sigma easy to understand and apply. We wrote it because we feel that Lean Six Sigma can help organisations of all shapes and sizes, both private and public, improve their performance in meeting their customers' requirements.

In particular, we wanted to draw out the role of the manager and provide a collection of concepts, tools and techniques to help him or her carry out the job more effectively. We also wanted to demonstrate the genuine synergy achieved through the combination of Lean and Six Sigma. For some reason unknown to the authors, a few people feel they can use only Lean or Six Sigma, but not both. How wrong they are!

In this book you can discover how to create genuine synergy by applying the principles of Lean and Six Sigma together in your day-to-day operations and activities.

Foolish Assumptions

In Lean Six Sigma, avoiding the tendency to jump to conclusions and make assumptions about things is crucial. Lean Six Sigma really is about managing by fact. Despite that, we've made some assumptions about why you may have bought this book:

- ✔ You're contemplating applying Lean Six Sigma in your business or organisation, and you need to understand what you're getting yourself into.

- ✔ Your business is implementing Lean Six Sigma and you need to get up to speed. Perhaps you've been lined up to participate in the programme in some way.

- ✔ Your business has already implemented either Lean or Six Sigma and you're intrigued by what you might be missing.

- ✔ You're considering a career or job change and feel that your CV or resume will look much better if you can somehow incorporate Lean or Six Sigma into it.

- ✔ You're a student in business, operations or industrial engineering, for example, and you realise that Lean Six Sigma could help shape your future.

We also assume that you realise that Lean Six Sigma demands a rigorous and structured approach to understanding how your work gets done and how well it gets done, and how to go about the improvement of your processes.

Icons Used In This Book

Throughout the book, you'll see small symbols called *icons* in the margins; these highlight special types of information. We use these to help you better understand and apply the material. Look out for the following icons:

This icon highlights an essential component of Lean Six Sigma.

Bear these important points in mind as you get to grips with Lean Six Sigma.

Keep your eyes on the target to find tips and tricks we share to help you make the most of Lean Six Sigma.

Throughout this book we share true stories of how different companies have implemented Lean Six Sigma to improve their processes. We also share true stories of when things go wrong so you learn from others' mistakes.

This icon highlights potential pitfalls to avoid.

Beyond This Book

In addition to the material in the print or e-book you're reading right now, this book also comes with some access-anywhere goodies on the web. Check out the free Cheat Sheet at http://www.dummies.com/cheatsheet/leansixsigma for helpful information that you can access on a regular basis.

You can find some free articles online that expand on some of the concepts in the book. You can find links to the articles on the parts pages and on the Extras page at http://www.dummies.com/extras/leansixsigma.

Where to Go From Here

In theory, when you read you begin with ABC, and when you sing you begin with doh-ray-me (apologies to Julie Andrews). But with a *For Dummies* book you can begin where you like. Each part and, indeed, each chapter is self-contained, which means you can start with whichever parts or chapters interest you the most.

That said, if you're new to the topic, starting at the beginning makes sense. Either way, lots of cross-referencing throughout the book helps you to see how things fit together and put them in the right context.

Part I
Getting Started with Lean Six Sigma

Go to www.dummies.com for more information about topics that interest you — everything from using Lean Six Sigma in your organization to holding effective meetings and from building teamwork to understanding quality control.

In this part . . .

✔ Grasp the basics of Lean Thinking and Six Sigma so you can understand what they mean and what they don't mean.

✔ Get a clearer picture of what the synergy created by merging the two disciplines into Lean Six Sigma looks like and understand the key principles underpinning the approach.

✔ Comprehend exactly what 'sigma' means and why the term is important in Lean Six Sigma.

✔ Examine in depth what the commonly used process improvement method known as DMAIC – Define, Measure, Analyse, Improve and Control – means in Lean Six Sigma.

Chapter 1

Defining Lean Six Sigma

In This Chapter

▶ Turning up trumps for the Toyota Production System

▶ Finding out the fundamentals of 'Lean' and 'Six Sigma'

▶ Applying Lean Six Sigma in your organisation

Throughout this book we cover the tools and techniques available to help you achieve real improvement in your organisation. In this chapter we aim to move you down a path of different thinking that gets your improvement taste buds tingling. We look at the main concepts behind Lean thinking and Six Sigma and introduce some of the terminology to help you on your way.

Introducing Lean Thinking

Lean thinking focuses on enhancing value for the customer by improving and smoothing the process flow (see Chapter 11) and eliminating waste (covered in Chapter 9). Since Henry Ford's first production line, Lean thinking has evolved through a number of sources, and over many years, but much of the development has been led by Toyota through the Toyota Production System (TPS). Toyota built on Ford's production ideas, moving from high volume, low variety, to high variety, low volume.

Although Lean thinking is usually seen as being a manufacturing concept and application, many of the tools and techniques were originally developed in service organisations. These include, for example, spaghetti diagrams, part of the organisation and methods toolkit, and the visual system used by supermarkets to replenish shelves. Indeed, it was a supermarket that helped shape the thinking behind the Toyota Production System. During a tour to General Motors and Ford, Kiichiro Toyoda and Taiichi Ohno visited Piggly Wiggly, an American supermarket, and noticed Just in Time and kanban being applied. This innovation enabled Piggly Wiggly customers to 'buy what they need at any time' and avoided the store holding excess stock. Kanban is simply a card providing the signal to order more stock. Incidentally, Piggly Wiggly was founded in 1916 in Memphis, Tennessee by the innovative Clarence Saunders, who was also the first to introduce the concept of a self-service grocery shop.

Lean is called 'Lean' not because things are stripped to the bone. Lean isn't a recipe for your organisation to slash its costs, although it will likely lead to reduced costs and better value for the customer. We trace the concept of the word 'Lean' back to 1987, when John Krafcik (who is joining Google to provide advice on the driverless car) was working as a researcher for MIT as part of the International Motor Vehicle Program. Krafcik needed a label for the TPS phenomenon that described what the system did. On a white board he wrote the performance attributes of the Toyota system compared with traditional mass production. TPS:

- ✔ Needed less human effort to design products and services.
- ✔ Required less investment for a given amount of production capacity.
- ✔ Created products with fewer delivered defects.
- ✔ Used fewer suppliers.
- ✔ Went from concept to launch, order to delivery and problem to repair in less time and with less human effort.
- ✔ Needed less inventory at every process step.
- ✔ Caused fewer employee injuries.

Krafcik commented:

> *It needs less of everything to create a given amount of value, so let's call it Lean.*

The Lean enterprise was born.

Bringing on the basics of Lean

Figure 1-1 shows the Toyota Production System, highlighting various tools and Japanese Lean thinking terms that we use throughout this book. In this chapter we provide some brief descriptions to introduce the Lean basics and the TPS.

Toyota's Taiichi Ohno describes the TPS approach very effectively:

> *All we are doing is looking at a timeline from the moment the customer gives us an order to the point when we collect the cash. And we are reducing that timeline by removing the non-value-added wastes.*

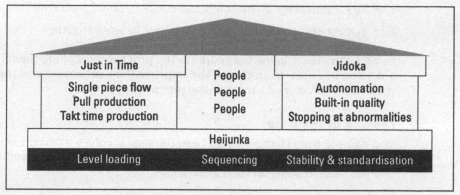

Figure 1-1:
The TPS
house.

The TPS approach really is about understanding how the work gets done, finding ways of doing it better, smoother and faster, and closing the time gap between the start and end points of our processes. And it applies to any process. Whether you're working in the public or private sector, in service, transactional or manufacturing processes really doesn't matter.

Think about your own processes for a moment. Do you feel that some unnecessary steps or activities seem to waste time and effort?

We must point out, however, that simply adopting the tools and techniques of the TPS isn't enough to sustain improvement and embed the principles and thinking into your organisation. Toyota chairperson Fujio Cho provides a clue as to what's also needed:

> *The key to the Toyota way is not any of the individual elements but all the elements together as a system. It must be practised every day in a very consistent manner – not in spurts. We place the highest value on taking action and implementation. By improvement based on action, one can rise to the higher level of practice and knowledge.*

Picking on people power

Figure 1-1 shows that people are at the heart of TPS. The system focuses on training to develop exceptional people and teams that follow the company's philosophy to gain exceptional results. Consider the following:

✔ Toyota creates a strong and stable culture wherein values and beliefs are widely shared and lived out over many years.

✔ Toyota works constantly to reinforce that culture.

- ✔ Toyota involves cross-functional teams to solve problems.
- ✔ Toyota keeps teaching individuals how to work together.

Being Lean means involving people in the process, equipping them to be able, and feel able, to challenge and improve their processes and the way they work. Never waste the creative potential of people!

Looking at the lingo

You can see from Figure 1-1 that Lean thinking involves a certain amount of jargon – some of it Japanese. This section defines the various terms to help you get Lean thinking as soon as possible:

- ✔ **Heijunka** provides the foundation. It encompasses the idea of smoothing processing and production by considering levelling, sequencing and standardising:

  - **Levelling** involves smoothing the volume of production in order to reduce variation, that is, the ups and downs and peaks and troughs that can make planning difficult. Amongst other things, levelling seeks to prevent 'end-of-period' peaks, where production is initially slow at the beginning of the month, but then quickens in the last days of a sale or accounting period, for example.

  - **Sequencing** may well involve mixing the types of work processed. So, for example, when setting up new loans in a bank, the type of loan being processed is mixed to better match customer demand, and help ensure applications are actioned in date order. So often, people are driven by internal efficiency targets, whereby they process the 'simple tasks' first to get them out of the way and 'hit their numbers', leaving the more difficult cases to be processed later on. This means tasks are not processed in date order, and people are reluctant to get down and tackle a pile of difficult cases at the end of the week, making things even worse for the customer and the business.

  - **Standardising** is the third strand of Heijunka. It seeks to reduce variation in the way the work is carried out, highlighting the importance of 'standard work', of following a standard process and procedure. It links well to the concept of process management, where the process owner continuously seeks to find and consistently deploy best practice. Remember, however, that you need to standardise your processes before you can improve them. Once they're standardised, you can work on stabilising them, and now that you fully understand how the processes work, you can improve them, creating a 'one best way' of doing them.

    In the spirit of continuous improvement, of course, the 'one best way' of carrying out the process will keep changing, as the people in the process identify better ways of doing the work. You need to ensure the new 'one best way' is implemented and fully deployed.

↙ **Jidoka** concerns prevention; it links closely with techniques such as failure mode effects analysis (FMEA), which are covered in Chapter 10. Jidoka has two main elements, and both seek to prevent work continuing when something goes wrong:

- **Autonomation** allows machines to operate autonomously, by shutting down if something goes wrong. This concept is also known as automation with human intelligence. The 'no' in auto*no*mation is often underlined to highlight the fact that no defects are allowed to pass to a follow-on process. An early example hails from 1902, when Sakichi Toyoda, the founder of the Toyota group, invented an automated loom that stopped whenever a thread broke. A simple example today is a printer stopping processing copy when the ink runs out.

  Without this concept, automation has the potential to allow a large number of defects to be created very quickly, especially if processing is in batches (see 'Single piece flow', below).

- **Stop at every abnormality** is the second element of Jidoka. The employee can stop an automated or manual line if he spots an error. At Toyota, every employee is empowered to 'stop the line', perhaps following the identification of a special cause on a control chart (see Chapter 7).

  Forcing everything to stop and immediately focus on a problem can seem painful at first, but doing so is an effective way to quickly get at the root cause of issues. Again, this can be especially important if you're processing in batches.

↙ **Just in Time (JIT)** provides the other pillar of the TPS house. JIT involves providing the customer with what's needed, at the right time, in the right location and in the right quantity. The concept applies to both internal and external customers. JIT comprises three main elements:

- **Single piece flow** means each person performs an operation and makes a quick quality check before moving his output to the next person in the following process. Naturally this concept also applies to automated operations where inline checks can be carried out. If a defect is detected, Jidoka is enacted: the process is stopped, and immediate action is taken to correct the situation, taking countermeasures to prevent reoccurrence. This concept is a real change of thinking that moves us away from processing in batches.

  Traditionally, large batches of individual cases are processed at each step and are passed along the process only after an entire batch has been completed. The delays are increased when the batches travel around the organisation, both in terms of the transport time and the length of time they sit waiting in the internal mail system. At any given time, most of the cases in a batch are sitting idle, waiting to be processed. In manufacturing, this is seen as costly excess inventory. What's more, errors can neither be picked up nor addressed quickly; if they occur, they often occur in volume. And, of course, this also delays identifying the root cause. With single piece flow, we can get to the root cause analysis faster, which helps prevent a common error recurring throughout the process.

- **Pull production** is the second element of JIT. Each process takes what it needs from the preceding process only when it needs it and in the exact quantity. The customer pulls the supply and helps avoid being swamped by items that aren't needed at a particular time.

  Pull production reduces the need for potentially costly storage space. All too often, overproduction in one process, perhaps to meet local efficiency targets, results in problems downstream. This increases work in progress, and creates bottlenecks. Overproduction is one of the 'seven wastes' identified by Ohno and covered in Chapter 9.

- **Takt time** is the third element of JIT, providing an important additional measure. It tells you how quickly to action things, given the volume of customer demand. Takt is German for a precise interval of time, such as a musical meter. It serves as the rhythm or beat of the process – the frequency at which a product or service must be completed in order to meet customer needs. Takt time is a bit like the beat of the drum on the old Roman galleys for synchronising the rowers.

Taking the strain out of constraints

Much of the focus in Lean thinking is on understanding and improving the flow of processes and eliminating non-value-added activities. The late Eliyahu Goldratt's *theory of constraints* (explained more fully in Chapter 11) provides a way to address and tackle bottlenecks that slow the process flow. Goldratt's theory proposes a five-step approach to help improve flow:

1. **Identify the constraint.**

   Data helps you identify the bottlenecks in your processes, of course, but you should be able to see them fairly easily, too. Look for backlogs and a build-up of work in progress, or take note of where people are waiting for work to come through to them. These are pretty good clues that demand is exceeding capability and you have a bottleneck.

2. **Exploit the constraint.**

   Look for ways to maximise the processing capability at this point in the process flow. For example, you may minimise downtime for machine maintenance by scheduling maintenance outside of normal hours.

3. Subordinate the other steps to the constraint.

You need to understand just what the bottleneck is capable of – how much it can produce, and how quickly it can do it. Whatever the answer is, in effect, that's the pace at which the whole process is working. The downstream processes know what to expect and when, and having upstream processes working faster is pointless; their output simply builds up as a backlog at the bottleneck. So, use the bottleneck to dictate the pace at which the upstream activities operate, and to signal to the downstream activities what to expect, even if that means these various activities are not working at capacity.

4. Elevate the constraint.

Introduce improvements that remove this particular bottleneck, possibly by using a DMAIC (Define, Measure, Analyse, Improve and Control) project (we delve into DMAIC in Chapter 2).

5. Go back to Step 1 and repeat the process.

After you complete Steps 1–4, a new constraint will exist somewhere else in the process flow, so start the improvement process again.

Considering the customer

The customer, not the organisation, specifies value. Value is what your customer is willing to pay for. To satisfy your customer, your organisation has to provide the right products and services, at the right time, at the right price and at the right quality. To do this, and to do so consistently, you need to identify and understand how your processes work, improve and smooth the flow, eliminate unnecessary steps in the process, and reduce or prevent waste such as rework.

Imagine the processes involved in your own organisation, beginning with a customer order (market demand) and ending with cash in the bank (invoice or bill paid). Ask yourself the following questions:

- How many steps are involved?
- Do you need all the steps?
- Are you sure?
- How can you reduce the number of steps and the time involved from start to finish?

Perusing the principles of Lean thinking

Lean thinking has five key principles:

- Understand the customer and his perception of value.
- Identify and understand the value stream for each process and the waste within it.
- Enable the value to flow.
- Let the customer pull the value through the processes, according to his needs.
- Continuously pursue perfection (continuous improvement).

We've covered these briefly in the preceding pages, but look at them again in more detail in Chapter 2, when we see how they combine with the key principles of Six Sigma to form *Lean Six Sigma*.

Sussing Six Sigma

Six Sigma is a systematic and robust approach to improvement, which focuses on the customer and other key stakeholders. Six Sigma calls for a change of thinking. When Jack Welch, former General Electric CEO, introduced Six Sigma, he said:

> *We are going to shift the paradigm from fixing products to fixing and developing processes, so they produce nothing but perfection or close to it.*

In the 1980s Motorola CEO Bob Galvin struggled to compete with foreign manufacturers. Motorola set a goal of tenfold improvement in five years, with a plan focused on global competitiveness, participative management, quality improvement and training. Quality engineer Bill Smith coined the name of the improvement measurements: Six Sigma. All Motorola employees underwent training, and Six Sigma became the standard for all Motorola business processes.

Considering the core of Six Sigma

A sigma, or standard deviation, is a measure of variation that reveals the average difference between any one item and the overall average of a larger population of items. Sigma is represented by the lower-case Greek letter σ.

Introducing a simple example

Suppose you want to estimate the height of people in your organisation. Measuring everyone isn't practical, so you take a representative sample of 30 people's heights. You work out the mean average height for the group – as an example – say this is 5 foot, 7 inches. You then calculate the difference between each person's height and the mean average height. In broad terms, one sigma, or standard deviation, is the average of those differences. The smaller the number, the less variation there is in the population of things you are measuring. Conversely, the larger the number, the more variation. In our example, imagine the standard deviation is one inch, though it might be any number in theory.

Figure 1-2 shows the likely percentage of the population within plus one and minus one standard deviation from the mean, plus two and minus two standard deviations from the mean, and so on. Assuming your sample is representative, you can see how your information provides a good picture of the heights of all the people in your organisation. You find that approximately two-thirds of them are between 5 foot 6 inches and 5 foot 8 inches tall, about 95 per cent are in the range 5 foot 5 inches to 5 foot 9 inches, and about 99.73 per cent are between 5 foot 4 inches and 5 foot 10 inches.

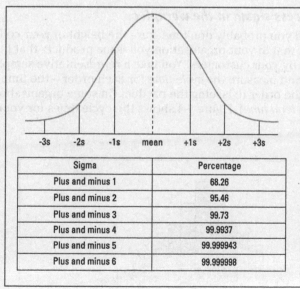

Sigma	Percentage
Plus and minus 1	68.26
Plus and minus 2	95.46
Plus and minus 3	99.73
Plus and minus 4	99.9937
Plus and minus 5	99.999943
Plus and minus 6	99.999998

Figure 1-2: Standard deviation.

© John Morgan and Martin Brenig-Jones

In reality, the calculation is a little more involved and uses a rather forbidding formula – as shown in Figure 1-3.

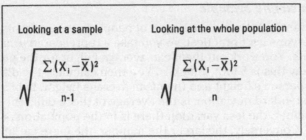

Figure 1-3:
Standard
deviation
formula.

© John Morgan and Martin Brenig-Jones

Using n – 1 makes an allowance for the fact that we're looking at a sample and not the whole population. In practice, though, when the sample size is over 30, there's little difference between using n or n – 1. When we refer to a 'population' this could relate to people or things that have already been processed, for example a population of completed and despatched insurance policies or hairdryers.

The process sigma values are calculated by looking at our performance against the customer requirements – see the next section.

Practising process sigma in the workplace

In the real world you probably don't measure the height of your colleagues. Imagine instead that in your organisation you issue products that have been requested by your customers. You take a representative sample of fulfilled orders and measure the *cycle time* for each order – the time taken from receiving the order to issuing the product (in some organisations this is referred to as *lead time*). Figure 1-4 shows the cycle times for your company's orders.

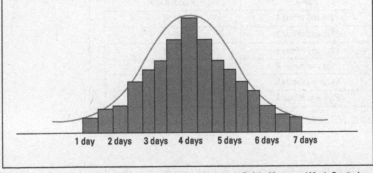

Figure 1-4:
Histogram
showing the
time taken
to process
orders.

© John Morgan and Martin Brenig-Jones

You can see the range of your company's performance. The cycle time varies from as short as one day to as long as seven days.

But the customer expects delivery in five days or less. In Lean Six Sigma speak, a customer requirement is called a CTQ – Critical To Quality. CTQs are referred to in Chapter 2 and described in more detail in Chapter 4, but essentially they express the customers' requirements in a way that is measurable. CTQs are a vital element in Lean Six Sigma and provide the basis of your process measurement set. In our example, the CTQ is five days or less, but the average performance in Figure 1-4 is four days. Remember that this is the average; your customers experience the *whole range* of your performance.

Too many organisations use averages as a convenient way of making their performance sound better than it really is.

In the example provided in Figure 1-4, all the orders that take more than five days are *defects* for the customer in Six Sigma language. Orders that take five days or less meet the CTQ. We show this situation in Figure 1-5. We could express the performance as the percentage or proportion of orders processed within five days or we can work out the *process sigma value*. The process sigma value is calculated by looking at your performance against the customer requirement, the CTQ, and taking into account the number of defects involved where you fail to meet it (that is, all those cases that took more than five days).

We explain the process sigma calculation in the next section.

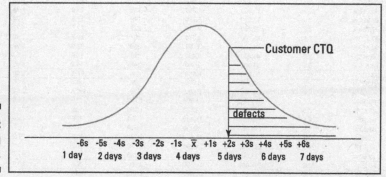

Figure 1-5: Highlighting defects.

© John Morgan and Martin Brenig-Jones

Calculating process sigma values

Process sigma values provide a way of comparing performances of different processes, which can help you to prioritise projects. The process sigma value represents the population of cases that meet the CTQs right first time. Sigma values are often expressed as defects per million opportunities (DPMO), rather than per hundred or per thousand, to emphasise the need for world-class performance.

Not all organisations using Six Sigma calculate process sigma values. Some organisations just use the number of defects or the percentage of orders meeting CTQs to show their performance. Either way, if benchmarking is to be meaningful, the calculations must be made in a consistent manner.

Figure 1-6 includes 'yield' figures – the right first time percentage. You can see that Six Sigma performance equates to only 3.4 DPMO.

Yield	Sigma	Defects per 1,000,000	Defects per 100,000	Defects per 10,000	Defects per 1,000	Defects per 100
99.99966%	6.0	3.4	0.34	0.034	0.0034	0.00034
99.9995%	5.9	5	0.5	0.05	0.005	0.0005
99.9992%	5.8	8	0.8	0.08	0.008	0.0008
99.9990%	5.7	10	1	0.1	0.01	0.001
99.9980%	5.6	20	2	0.2	0.02	0.002
99.9970%	5.5	.30	3	0.3	0.03	0.003
99.9960%	5.4	40	4	0.4	0.04	0.004
99.9930%	5.3	70	7	0.7	0.07	0.007
99.9900%	5.2	100	10	1.0	0.1	0.01
99.9850%	5.1	150	15	1.5	0.15	0.015
99.9770%	5.0	230	23	2.3	0.23	0.023
99.670%	4.9	330	33	3.3	0.33	0.033
99.9520&	4.8	480	48	4.8	0.48	0.048
99.9320%	4.7	680	68	6.8	0.68	0.068
99.9040%	4.6	960	96	9.6	0.96	0.096
99.8650%	4.5	1,350	135	13.5	1.35	0.135
99.8140%	4.4	1,860	186	18.6	1.86	0.186
99.7450%	4.3	2,550	255	25.5	2.55	0.255
99.6540%	4.2	3,460	346	34.6	3.46	0.346
99.5340%	4.1	4,660	466	46.6	4.66	0.466
99.3790%	4.0	6,210	621	62.1	6.21	0.621
99.1810%	3.9	8,190	819	81.9	8.19	0.819
98.930%	3.8	10,700	1,070	107	10.7	1.07
98.610%	3.7	13.900	1.390	139	13.9	1.39
98.220%	3.6	17,800	1,780	178	17.8	1.78
97.730%	3.5	22.700	2,270	227	22.7	2.27
97.130%	3.4	28,700	2,870	287	28.7	2.87
96.410%	3.3	35,900	3,590	359	35.9	3.59
95.540%	3.2	44,600	4,460	446	44.6	4.46
94.520%	3.1	54,800	5,480	548	54.8	5.48
93.320%	3.0	66,800	6,680	668	66.8	6.68
91.920%	2.9	80,800	8,080	808	80.8	8.08
90.320%	2.8	96,800	9,680	968	96.8	9.68
88.50%	2.7	115,000	11,500	1,150	115	11.5
86.50%	2.6	135,000	13,500	1,350	135	13.5
84.20%	2.5	158,000	15,800	1,580	158	15.8
81.60%	2.4	184,000	18,400	1,840	184	18.4
78.80%	2.3	212,000	21,200	2,120	212	21.2
75.80%	2.2	242,000	24,200	2,420	242	24.2
72.60%	2.1	274,000	27,400	2,740	274	27.4
69.20%	2.0	308,000	30,800	3,080	308	30.8
65.60%	1.9	344,000	34,400	3,440	344	34.4
61.80%	1.8	382,000	38,200	3,820	382	38.2
58.00%	1.7	420,000	42,000	4,200	420	42
54.00%	1.6	460,000	46,000	4,600	460	46
50%	1.5	500,000	50,000	5,000	500	50
46%	1.4	540,000	54,000	5,400	540	54
43%	1.3	570,000	57,000	5,700	570	57
39%	1.2	610,000	61,000	6,100	610	61
35%	1.1	650,000	65,000	6,500	650	65
31%	1.0	690,000	69,000	6,900	690	69
28%	0.9	720,000	72,000	7,200	720	72
25%	0.8	750,000	75,000	7,500	750	75
22%	0.7	780,000	78,000	7,800	780	78
19%	0.6	810,000	81,000	8,100	810	81
16%	0.5	840,000	84,000	8,400	840	84
14%	0.4	860,000	86,000	8,600	860	86
12%	0.3	880,000	88,000	8,800	880	88
10%	0.2	900,000	90,000	9,000	900	90
8%	0.1	920,000	92,000	9,200	920	92

Figure 1-6: Abridged process sigma conversion table.

© *John Morgan and Martin Brenig-Jones*

Recognising that you're looking at 'first pass' performance is important. If you make an error but correct it before the order goes to the customer, you still count the defect because the rework activity costs you time and effort. And remember that you're looking at defects. Your customer may have several CTQs relating to an order – for example, speed, accuracy and completeness – thus more than one defect may exist in the transaction.

So, for example, you could have a situation whereby the speed of delivery CTQ was met, but the accuracy and completeness CTQs were missed. The outcome would be one *defective* (see the bullet list below) as a result of these two *defects*. In calculating sigma values for your processes, you need to understand the following key terms:

- ✓ **Unit:** The item produced or processed.

- ✓ **Defect:** Any event that does not meet the specification of a CTQ.

- ✓ **Defect opportunity:** Any event that provides a chance of not meeting a customer CTQ. The number of defect opportunities will equal the number of CTQs.

- ✓ **Defective:** A unit with one or more defects.

In manufacturing processes you may find that the number of defect opportunities is determined differently, taking full account of all the different defects that can occur within a part. The key is to calculate the process sigma values in a consistent way.

You can work out your process sigma performance against the CTQs as shown in Figure 1-7. We have a sample of 500 processed units. The customer has three CTQs, so we have three defect opportunities. The CTQs are related to speed, accuracy and completeness. We find 57 defects. With software, you can determine a precise process sigma value, but with the abridged table in Figure 1-6, find the sigma value that's closest to your DPMO number of 38000. As you can see, this is 3.3.

A difference exists between process sigma and standard deviation (see the 'Introducing a simple example' section earlier in this chapter for how to work out standard deviations). This results from Motorola adjusting the tables to reflect the variation being experienced in its processes. This adjustment is referred to as a 1.5 sigma shift, reflecting the extent of the adjustment. Although this adjustment related to *its* processes, rightly or wrongly, everyone adopting Six Sigma has apparently also adopted the adjusted sigma scale. Incidentally, without this adjustment, Six Sigma would equate to 0.002 DPMO as opposed to 3.4 DPMO – so, even harder to achieve.

✿ Number of units processed	N=500	
✿ Total number of defects made (include defects made and later fixed)	D=57	
✿ Number of defect opportunities per unit (equate to CTQs)	O=3	
✿ Calculate # defects per million opportunities	DPMO $= 1{,}000{,}000 \times$	$\dfrac{D}{(N \times O)}$
	$= 1{,}000{,}000 \times$	$\dfrac{57}{(500) \times (3)}$
	$= 38000$	
✿ Look up process sigma in sigma conversation table (see Figure 1-6)	Sigma $= 3.3$	

© John Morgan and Martin Brenig-Jones

Figure 1-7: Calculating process sigma values.

When we talk about Six Sigma performance before the adjustment, we're talking about plus and minus six standard deviations, which embrace 99.999998 per cent of the data. And we are talking about the percentage of cases that are right first time in terms of meeting the requirements of the customer. Taking account of the adjustment, we're still looking at a truly demanding standard, with 99.999666 per cent of cases right first time in meeting the CTQs.

Clarifying the major points of Six Sigma

The five key principles of Six Sigma are:

✔ **Understand the CTQs of your customers and stakeholders.** To deliver the best customer experience, you need to know what your customer wants – his requirements and expectations. You need to listen to and understand the *voice of the customer* (VOC), which we talk about in Chapter 4.

✔ **Understand your organisation's processes and ensure they reflect your customers' CTQs.** You need to know how your processes work and what they're trying to achieve. A clear objective for each process should exist, focused on the customer requirements – the CTQs.

✔ **Manage by fact and reduce variation.** Measurement and management by fact enables more effective decision-making. By understanding variation, you can work out when and when not to take action.

✔ **Involve and equip the people in the process.** To be truly effective you need to equip the people in your organisation to be able, and to feel able, to challenge and improve their processes and the way they work.

> ✔ **Undertake improvement activity in a systematic way.** Working systematically helps you avoid jumping to conclusions and solutions. Six Sigma uses a system called DMAIC (Define, Measure, Analyse, Improve and Control) to improve existing processes. We cover DMAIC in Chapter 2. In designing new processes, we use DMADV.

A natural synergy exists between Lean and Six Sigma – your organisation needs both. Many people think of Lean as focusing on improving the efficiency of processes, and Six Sigma as concentrating on their effectiveness. The reality is that both approaches tackle efficiency and effectiveness.

Chapter 2

Understanding the Principles of Lean Six Sigma

In This Chapter
▶ Merging Lean and Six Sigma to make Lean Six Sigma
▶ Undertaking DMAIC to make things better
▶ Reviewing what you do in order to do it better

*I*n this chapter we look at the synergy produced by combining the approaches of Lean and Six Sigma to form Lean Six Sigma. The merged approach provides a comprehensive set of principles, and supporting tools and techniques, to enable genuine improvements in both efficiency and effectiveness for organisations.

Considering the Key Principles of Lean Six Sigma

Lean Six Sigma takes the features of Lean and of Six Sigma and integrates them to form a magnificent seven set of principles. The principles of each approach aren't dissimilar (check out Chapter 1 to read more about the individual components), and the merged set produces no surprises. The seven principles of Lean Six Sigma are:

> ✔ **Focus on the customer.** The customer's CTQs describe elements of your service or offering they consider Critical To Quality (see Chapter 1 for more on those). Written in a way that ensures they're measurable, the CTQs provide the basis for determining the process measures you need to help you understand how well you perform against these critical requirements. Focusing on the customer and the concept of value-add is important because typically only 10–15 per cent of process steps

add value and often represent only 1 per cent of the total process time. These figures may be surprising, but they should grab your attention and help you realise the potential waste that's happening in your own organisation. As you improve your performance in meeting the CTQs, you're also likely to win and retain further business and increase your market share. The concept of value-added process steps is covered in Chapter 9, and Chapters 3 to 5 consider the customer in more detail.

✔ **Identify and understand how the work gets done.** The *value stream* describes all of the steps in your process – for example, from a customer order to the issue of a product or the delivery of a service, through to payment. By drawing a map of the value stream, you can highlight the non-value-added steps and areas of waste and ensure the process focuses on meeting the CTQs and adding value. To undertake this process properly, you must 'go to the Gemba'. The Japanese word *Gemba* means the place where the work gets done – where the action is – which is where management begins. Process stapling (which we introduce in Chapter 5) involves you spending time in the workplace to see how the work really gets done, not how you think it gets done or how you'd like it to be done. You see the real process being carried out and collect data on what's happening. Process stapling helps you analyse the problems that you want to tackle and determine a more effective solution for your day-to-day activities.

The value stream reveals all of the actions, both value-creating and non-value-creating, that take your product or service concept to launch and your customer order through the supply chain to delivery. These value-creating and non-value-creating actions include those to process information from the customer and those to transform the product on its way to the customer. Chapter 5 covers the value stream.

✔ **Manage, improve and smooth the process flow.** This concept provides an example of different thinking. If possible, use single piece flow, moving away from batches, or at least reducing batch sizes. Either way, identify the non-value-added steps in the process and try to remove them – certainly look to ensure they do not delay value-adding steps. The concept of pull, not push (see Chapter 1), links to your understanding the process and improving flow. And it can be an essential element in avoiding bottlenecks. Overproduction or pushing things through too early is a waste.

✔ **Remove non-value-adding steps and waste.** Doing so is another vital element in improving flow and performance, generally. The Japanese refer to waste as *Muda*; they describe two broad types and seven categories of waste. Of course, if you can prevent waste in the first place, then so much the better (see Chapters 9 and 10 on how to do this).

✔ **Manage by fact and reduce variation.** Managing by fact, using accurate data, helps you avoid jumping to conclusions and solutions. You need the facts! And that means measuring the right things in the right way. Data collection is a process and needs to be managed accordingly. Using control charts (Chapter 7 has more on these) enables you to interpret the data correctly and understand the process variation. You then know when to take action and when not to.

✔ **Involve and equip the people in the process.** You need to involve the people in the process, equipping them to both feel and be able to challenge and improve their processes and the way they work. Involving people is what has to be done if organisations are to be truly effective, but, like so many of the Lean Six Sigma principles, it requires different thinking if it's to happen. (See Chapter 18 for more on understanding the 'people issues'.)

✔ **Undertake improvement activity in a systematic way.** DMAIC comes into play here: Define, Measure, Analyse, Improve and Control. One of the criticisms sometimes aimed at 'stand-alone' Lean is that improvement action tends not to be taken in a systematic and standard way. In Six Sigma, DMAIC is used to improve existing processes, but the framework is equally applicable to Lean and, of course, Lean Six Sigma. Where a new process needs to be designed, the DMADV method is used.

Less is usually more. Tackle problems in bite-sized chunks and never jump to conclusions or solutions.

The focus in the following section is on improving existing processes with DMAIC using the appropriate tools and techniques from the Lean Six Sigma toolkit. But these tools, and the seven principles, identified earlier in this chapter also provide a framework to improve the day-to-day management and operation of processes. We look at this aspect of Lean Six Sigma, which we refer to as 'Everyday Operational Excellence', in Chapter 17.

Improving Existing Processes: Introducing DMAIC

DMAIC (Define, Measure, Analyse, Improve and Control) provides the framework to improve existing processes in a systematic way. DMAIC projects begin with the identification of a problem, and in the Define phase you describe what you think needs improving. Without data this might be based on your best guess of things, so in the Measure phase you use facts and data to understand how your processes work and perform so that you can describe the problem more effectively.

Now you can Analyse the situation by using facts and data to determine the root cause(s) of the problem that's inhibiting your performance. With the root cause identified, you can now move to the Improve phase, identifying potential solutions, selecting the most suitable, and testing or piloting it to validate your approach, using data where appropriate. You're then ready to implement the solution in the Control phase.

The Control phase is especially important. You need to implement your solution, checking that your customers feel the difference in your performance. You'll need to use data to determine the extent of the improvement and to help you hold the gains. After all your hard work, you don't want the problem you've solved to recur. With the right ongoing measures in place, you should also be able to prompt new opportunities (see Chapter 8 for more on getting the right balance of measures).

The following sections provide a little more detail about the five DMAIC phases. Figure 2-1 shows how the phases link together, though the process is not necessarily linear. It could be that in the Define phase, for example, the problem that you are planning to tackle can't be adequately quantified. In the Measure phase, you'll be collecting data that enables you to go back to Define and update your description of the problem.

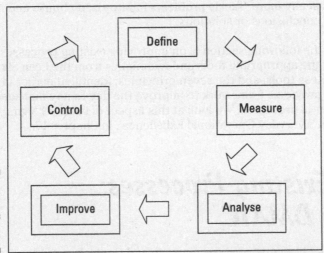

Figure 2-1:
The five
phases of
DMAIC.

© John Morgan and Martin Brenig-Jones

Defining your project

When you start an improvement project, ensuring that you and your team understand why you're undertaking the project and what you want to achieve is an essential ingredient for success. With a DMAIC project, you start with a problem that needs to be solved. Before you can solve the problem, you need to define it – not always as straightforward a process as you may think. One of the key outputs from the Define phase is a completed *improvement charter*.

The improvement charter is an agreed document defining the purpose and goals for an improvement team. It can help address some of the elements that typically go wrong in projects by providing a helpful framework to gain commitment and understanding from the team. Keep your charter simple and try to contain the document to one or two sides of A4 in line with the example shown in Figure 2-2.

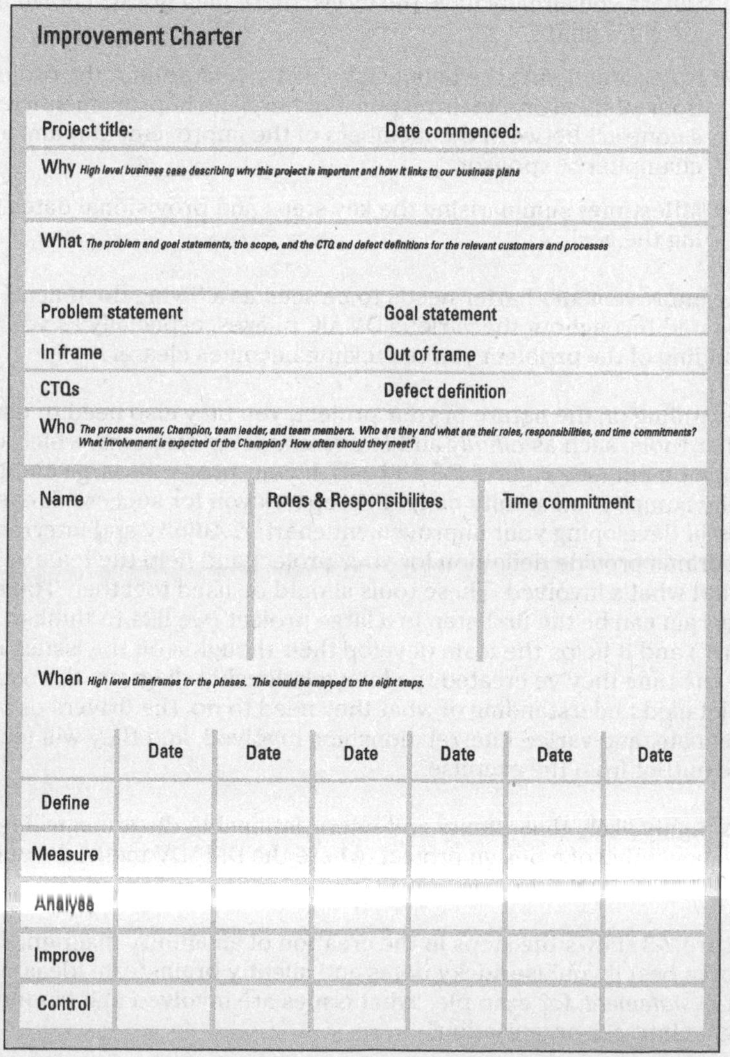

Improvement Charter

Project title: Date commenced:

Why *High level business case describing why this project is important and how it links to our business plans*

What *The problem and goal statements, the scope, and the CTQ and defect definitions for the relevant customers and processes*

Problem statement	Goal statement
In frame	Out of frame
CTQs	Defect definition

Who *The process owner, Champion, team leader, and team members. Who are they and what are their roles, responsibilities, and time commitments? What involvement is expected of the Champion? How often should they meet?*

Name	Roles & Responsibilites	Time commitment

When *High level timeframes for the phases. This could be mapped to the eight steps.*

	Date	Date	Date	Date	Date	Date
Define						
Measure						
Analyse						
Improve						
Control						

© John Morgan and Martin Brenig-Jones

Figure 2-2:
A sample improvement charter.

The improvement charter contains the following key elements:

- **A high-level business case** providing an explanation of why undertaking the project is important.

- **A problem statement** defining the issue to be resolved.

- **A goal statement** describing the objective of the project.

- **The project scope** defining the parameters and identifying any constraints.

- **The CTQs** specifying the problem from the customer's perspective. Unless you already have the CTQs, these may not be known until the Measure phase.

- **Roles** identifying the people involved in and around the project, expectations of them and their responsibilities. The improvement charter forms a contract between the members of the improvement team, and the champion or sponsor.

- **Milestones** summarising the key steps and provisional dates for achieving the goal.

The improvement charter needs to be seen as a 'living document' and be updated throughout the various DMAIC phases, especially as your understanding of the problem you're tackling becomes clearer.

Depending on the nature of your project, you may also need to use some other tools, such as *affinity* and *interrelationship diagrams*, which we describe in a moment (see Figures 2-3 and 2-4). If your project is large and potentially complex, an affinity diagram prepares you for success. It can also aid you in developing your improvement charter. Affinity and interrelationship diagrams provide definition for your project and help the team really understand what's involved. These tools should be used together. The affinity diagram can be the first step in a large project (we like to think of it as 'step zero') and it helps the team develop their thoughts on the issues involved. By the time they've created the interrelationship diagram, the team will have a detailed understanding of what they need to do, the drivers of success and the many and varied interrelationships involved, and they will feel they own the output from the exercise.

It's highly likely that affinity and interrelationship diagrams will be used at the beginning of a design project, where the DMADV method would be used rather than DMAIC.

Figure 2-3 shows the steps in the creation of an affinity diagram. The process works best if you use sticky notes and silently brainstorm ideas on an agreed *issue statement*; for example, 'what issues are involved in introducing Lean Six Sigma into our organisation?'

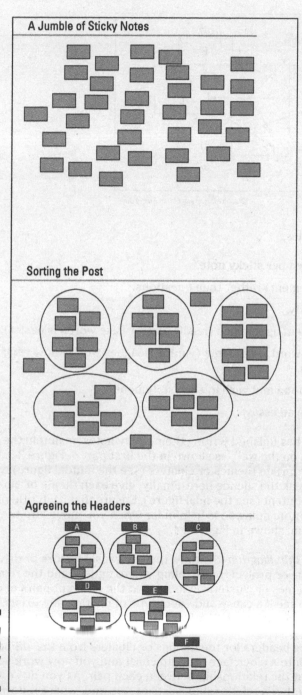

Figure 8-0:
Creating
an affinity
diagram.

© John Morgan and Martin Brenig-Jones

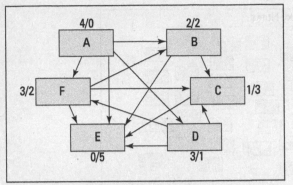

© John Morgan and Martin Brenig-Jones

Figure 2-4:
A sample interrelationship diagram.

Follow these rules:

- ✔ Use one idea per sticky note.
- ✔ Write statements rather than questions.
- ✔ Write clearly.
- ✔ Don't write in upper case (reading lower-case words is easier).
- ✔ Avoid one-word statements (your colleagues won't know what you mean).
- ✔ Include a noun and verb in each statement.
- ✔ Don't write an essay.

After everyone has finished writing their sticky notes, maintain the silence and place them on the wall, as shown in the first part of Figure 2-3. Move the notes into appropriate themes or clusters (see the middle figure), you'll probably need to break the silence here. Finally, give each theme or cluster a title describing its content (see the final figure). Ensure that each title provides enough description; doing so is helpful for when you move into the interrelationship diagram, shown in Figure 2-4.

An *interrelationship diagram* identifies the key causal factors or drivers for your programme or project, by enabling you to understand the relationships between the themes or clusters. In looking at the different pairs of clusters you're trying to see if a cause and effect type of relationship exists, so does 'this' have to be done before 'that', or does 'this' drive 'that'.

In Figure 2-4, the headers for the themes or clusters from the affinity diagram have been put into a clock face on a flip chart and you now work your way round looking at the relationship between each pair. As you do so, you need to consider whether a relationship exists or not, and, where it does, determine which has a greater effect on the other – for example, 'must this happen before this does?'

If a relationship does exist between two clusters, connect them with a line. Importantly, either there is a relationship or there isn't, so don't use dotted lines – you might start with a pencil, though! Agreeing some ground rules is sensible to ensure the relationships are tangible.

After you've determined the 'causal' cluster, draw an arrow into the 'effect' cluster. Some discussion is likely to take place about which way the arrow faces, but it has to go one way or the other – two-headed arrows are not allowed! In Figure 2-4, you can see that A drives B, but that B is the driver of C. The numbers represent arrows out over arrows in.

The finished diagram can be presented as shown in Figure 2-5, and you can clearly see the key driver is A, whereas E is probably the outcome of the project. You need to particularly focus on A to ensure your project or programme is successful.

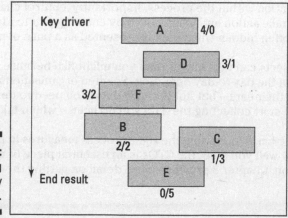

Figure 2-5: Identifying the key drivers.

© John Morgan and Martin Brenig-Jones

TIP

Throughout your project, developing a storyboard summary of the key decisions and outputs helps you review progress and share what you've learnt. A storyboard builds up as you work your way through your project by capturing the key outputs and findings from the DMAIC phases. A storyboard would include, for example, your improvement charter and process map (see Chapter 5). The storyboard also helps your communication activities. Developing and reviewing a communication plan is an essential activity. You really need to keep your team and the people affected by your project informed about the progress you're making in solving the problem you're tackling. Communication begins on day one of your project.

Measuring how the work is done

After you've defined the problem, at least based on your current understanding, you need to clarify how, and how well, the work gets done. To understand the current situation of your process, knowing what it looks like and how it's performing is important. You need to know what's meant to happen, and why. Understanding how your process links to your customer and his CTQs is also helpful. What does the bigger picture of the process look like?

Knowing the current performance of your process is essential – this knowledge becomes your baseline – but knowing what's happened in the past is also useful. Measure what's important to the customer, and remember also to measure what the customer sees. Gathering this information can help focus your improvement efforts and prevent you going off in the wrong direction. Using control charts (see Chapter 7) can help you make better sense of the data, as they provide a visual picture that demonstrates performance and shows you the variation within the process. Importantly, control charts help you know when to take action and when not to by enabling you to identify the key signals so often hidden when data is presented as a page of numbers.

Lean Six Sigma projects can take longer than you might like because the right data isn't in place in the day-to-day operation. So often organisations have data coming out of their ears – but not the *right* data. You need to develop the right measures and start collecting the data you do need – which takes time.

 Use the CTQs as the basis for getting the right process measures in place. Understanding how well you meet the CTQs is an essential piece of management information. Chapter 8 provides more detail on getting the right measures.

Analysing your process

In the Measure phase, you discovered what's really happening in your process. Now you need to identify why it's happening, and determine the root cause. You need to manage by fact, though, so you must verify and validate your ideas about possible suspects. Jumping to conclusions is all too easy.

Carrying out the Analyse phase properly helps you in determining the solution when you get to the Improve phase. Clearly, the extent of analysis required varies depending on the scope and nature of the problem you're tackling, and, indeed, what your Measure activities have identified. Essentially, though, you're analysing the process and the data.

Checking the possible causes of your problem using concrete data to verify your ideas is crucial. In checking the vital few, you may find the 'usual suspects' aren't guilty at all! Identifying and removing the root causes of a problem prevents it happening again.

Improving your process

Most people want to start at this point. Now you've identified the root cause of the problem, you can begin to generate improvement ideas to help solve it. Improve, however, involves three distinct phases:

1. **Generate ideas about possible solutions.**

   The solution may be evident from the work done in the previous two steps. Make sure that your proposed solutions address the problem and its cause.

2. **Select the most appropriate solution.**

   Take account of the results from any testing or piloting, and the criteria you've identified as important, such as customer priorities, cost, speed or ease of implementation. Ensure your solution addresses the problem and that customers will see a difference if you adopt it.

3. **Plan and test the solution.**

   This step seeks to ensure the smooth implementation of your chosen solution. The main focus, though, is on prevention – causing something *not* to happen. Carrying out a more detailed pilot is likely to be helpful.

Coming up with a control plan

After all your hard work, you need to implement the solution in a way that ensures you make the gain you expected and hold onto it! If you're to continue your efforts in reducing variation and cutting out waste, the changes being made to the process need to be consistently deployed and followed.

If the improvement team is handing over the 'new' process to the process team, the handover needs to ensure that everyone understands who's responsible for what and when. Misunderstandings are all too easy and a clear cut-off point must exist signalling the end of the improvement team's role. A control plan needs to be developed to ensure that the gain is secured and the new process effectively deployed – see Figure 2-6.

Process	Performance	Action
Deployment Flowchart	**Checks and Measures**	**Corrective Actions**
	Plot time on each step; should be two hours or less; check for special causes	If time exceeds two hours, alert team leader and organize investigation
	Count errors	If more than one per oder, stop process, contact team leader and investigate

© John Morgan and Martin Brenig-Jones

Figure 2-6:
A control plan helps to make the handover process run smoothly.

The *control plan* helps to ensure that the process is carried out consistently. It also identifies key points in the process where measurement data is needed, plus highlights what action is required depending on the results. Ensuring you have the right ongoing measures in place is extremely important.

Your various DMAIC projects help the organisation move towards a situation where processes are completely understood, and are focused on meeting customer CTQs involving the minimum possible non-value-added activity.

Reviewing Your DMAIC Phases

Informal reviews of the progress of your improvement project on a weekly or even daily basis may be very sensible. These reviews involve the improvement team and the champion or sponsor.

But, as a minimum, you should conduct a formal tollgate review at the end of each DMAIC phase. A *tollgate review* checks that you have completed the current phase properly and reviews the team's various outputs from it. The improvement team leader and the management sponsor or champion of the improvement activity should conduct this review. In effect, you're passing through a tollgate.

Before moving from one phase to another, stepping back, assessing progress and asking some key questions is crucial. For example:

- How are things going? For instance, is the team working well together?
- Are we on course?
- What have we discovered?
- What went well? Why?
- What conclusions can we draw?

The tollgates also provide an opportunity to update your improvement charter and storyboard. Doing so pulls together some of the key elements of your project; for example, a picture of the process and a control chart showing performance. The tollgate also enables you to take stock of the benefits accruing and the financial details; for example, reductions in errors, improvements in processing time and customer satisfaction. In determining the benefits and financial details, ensure you record the assumptions behind your estimates or calculations, as you may need to explain these to others in the organisation.

At the end of the Analyse phase, the review is of particular importance. It provides an opportunity to review the scope of your project; that is, how much improvement you're seeking to achieve from it.

Before the project began, you may well have best-guessed a business case that justifies starting the work. By the end of this phase, you should be able to *quantify the opportunity* – to really understand the extent of non-value-adding activities and waste, and the potential for improvement. On completion of the Measure phase, you're able to understand the current situation and level of performance. Following the Analyse phase, your level of understanding will have increased significantly and you'll understand the root cause of the problem:

- You know why performance is at the level it is.
- You understand the costs involved in the process, both overall and at the individual step level.
- You have identified the waste and the non-value-adding steps, including the extent of rework, and understood their impact on your ability to meet the CTQs.

In quantifying the opportunity, you first need to calculate the saving if all this waste and non-value-added work were eliminated, making sure you document your assumptions. You may feel the opportunity is too small to bother about, or so large it justifies either widening the scope of the project or developing a phased approach, by breaking the task into several smaller projects, for example. Either way, review and agree your project goals now, sensibly estimating what's possible for your project.

The benefits are reviewed again closely following your completion of the Improve phase. You're looking to confirm the deliverables from the project, and secure authority for the solution to be fully implemented. As with quantify the opportunity, the post-Improve review also provides an opportunity to look at the project more generally, and key questions include:

- Are we on course?
- What have we discovered? And forgotten?
- What went well? Why?
- Can we apply the solution elsewhere?
- What conclusions can we draw?

Confirming the benefits you expect to achieve is the main focus of this second benefits review; for example, in reduced rework or improved processing speeds. In completing the phase, you should feel confident that the chosen solution addresses the root cause of the identified problem, and ensures you meet the project goals. Management by fact is a key principle of Lean Six Sigma, so you should have appropriate measurement data and feel confident that your solution will deliver.

Quite a range of differing benefits may occur, including:

- Reduced errors and waste.
- Faster cycle time.
- Improved customer satisfaction.
- Reduced cost.

In assessing how well these benefits match the project objectives, bear in mind that quantifying the softer benefits of enhanced customer satisfaction may be difficult. And in projecting when the benefits are likely to emerge, don't lose sight of the fact that a time gap will probably exist between the cause and effect, especially where customer satisfaction feedback and information is concerned.

As well as looking at the benefits, this review also confirms any costs associated with the solution and its implementation. The piloting or testing activity carried out in the Improve phase (see 'Improving your process' earlier in this chapter) should have helped you pull this information together, provided you treated it as though it were a full-scale implementation. Internal guidelines will probably be available to help you assess and present the benefits and costs, but ensure you've documented the assumptions behind your benefits assessment.

A third and final benefit review follows the Control phase, enabling you to confirm the actual costs and benefits and whether any unexpected debits or credits have occurred. And you should know the answers to these questions:

- ✔ Do our customers feel an improvement has occurred? How do we know?

- ✔ Can we take any of the ideas or 'best practices' and apply them elsewhere in the business?

This review is the formal post-implementation phase involving the project sponsor or champion. In some organisations you may find a wider team of managers forming a 'project board' or 'steering committee', which provides overall guidance for improvement teams and helps prevent duplication of effort with different teams tackling the same or similar problems. This review is likely to involve your team presenting their storyboard, as described in the 'Defining your project' section earlier in this chapter.

Taking time for these reviews and tollgates is an important element in developing a culture that manages by fact. Maintaining an up-to-date storyboard as you work your way through the DMAIC phases helps you prepare for the reviews and share discoveries. The storyboard is created by the team and should present the important elements of its work – the key outputs from the DMAIC process.

Taking a Pragmatic Approach

Six Sigma and DMAIC have been criticised by some for being too complex, and for projects taking too long. Be pragmatic. Projects need to take as long as is appropriate and often only a few simple tools and techniques are needed to secure quick and successful improvements.

Some say that Lean doesn't always ensure a systematic and controlled approach to achieving and holding on to improvement gains – this is where the Control phase of DMAIC is so important. For relatively straightforward problems, *rapid improvement events* can be utilised. These can be run in one-week sessions – sometimes known as *Kaizen blitz events*. Kaizen is the Japanese word for continuous improvement; it means 'change for the better'. The implementation of the improvement may take a further month or so, and some pre-event planning and data collection is necessary.

Wax on, wax off: Lean Six Sigma and martial arts

The different levels of training in Lean Six Sigma are often referred to in terms of the coloured belts acquired in martial arts. Think about the qualities of a martial arts Black Belt: highly trained, experienced, disciplined, decisive, controlled and responsive, and you can see how well this metaphor translates into the world of making change happen in organisations. Thankfully, no bricks need to be broken in half by hand . . .

✔ Some organisations develop a pool of **Yellow Belts**, who typically receive two days of practical training to a basic level on the most commonly used tools in Lean Six Sigma projects. They work either as project team members or carry out mini-projects themselves in their local work environment under the guidance of a Black Belt.

✔ **Green Belts** are trained on the basic tools and lead fairly straightforward projects. The extent of training varies somewhat. In the USA, for example, it's typically 10 days, whereas in the UK some organisations break the training along the following lines – Foundation Green Belt level (four to six days' training) covers Lean tools, process mapping techniques and measurement, as well as a firm grounding in the DMAIC methodology and the basic set of statistical tools. Advanced Green Belts (an additional six days' training) receive further instruction on more analytical statistical tools and start to use statistical software. This helps ensure the training is delivered 'just in time', since early projects can be relatively simple, often involving an assessment of how the work gets done, enabling the identification and elimination of non-value-added steps, without the need for detailed statistical analysis.

Green Belts typically devote the equivalent of about a day a week (20 per cent of their time) to Lean Six Sigma projects, usually mentored by a Black Belt.

✔ An expert Lean Six Sigma practitioner is trained to **Black Belt** level, which means attending several modules of training over a period of months. Most Black Belt courses involve around 20 days of full-time training as well as working on projects in practice under the guidance of a Master Black Belt. The role of the Black Belt is to lead complex projects and give expert help with the tools and techniques to the project teams.

Black Belts are often from different operational functions across the company, coming into the Black Belt team from customer service, finance, marketing or HR, for example. The Black Belt role is usually full time, often for a term of two to three years, after which they return to operations. In effect, they become internal consultants working on improving the way the organisation works; changing the organisational systems and processes for the better.

✔ The **Master Black Belt (MBB)** receives the highest level of training and becomes a full-time professional Lean Six Sigma expert. The MBB will have extensive project management experience and should be fully familiar with the importance of the soft skills needed to manage change. An experienced MBB is likely to want to take on this role as a long-term career path, becoming a trainer, coach or deployment advisor, and working with senior executives to ensure the overall Lean Six Sigma programme is aligned to the strategic direction of the business. MBBs tend to move around from one major business to another after typically three or four years in one organisation. MBBs are likely to have been a Black Belt for at least two years before moving into this role.

Certification processes are operated in many organisations to ensure a set standard is reached through exams and project assessments. Certification processes are established in many countries, such as the British Quality Foundation and the American Society of Quality. Many large corporate businesses set up their own internal certification processes, with recognition given at high-profile company events to newly graduated 'belts'.

Where people are provided with an introduction to the topic – an Awareness programme – the term 'White Belt' has recently been utilised. No certification process is involved and these programmes vary in length from an hour or two through to a full day.

These events bring together the powerful concepts of Kaizen to involve people in continuously seeking to improve performance within the framework of DMAIC. That improvement comes from focusing on how the work gets done and how well.

Rapid improvement events can also be run as a series of half- or one-day workshops, over a period of five or six weeks. They follow the DMAIC framework, and particular emphasis is placed on the Define and Control phases. So, for example, the first workshop focuses on getting a clear definition of the problem to be tackled (Define), and so on. The aim is to tackle a closely scoped bite-sized problem using the expertise of the people actually involved in that process to solve it. They'll need someone with Lean Six Sigma experience as a facilitator, because they may need help using some of the tools and techniques required (for example, value stream maps – see Chapter 5). So often, the people doing the job know what's needed to put things right. You may well find that the solution is already known by the team, but historically they haven't been listened to. Implementation of the solution can thus be actioned quickly, much of it during the actual event. Rapid improvement events can provide the people doing the job with the opportunity to use their skills and knowledge.

In terms of time, the short duration of rapid improvement events compares to perhaps four months part time in a traditional DMAIC project, though the actual team hours may be similar.

As with a traditional DMAIC project, the Control phase is vital to ensure the improvement gain is maintained. Typical Lean improvement activities often neglect it.

Part II
Working with Lean Six Sigma

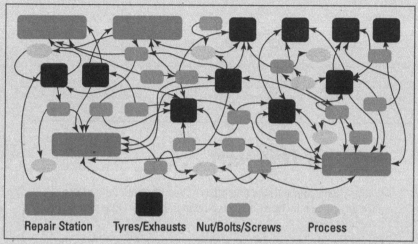

Repair Station   Tyres/Exhausts   Nut/Bolts/Screws   Process

© John Morgan and Martin Brenig-Jones

In this part . . .

✔ Know who your various and often quite different customers are or who they may be and how you can then determine their requirements.

✔ Use the information about who your customers are to form the basis of the measurement for your processes.

✔ Look at your processes, through either a process or value stream map or both, to see what the process really looks like and understand who does what, when, where and why.

Chapter 3

Identifying Your Customers

In This Chapter

▶ Finding out the fundamentals of processes

▶ Engaging with internal and external customers

▶ Creating a map of your processes

A ll organisations have a whole range of different customers – internal and external, large and small. Each organisation's processes should be designed and managed in a way that meets its customers' various needs. In this chapter we help you understand some process fundamentals necessary to focusing on your customers and their requirements.

Understanding the Process Basics

A process is a series of steps and actions that produce an output in the form of a product or service. Ideally, each process should add value in the eyes of the customer.

All work is a process, and a process is a blend of PEMME:

- ✔ **People:** Those working in or around the process. Do you have the right number in the right place, at the right time and possessing the right skills for the job? And do they feel supported and motivated?

- ✔ **Equipment:** The various items needed for the work. Items can be as simple as a stapler or as complicated as a lathe used in manufacturing. Consider whether you have the right equipment, located in an appropriate and convenient place, and being properly maintained and serviced.

- ✔ **Method:** How the work needs to be actioned – the process steps, procedures, tasks and activities involved.

✔ **Materials:** The things necessary to do the work – for example, the raw materials needed to make a product.

✔ **Environment:** The working area – perhaps a room or surface needs to be dust-free, or room temperature must be within defined parameters.

Focusing on PEMME helps you think differently when considering what a process actually is. (All the elements of PEMME also combine to influence the results from your processes in relation to variation – as covered in Chapter 7.)

PEMME tends to be the recognised format for considering processes, but the importance of 'information' should never be overlooked, and the extension of PEMME to PEMMIE can be helpful, especially when you're developing a value stream map – see Chapter 5.

Pinpointing the elements of a process

The concept of processes and PEMME applies to everything you do, from getting up in the morning, to making a cup of tea, to paying a bill. All of these activities can be broken down into a series of steps. The process model shown in Figure 3-1 has PEMME at its heart (the 'process'), but it also builds on PEMME and helps you think about the wider requirements of the process. To meet your customers' requirements (the CTQs – Critical to Quality – see Chapters 2 and 4), the process elements must be addressed.

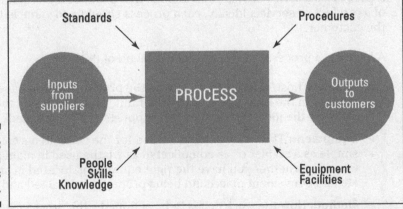

Figure 3-1:
Using a process model.

© John Morgan and Martin Brenig-Jones

Ensuring that the CTQs are understood and agreed on is the first require-ment of a process. More often than not, a lack of quality or rework is the direct result of not defining the customer's requirements properly. Even on apparently simple things, a little extra time spent in translating the voice of the customer and clarifying requirements can help save time and potential upset later on. Once the customer's requirements have been agreed, deter-mining your own requirements from suppliers is the next step. Now you're the customer, so spend time with your suppliers to ensure your needs are properly understood and agreed.

Make sure you have the right number of people working in the process, and that they have the necessary knowledge and skills. If they don't, appropriate training needs to be delivered.

You need procedures, too. These should describe precisely how the work gets done – the method – and must be developed, agreed, appropriately documented and kept up to date, especially in a culture of continuous improvement, where enhancements are regularly being made to the process. Importantly, they should be simple to follow and understand. Clear language and diagrams help ensure they're used to good effect.

Properly describing relevant standards is also sensible. They may well form part of the method, applying, for example, to regulatory requirements or service-level agreements that need to be followed. Like procedures, the standards should be documented in an easily accessible manner. Similarly, if budget constraints or authority limits on certain actions apply, management must ensure the people in the process know the details.

Equipment and facilities are needed to operate the process, and need to be capable of meeting or exceeding the customer requirements. These must be appropriate from day one, located in the right place and correctly maintained thereafter. Also ensure the environment is appropriate for the activity. The facilities link to the environment element of PEMME and could include having the right workspace, for example.

Identifying internal and external customers

All of your processes are likely to involve other people. Some of them prob-ably work in your organisation – your internal customers and suppliers. They're the people involved in the different steps of your process – they may be members of your team or department, but could also be in other depart-ments or functions. An internal supplier provides you with the inputs you need to start your work; for example, information, perhaps a schedule of available products, or an approved order. You're their internal customer.

Knowing who the internal customers and suppliers are, and how they fit into the picture, is important because together you form the end-to-end process, the value stream that ultimately provides the external customer with the service or product he's looking for. The external customer is someone outside of your organisation. He looks to you to meet his requirements and pays you accordingly.

Consider Figure 3-2. Department A produces output for Department B, which produces output for Department C, which provides the answer to an external customer enquiry. Each of these departments is involved in the process and needs to understand the objectives of the 'big process'.

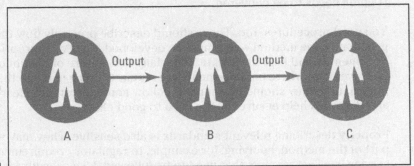

Figure 3-2: Identifying your internal customers.

© John Morgan and Martin Brenig-Jones

All too often, departments work in a vacuum, doing their own thing without regard for its impact on the end-to-end process. They may have their own targets, measures and priorities, for example. Possibly, the end-to-end process or value stream isn't even known; each team or department involved works as though their step in the process is independent of any others. In reality, the end-to-end process is a series of interdependent steps.

Internal customers and suppliers must understand their relationship and their different roles. If they don't, the external customers will experience poor service – the very people who should be viewed as the most important because they're paying an organisation for the services or products they provide.

Even if you're not directly dealing with the external customer, you're quite likely to be dealing with someone who is. So, understanding the bigger picture is important, and meeting the requirements of your internal customers could well be the key to successfully meeting the external customers' CTQs. Quality Function Deployment (QFD) is helpful here. QFD establishes a clear link between each process requirement and the end customer, making it easier for each employee to see the role that he plays in meeting customer requirements. We cover QFD in Chapter 12.

Getting a High-Level Picture

To really understand how the work gets done, and to identify just who the internal and external customers are, you need to draw a picture of the process. These pictures are known as *process* or *value stream maps* (covered in detail in Chapter 5). Often, however, organisations map their processes in minute detail. You can get lost in too much information. Keep it simple.

Also, the pictures or process maps tend to be based on what people think is happening in their organisation rather than on the reality of the *Gemba* – 'the place where the work gets done' (see Chapter 5 for more on this concept).

Before developing a process map, recognising that different process levels exist in an organisation is important. Right at the top of an organisation are some very high-level processes, such as 'business development'. These Level 1 processes break down into a number of sub-processes. Level 2 and 3 processes gradually increase the amount of detail. You move from the high-level 'what' to the increasingly detailed 'how'. Levels 4 or 5 cover the step-by-step procedural tasks and elements.

Our example in Figure 3-3 has 'business development' at Level 1 and shows the various sub-processes down to Level 3.

Figure 3-4 provides another example of Level 1 processes.

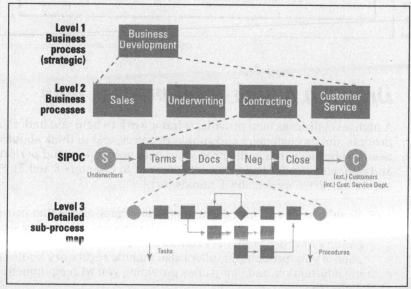

Figure 3-3: Process levels.

© John Morgan and Martin Brenig-Jones

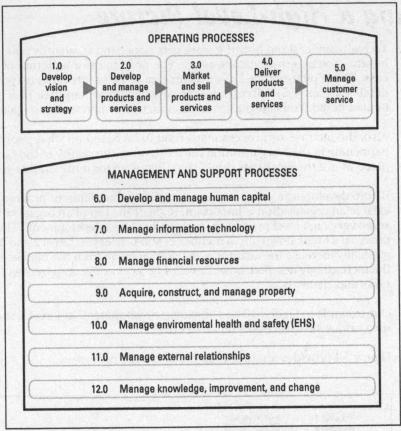

OPERATING PROCESSES

| 1.0 Develop vision and strategy | 2.0 Develop and manage products and services | 3.0 Market and sell products and services | 4.0 Deliver products and services | 5.0 Manage customer service |

MANAGEMENT AND SUPPORT PROCESSES

6.0   Develop and manage human capital

7.0   Manage information technology

8.0   Manage financial resources

9.0   Acquire, construct, and manage property

10.0   Manage enviromental health and safety (EHS)

11.0   Manage external relationships

12.0   Manage knowledge, improvement, and change

Figure 3-4: The APQC generic process framework.

Drawing a high-level process map

A high-level process map provides a framework to help you understand your process and its customers and suppliers better, and to think about what needs to be measured in the process to help you understand performance and opportunities for improvement (covered in Chapters 6 and 7). Figure 3-5 shows the *SIPOC model*. SIPOC stands for:

✔ **Suppliers:** The people, departments or organisations that provide you with the 'inputs' needed to operate the process. When they send you an enquiry or order form, the external customer is also included as a supplier in your process. Suppliers also include regulatory bodies providing information, and companies providing you with equipment or raw materials.

✔ **Inputs:** Forms or information, equipment or raw materials, or even the people you need to carry out the work. For people, the supplier may be the human resources department or an employment agency.

✔ **Process:** In the SIPOC diagram, the P presents a picture of the process steps at a relatively high level, usually Levels 2 or 3, as shown in Figure 3-3.

✔ **Outputs:** A list of the things that your process provides to the internal and external customers in seeking to meet their CTQs. Your outputs will become inputs to their processes.

✔ **Customers:** The different internal and external customers who'll receive your various process outputs.

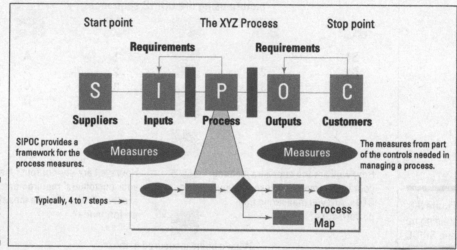

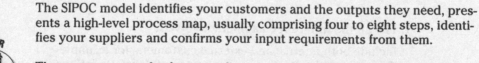

Figure 3-5:
The SIPOC
model.

© John Morgan and Martin Brenig-Jones

The SIPOC model identifies your customers and the outputs they need, presents a high-level process map, usually comprising four to eight steps, identifies your suppliers and confirms your input requirements from them.

The customer can also be a supplier, particularly of information needed by you.

In many ways, SIPOC should really be called COPIS, because when you create the diagram you start with the customer on the right-hand side of the model, before listing the outputs that go to him. Well, you almost start with the customer. First, you and the process team need to agree a start and stop point for the process, so that everyone in the team is clear about the parameters.

For example, your process may start with the external customer sending you an order form for one of your products and end when the product has been sent to him or you've issued an invoice. Once the process parameters are agreed, you next consider the customer – which is easier if you have a clear understanding of their CTQs.

The best way to create your SIPOC diagram is to gather your team around a large sheet of paper and follow these steps (Figure 3-6 provides an example of how it might look):

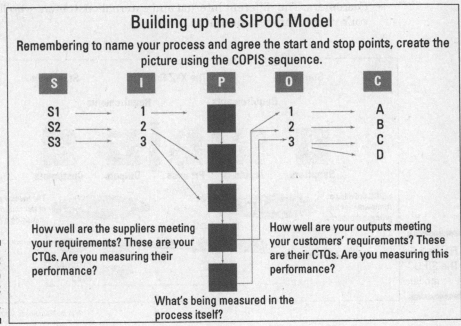

Building up the SIPOC Model

Remembering to name your process and agree the start and stop points, create the picture using the COPIS sequence.

How well are the suppliers meeting your requirements? These are your CTQs. Are you measuring their performance?

How well are your outputs meeting your customers' requirements? These are their CTQs. Are you measuring this performance?

What's being measured in the process itself?

© John Morgan and Martin Brenig-Jones

Figure 3-6: Building up the SIPOC model.

1. **List all the different customers involved.**

   Include both internal and external customers, for example 'Management', who may need reports or information. Consider third parties, such as regulatory bodies, where relevant. Segment external customers by the different outputs they receive.

2. **List all the outputs you send your customers.**

   Now you have your list of customers, what is it that you need to provide them with? Under the 'O' for outputs, make a list of the things you send them. Drawing arrows showing who receives what output can be useful.

3. Set out the steps in the process.

Use sticky notes to construct a high-level picture of the process. Typically, it involves four to eight steps. Don't go beyond eight steps because you'll be dealing with too much detail, too soon (Chapter 5 covers process and value stream mapping in detail, but the map starts here in the P of SIPOC). Again, as shown in Figure 3-6, using arrows to show which process steps produce outputs can be helpful, especially because not all of the outputs will come from the last step in the process.

Involving the step-by-step procedures of a process in your SIPOC diagram can make you lose your way in the various twists and turns that can occur. As a result, you may not be able to see the non-value-added steps. Spotting unnecessary activities is easier with high-level process documentation tools such as the SIPOC.

In Figure 3-5, the start and stop points are represented with the oval shapes, the process steps with the rectangular boxes, and points in the process involving questions with the diamond shapes. Diamonds are decision points, for example showing the need to do something different if you're dealing with product A or product B, or where different authority levels may come into operation in underwriting a loan, perhaps based on the loan value. Diamonds tend to be not so relevant in the SIPOC diagram, though there will be times when you need to use them. In Figure 3-5, we include one purely for reference. Figure 3-6 simply uses the square boxes.

4. List all the inputs you receive.

Include order forms and information, but also consider equipment or even personnel, depending on whether this is a new or existing process. Use the arrows to show where in the process these inputs go.

5. Identify where all your inputs come from.

Under the 'S' for supplier, list the sources of all your inputs; again, use the arrows to clarify who's supplying what. Remember that some of your customers will also be your suppliers.

SIPOC provides a helpful checklist, identifying who your customers are and the outputs that go to them. It highlights areas where greater clarity is needed, especially in relation to requirements and outputs. It also helps you focus on what needs to be measured; for example, how well are you delivering the outputs to your customers, and how well are your suppliers meeting your requirements of them? (Measurement is covered in more detail in Chapters 6 and 8, with Chapter 7 focusing on how you present your data and understand variation in your results.)

Creating a SIPOC process map provides an opportunity to begin thinking about the various elements involved in your process, whether you have all the information you need and if segmenting your customers is necessary.

Segmenting customers

In developing your SIPOC process map, you need to identify your customers and the outputs that go to them. Possibly, you classify or segment your customers in some way, for example by size or geographical location.

Think carefully about these different customers. Do they actually have different CTQs? Will the process outputs be the same for each segment, or will these vary to some degree?

We look at segmentation in a little more detail in Chapter 4, but ensure your SIPOC map and the thinking that accompanies it takes appropriate account of your different customer segments.

Chapter 4

Understanding Your Customers' Needs

In This Chapter

▶ Introducing Kano

▶ Hearing the voice of the customer

▶ Putting your customers first

▶ Gauging how well you do

*I*n focusing on our customers, we're looking to provide value for them. Amongst other things, this means the right products and services, at the right time, the right price and the right quality. And, of course, in the right place.

Throughout this book we make several references to the 'voice of the customer' and to CTQs (critical to quality requirements). The voice of the customer (VOC) helps you understand customer requirements. This expression describes information coming from the customer, perhaps through market research or face-to-face discussion, which enables you to determine your customers' CTQs and what value means to them. The CTQs are vital elements in Lean Six Sigma, providing you with the basis to assess how well you're performing in meeting your customers' requirements. This chapter looks at how to obtain the VOC and develop the CTQs.

Considering If You Can Kano

In striving to understand customers' requirements and their perception of value, it's useful to understand the Kano model, as shown in Figure 4-1.

Developed by Professor Kano at the University of Tokyo, the model looks at customer requirements and helps you understand how your customers will perceive the service and products you provide. The Kano model involves three main categories:

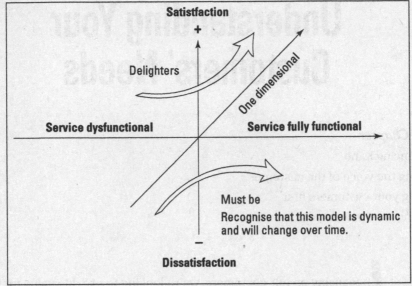

Figure 4-1:
Can you Kano? You must know the must-be requirements.

✔ **Must-bes:** These are sometimes referred to as the unspoken customer requirements. To the customer, they're so obviously required that she doesn't expect to have to spell them out. Meeting these requirements will not increase customer satisfaction; they're the absolute minimum the customer is expecting – so miss them at your peril. The must-be requirements are also sometimes referred to as *dissatisfiers*.

✔ **One-dimensionals:** The more of these requirements that are met, the higher the customer satisfaction. The requirements might relate to product features or elements of service delivery, or both. One-dimensionals are sometimes referred to as *satisfiers*.

✔ **Delighters:** Here, the customer is surprised and delighted by something you've done, a wow factor, and her satisfaction increases, even if some other elements haven't been delivered as well as they might.

Do remember, though, that over time things will change. A one-dimensional satisfier will become a must-be and delighters will become one-dimensionals.

Let's put all of this information into a context. What are your must-be requirements when your car is serviced? For me (John), I like to feel certain that the service has been carried out correctly – the oil, plugs and filters changed, and so on. Some years ago that would have been all I'd have expected and hoped for. But delighters started to appear. The car was cleaned inside and out! The garage offered to collect and return the car or provide a courtesy car while mine was being serviced. Other garages offered a while-you-wait service with complimentary coffee and biscuits.

Very quickly, these delighters became one-dimensionals. And, for some customers, they became must-be requirements! The model is dynamic. However, bear in mind that other customers will also exist who only want a basic, no-frills service. They'll see no value in the extras they're paying for, albeit in the hidden costs linked to the service charge. Understanding your different customer segments is vital if you're to deliver value and meet their CTQs (see Chapter 2).

Obtaining the Voice of the Customer

We find out what our customers want by talking with, listening to and observing them. You can source the customer's voice in lots of places, such as market research results, focus group discussions, survey results hits on your organisation's website and customer complaints. The trick is to translate what the customer says into a measurable requirement – the critical to quality (CTQ) customer requirement. You gather input from your customers in order to understand their needs, identify the key issues and translate them into terms that mean something to your organisation and that you can measure.

Listening to the voice of the customer (VOC) is about determining your customer requirements, not determining solutions to meet those requirements – it isn't about jumping to conclusions about what they mean, either!

Doing things properly usually involves a number of conversations with your customer, the process owner and all the other people involved in the process. The *process owner* is the person responsible for the process, for example a manager or director; she needs to ensure the process is designed and managed to meet the CTQs so she must understand what the customer is saying.

On occasion, the customer may not be totally clear about her requirements. Reflect back your interpretations to ensure they're correct.

Taking an outside-in view

Many organisations assume they know what their customers want – but this isn't always the case. Even when you try to be objective, the fact that you know your products and services so well, and understand your workplace's jargon, means seeing things from your customers' perspective is actually quite difficult.

Customers aren't all the same. They come in all sorts of different shapes and sizes, and your customers have different requirements, even for the 'same' product or service. Identifying the different customer segments that your organisation deals with, and recognising that each segment may have different CTQs, is essential. For example, a small company may be happy to receive your products on a monthly basis, whereas a larger business may need daily deliveries of those same products.

Segmenting your customers

Grouping your customers into segments helps you see your customers' different requirements. By segmenting them, you can develop the right products and services for each group, and create specific measures that help you understand your performance in meeting their differing requirements. To help you segment your customers, list some categories that describe both your current customers and the people or organisations that you consider to be potential customers. You might also look at past customers in this way, too.

Consider the following segmentation categories in relation to your customers:

- Industry
- Size
- Spend
- Geographical location
- End use
- Product characteristics
- Buying characteristics
- Price/cost sensitivity
- Age
- Gender
- Socioeconomic factors
- Frequency of purchase/use

- ✔ Impact/opinion leader
- ✔ Loyalty
- ✔ Channel
- ✔ Technology

Naturally, you need to determine the categories that are relevant to your own organisation, but this list provides a good starting point. If appropriate, you can also create umbrella customer segments to include, for example, frequency of purchase and spend.

Prioritising your customers

Every customer is important, but some customers use your services more frequently or are more critical to your business than others. You may need to devote more time and resources to these particular customers.

Italian economist Vilfredo Pareto developed the idea of the 80:20 rule, when he described how 80 per cent of the wealth of his country was in the hands of 20 per cent of the population. Your organisation may well have a 'vital few' customers, perhaps 20 per cent who provide you with 80 per cent of your margin. If that's the case, those customers are very important to the ongoing success of your business and understanding their requirements and their perceptions of your performance in some detail is crucial.

You could prioritise by customer segment, but you need to understand how best to prioritise your customers for your organisation. For many organisations, the priority may be revenue, but more sensibly it should be profit. As your understanding of your customers increases, you'll find it easier to determine your organisation's priorities.

Truly focusing on customers, as opposed to simply saying you are, requires real investment in understanding your customers' needs. Knowing who your customers are, how they're segmented and which ones are your priority is a vital prerequisite to your research and data gathering. Identifying the wrong customers, or not being aware of the different segments, can mean you collect information on requirements or customers that aren't related to the process or service you're designing.

Your customers may be both internal and external. Thinking in terms of processes helps you identify where you need to focus and highlights who your internal customers are.

Researching the Requirements

Researching your customers follows a natural progression. You start with potentially no information about customers, and end up with a collection of quantified, prioritised customer needs and expectations. You might also gain information about how your competitors succeed in meeting their – and your! – customers' needs.

Start by investigating what information you already have and then determine the gaps in your customer information. For example, if your proposed product or service is a variation on something you've done before, you may have a lot of information in your organisation's files. Likewise, if one of your competitors already offers the product or service, you may find some useful industry information.

You then need to develop a customer research plan that moves you from where you are right now to where you need or want to be, so you can close the gaps.

Use Table 4-1 to help you determine the sequencing of your research plan.

Table 4-1	Researching the Requirements	
Input	*Research Method*	*Output: What You Get*
No information	Interview/focus group What is important?	Customer wants and needs (general ideas, unprioritised, not clarified, all qualitative)
Known preliminary customer wants and needs	Interview/focus group Which are most important?	Customer wants and needs (clarified, more specific, preliminary prioritisation) Customer input to list of competitors, best-in-class
Qualitative, prioritised customer wants and needs	Survey Face-to-face Written mail Telephone Electronic	Quantified prioritised customer wants and needs Competitor comparative information

Table 4-1 helps you think about the information you currently have, and the information you need to get and how to go about getting it.

If you have no information to begin with, the first step is interviewing some representative customers, perhaps in a focus group, to help you understand what's important to them about the service or product you're offering. You should be able to capture some general ideas about their wants and needs; though these are unlikely to be totally clear, and you probably won't be able to prioritise them yet. This first step helps you determine your customers' preliminary needs and enables you to now undertake some more detailed interviews or focus groups.

The second row in Table 4-1 shows how more detailed analysis should lead you to a clearer picture of customer requirements, and at least a preliminary prioritisation of them. This stage also gives you the opportunity to ask the customers about their experience of your competitors.

With this clear picture, you can move to the third row in the table. Your interviews and focus groups will have been run with a relatively small number of customers. This approach is described as *qualitative* research. You now need to test their views and opinions by conducting research with a larger number of customers. This approach is described as *quantitative* research, involving a survey.

Quantitative research is important – it enables you to feel confident that you have a true picture of customer wants and needs. The results from the qualitative research may have been skewed in some way if you had inadvertently included unrepresentative customers. For example, you may have carried out research on a product aimed at the high end of the market, but interviewed customers from a different market segment by mistake. The same issue can occur where customers fail to respond to your survey. Is there a particular reason why they haven't, but others have? This situation is known as 'non-response bias' and can be just as troublesome.

As you plan your research, be aware of the following issues:

✔ The customer may offer you a 'solution' rather than express her real needs. Ask the customer 'Why do you want this?' until you truly understand the real need.

By asking its customers to express their real wants, Xerox refocused its entire business on its customers' need for documents rather than just photocopiers.

✔ Different customers may perceive the same product or service differently. For example, a shirt that shows off the designer's logo may command a premium price over a similar article without the logo – but only for some customers.

Toyota offers the Lexus version of many of its cars to appeal to its more luxury-conscious customers, and uses the slogan 'The relentless pursuit of perfection' to describe this brand.

✔ Remember that how your customers say they'll use a product or service isn't always the same as how they actually use it!

✔ External customers generally express *effectiveness needs* – needs that relate to the value they receive from the product or service. Internal customers, on the other hand, tend to express *efficiency needs* – needs that relate to the amount of resources allocated to or consumed in meeting customers' needs.

Interviewing your customers

Customer interviews are helpful as a research technique. The aims of customer interviews are to *understand* a specific customer's needs and requirements, values and points of view on service issues, product/service attributes and performance indicators/measures. Customer interviews are useful and enable you to explore issues with them during your customer research:

✔ At the beginning, to learn what's important to customers, which supports the development of hypotheses about customer values.

✔ In the middle, to clarify points or to better understand why a particular issue is important to customers.

✔ At the end, to clarify findings, to get ideas and suggestions, or to test ideas with customers.

The advantages of customer interviews are:

✔ Flexibility – you can obtain more detailed explanations by probing and clarifying.

✔ Greater complexity – you can administer highly complex questionnaires/surveys and can explain questions to interviewees.

✔ Ability to reach all customer types – you can interview populations that are difficult or impossible to reach by other methods.

✔ High response rate – the degree to which the information collection process reaches all targets is higher.

✔ Assurance that instructions are followed – because the interview is taking place in person, you can ensure that all steps are followed.

The disadvantages of customer interviews are:

✔ They're costly to administer.

✔ They're the least reliable form of data collection because the interviewer may influence the responses to the questionnaire.

✔ Less anonymity is possible.

- Interview time is limited to 15–20 minutes (business-to-business customer interviews are generally of 45–50 minutes' duration).

- Generating supportable quantitative evidence can be difficult.

- Results can be difficult to analyse.

- The sample size may not be sufficient to draw supportable conclusions.

- Use of different interviewers asking questions in a particular way may result in bias (see the 'Avoiding Bias' section later in this chapter).

- Positive response bias may occur, whereby people give higher ratings in personal interviews.

Ask open questions to get the interviewee talking, rather than asking a series of closed questions that simply elicit a yes or no response. The key is to listen to what the customer is saying – her responses often provide the answers to some of the specific issues you need information on.

Focusing on focus groups

Focus groups are interviews, usually involving between six to ten people at the same time in the same group. Typically, they run for two to three or four hours. Focus groups are a powerful means to capture views and opinions, to evaluate services or test new ideas, or (in the context of this chapter) to clarify and prioritise customer requirements.

Essentially, a focus group is a carefully planned discussion designed to obtain perceptions concerning a defined area of interest in a non-threatening environment. Listening to the members of the focus group is key!

The focus group participants should share characteristics that relate to the focus group topic; all being in the same customer segment, for example. To avoid bias, running more than one focus group is sensible; run three as a minimum.

Focus groups are used:

- To clarify and define customer needs.

- To gain insights into the prioritisation of needs.

- To test concepts and receive feedback.

- As a next step after customer interviews or a preliminary step in a survey process.

The participants will be asked to thoroughly discuss very few topics, and often only three or four questions will be posed during the focus group. These will be very general questions, such as 'What do you find important in service delivery, generally?' or 'What is it that makes you feel you have received good or bad service?'

Focus groups aim to get the participants talking and you listening, ideally recording the discussion for subsequent analysis. Table 4-2 lists the advantages and disadvantages of using focus groups.

Table 4-2	Pros and Cons of Using Focus Groups
Use Focus Groups When:	*Don't Use Focus Groups When:*
You need to make or confirm market segmentation decisions.	The environment is emotionally charged and more information of any type is likely to intensify the conflict.
Hypotheses about the market and customer values need to be developed or tested in exploratory or preliminary studies.	Highly valid, quantitative data is needed.
A communication gap appears to exist between your company and the market segment.	Other methodologies can produce either better quality or more economical information.
Insight is needed into customer perceptions of potentially complicated topics where their opinions and attitudes may influence your course of action, perhaps in launching a new product.	The researcher can't ensure the confidentiality of sensitive information.
Synergy among individuals will be useful in creating ideas.	You're trying to sell products.
Hypotheses need to be developed in preparation for a broad survey or large-scale study.	
A higher value is placed on capturing open-ended comments than data from the target audience.	

Considering customer surveys

You can run customer surveys in a number of ways, including by postal questionnaire or electronically by email or the Internet. They enable you to measure the importance or performance of customer needs and requirements. You can check out your focus group findings with a larger group of customers.

The pros and cons of customer surveys are shown in Table 4-3.

Table 4-3	Pros and Cons of Customer Surveys
Advantages	*Disadvantages*
Low cost	Low rate of return
Efficiency of large samples	Non-responsive bias
Ready access to hard-to-reach respondents	Little control
No interviewer bias (though beware of the questions)	Limitations on questions
Potential for exhibits	Potential misunderstanding of questions or rating scale
High reliability and validity	Oversimplification of format
	Slowness – requires development
	Requires pre-testing
	Difficulty of obtaining names

Using observations

Observations are another way of identifying your customers' needs and CTQs. Observing a customer is an effective way to understand how she uses and views your products and services. For example, by observing the purchasing patterns of customers, supermarkets can strategically position the products in their store to increase sales. Key products appealing to elderly customers are positioned on middle shelves so they don't have to bend or stretch to reach them. The CTQs for this particular customer segment have then been met.

Toyota allocates some of its engineers to ride as passengers in customers' cars, enabling them to observe their customers' driving first-hand. One result of such observations was the introduction of drink holders in Toyota's cars. The engineers observed children in the back seats holding drinks but having nowhere to put them. The inclusion of drink holders may not have increased sales as such, but they're now a standard requirement for most buyers, and their inclusion in a car as 'standard' helps maintain or enhance the general level of customer satisfaction. Drink holders are a good example of Kano in practice, where their introduction was a delighter or wow factor, but their inclusion in cars and vans quickly became a 'must be'.

Avoiding Bias

Whichever approach you take to collecting voice of customer (VOC) information (see the earlier sections in this chapter), you need to recognise the potential for bias. Possibly you may ask the wrong questions, or ask the wrong customers because you haven't segmented them properly, or simply misinterpret, deliberately or otherwise, what the customer says.

You need to really listen to what the customer says – not to what you think they're saying or you'd like them to say! In a focus group, asking very open questions is best. Then make sure you listen to the responses. Leading customers through a series of closed questions results in closed answers, which are then open to interpretation and bias.

On questionnaires, the wording of questions is vital. Each question should ask only one question. So, for example, you may ask the customer to rate your performance on a scale of one to five, where one is poor and five is super. If you pose a question such as, 'How well do you feel we perform in terms of speed and accuracy?', you may receive a response relating to only speed or accuracy, not both.

The fictional British television series *Yes, Prime Minister* provides a great example of how asking closed questions can lead to two different answers to the question: 'Would you be in favour of reintroducing National Service?' In the first survey, the questions include 'Are you worried about the number of young people without jobs?', 'Are you worried about the rise in crime among teenagers?' and 'Do you think young people welcome some authority and leadership in their lives?'.

Given the previous questions, the respondent is almost obliged to say yes to reintroducing National Service. The bias is increased if the results are published without reference to the previous questions.

Asking a different set of questions elicits the opposite response. Questions include 'Are you worried about the danger of war and the growth of armaments?', 'Do you think there's a danger in giving young people guns and teaching them to kill?' and 'Do you think it's wrong to force people to take up arms against their will?'. This time the respondent can only answer that she *opposes* the reintroduction of National Service.

Beware of the huge potential for bias, be it innocently introduced or deliberately created.

Considering Critical To Quality Customer Requirements

When you've collected the VOC information (see the earlier sections of this chapter), you need to develop the CTQs. Write the CTQs in a measurable form: they provide the basis for your process measurement set. This set will enable you to put the right measures in place to assess your performance (see Chapter 6).

CTQs help you focus on your customer requirements and provide the foundation for your measurement data. Figure 4-2 provides a framework to help you define your CTQs. You can identify two key issues – getting through to the right person and speed. Looking at the first example, the CTQ for getting through to the right person first time is straightforward to understand and to measure, but to define the CTQ covering speed you need to go back to the customer and agree what 'quickly' means. You might then define a second measurable requirement as 'The call is answered within 10 seconds'.

Voice of the Customer	Key issues(s)	CTQ
You either put me on hold, or put me through to the wrong department or person	The customer wants to be put through quickly to the right person	• Customer gets through to the correct person the first time
You send me an invoice at different times of the month	Consistent monthly billing	• Customer bill received same day of the month
It takes too long to process my mortgage application and get me the money when it's needed	Speed up loan so I get the money on time	• Customer receives cheque on customer request date

Figure 4-2: Determining the CTQs.

© John Morgan and Martin Brenig-Jones

Without this type of data, you won't know how you're performing in meeting the customer requirements – information that determines where improvement actions are required.

A CTQ shouldn't prescribe a solution. A CTQ should be measurable and, where appropriate, have upper and lower specification limits and a target value. A CTQ should be a positive statement about what the customer wants rather than a negative statement about what the customer doesn't want.

Say you agree an arrival time window for a customer's boiler to be repaired. The upper specification limit might be midday, the lower specification 8 a.m. and the target time 10 a.m., for example. So you aim to be there for 10 a.m. plus or minus two hours, but, of course, you also aim to repair the boiler and restore heat for the customer!

The affinity diagram (see Figure 2-3 in Chapter 2) provides a useful format for sorting VOC information into themes. These themes can then be broken down into more detailed elements, as a CTQ tree, as shown in Figure 4-3.

First level	Second level	
Friendly staff	Willing to answer question Shows respect	
Knowledgeable staff	Knows the loan process	
	Knows the market	You will probably need to go down to more levels. And remember the CTQs need to be measureable
	Understands my situations	
Speed	Money when I need it	
	Application fast to fill out	
Accurate	Don't make mistakes	
	Give me the right rate	

Figure 4-3: Developing a CTQ tree.

© John Morgan and Martin Brenig-Jones

The example in Figure 4-3 is from a bank that has taken the various customer statements and comments from a survey and sorted them into themes using an affinity diagram. The high-level themes are shown in the first level; the second level shows some of the comments within the theme. These comments break down into another level of detail (rather like the branches on a tree) to ensure the requirements are properly understood – thus a CTQ tree.

When you develop CTQs, you can usually group customer requirements under common sets of headings. We do this, and show a selection of examples and potential measures, in Table 4-4.

This common list allows you to structure the process of gathering requirements and reduces the risk of you missing a CTQ.

Table 4-4	Some Common CTQs	
CTQ grouping	*Examples*	*Measures*
Speed	Bills paid on time (in and out)	Elapsed times and deviation from target
	Deliveries made on time	Turn-around times
	Time to answer calls	Call answer rate
	Turn-around time on IT project delivery	Call abandon rate
Accuracy	Orders containing the correct information	Number of defects in orders, deliveries, products or software
	Computer system that works	Number of calls to helpdesk
		Number of bugs reported by users testing a new computer system or a program change
Capacity	Needs to cope with the right volume of orders/number of simultaneous enquiries	Number of items per order
		Number of clients
		Number of concurrent users
		Number of orders per day
Data/information	Easy access to order details and status	Salesperson can access order details and status within five minutes of request while on the road
	Software developer needs to understand how a software module works before changing it	Time spent converting data and cleansing data
		Percentage of software modules not meeting development standards
Safety	No customers or staff injured on company premises	Score on monthly safety audit, so, for example, number of injuries, near misses, and time between these incidents
Compliance	Data Protection Act	Complies
	Consumer Credit Act	
	Health and Safety at Work Act	

(continued)

Table 4-4 *(continued)*

CTQ grouping	Examples	Measures
Security	Very difficult to defraud the company either from within or externally	Customers' or suppliers' risk rating
		Score on six-monthly security audit
		Maximum Risk Priority Number (RPN) rating from a Failure Modes Effects Analysis (FMEA) – a prevention technique covered in Chapter 10
		Time since last FMEA performed
Money	Cost of supplies	Ratio of size of order in cost terms to customer's risk rating
	Commissions paid	
	Limits on size of order	
People	Staff need to be adequately trained	Approval review scores on requirements documents
	Need access to key staff to assist with requirements, design, testing and so on	Approval review scores on design documents
		Scores employees achieved on post-training exams
	All functions properly consulted on requirements and participate fully in requirements review and design reviews	Hours worked on project with day job
		Employees' scores on quarterly HR questionnaire
Professionalism	Integrity	Scores on knowledge tests
	Knowledge	Scores on post-delivery follow-up calls to customers
	Courtesy	Scores on HR psychometric tests
	Availability	
		Number of calls not answered first time by the first point of contact
		Call answer rate
		Call abandon rate

CTQ grouping	Examples	Measures
Social conscience	Ethnic mix	Percentage of turnover given to charitable causes
	Equal salary structures for men and women	
	Contributions to charity	
Environment	Recycling policy	Percentage of offices with recycling containers in daily use
	Biodegradable packaging	
	Emissions	
Changes/ re-schedules to original order or contract	Conflicting requirements between customer and supplier	Ratio of cost of change to extra charge to the customer

Establishing the Real CTQs

Interpreting a customer's wants and needs to form an appropriate and realistic CTQ that can be measured presents a big challenge. Often, customers jump to preconceived solutions and prescribe those solutions as part of their requirements. If you take these customers' requirements literally, several problems can occur, including missing their real requirements. The product or service you provide them with may then not be quite right. In turn, misunderstanding could then lead to you delivering more expensive or less efficient solutions than the particular CTQs require.

The secret to finding the real CTQs is to keep challenging the customer by asking 'Why?' until the need falls into one of the general categories in Table 4-4 or is otherwise clear. Below are two, disguised, real-life examples:

✔ An internal customer said, 'We need one integrated SAP system handling all orders instead of splitting orders between our different European divisions.' But *why* do we need this?

The internal customer responded: 'Because customers think we are unprofessional.' But *why* do customers think that? The internal customer's answer explained that customers get more than one order acknowledgement if the order is split between divisions.

This answer gives us the real CTQ: 'Customers require single order acknowledgement for all orders.' In Table 4-4, this CTQ comes under the Data/information category. You may find several solutions to meet this requirement without going to the expense of a single integrated SAP system.

✔ An internal customer asks for a web-based order enquiry system. But *why* does she need this? She responds that enquiries currently take ages.

But why do enquiries take so long? The current process involves having to go to four different screens to get the information needed. By asking why speed is important, we discover that the customer is left waiting on the phone, but she expects the answer within 30 seconds.

The real CTQ becomes: 'Customers' order enquiries by telephone should be satisfied within 30 seconds', which comes under the Speed category in Table 4-4. As with the first example, there could be several solutions to meeting the CTQ – the web-based idea may not be the most appropriate or economical.

Prioritising the requirements

Clarifying your customers' CTQs (which we describe in the previous section) is vital, but you also need to find out which of the CTQs are especially important.

You can prioritise your CTQs in a number of ways. You can simply ask your customers to weight their own CTQs, or you can use a simple tool such as *paired comparisons*.

The paired comparisons technique provides a way to determine priorities and weight the importance of criteria. Using the paired comparisons tool forces you to make choices by looking at each pair from a list of options – in this case, a list of CTQs. Instead of asking your customers to identify their top choice, you ask them to select their preference from each pair.

For example, if you have five CTQs, you ask: 'Do you prefer A or B? A or C? A or D? A or E?' After A, you compare B and C, B and D, and B and E and so on.

You can use this technique face-to-face, over the phone or by using a 'voting grid' like that shown in Figure 4-4, where participants circle their choices for each comparison. In the example, ten preferences will be expressed. Imagine that A comes out with 4 votes, C gets 3, E has 2, but B receives only 1, and D none at all. It's clear that the most important CTQs are A and C, with E reasonably important in the middle, whereas B and D are of little consequence by comparison. In these circumstances you now know how especially important it is to get A and C right for the customer.

Item	Description				
A		A/B	A/C	A/D	A/E
B			B/C	B/D	B/E
C				C/D	C/E
D					D/E
E					

© John Morgan and Martin Brenig-Jones

Figure 4-4: Paired comparisons: Do you prefer this or that?

Measuring performance using customer-focused measures

Talking about being customer-focused is much easier than actually *being* customer-focused. Using *outside-in* thinking and measures to assess your CTQ performance is one way to help you think differently and focus on the customer.

Determining your CTQs provides a basis for your measures. In Chapter 6 we look at measurement and data collection in some detail, but here we take a brief look at some of the different thinking you need in order to focus on your customers.

Think about what your customer sees and experiences in terms of your organisation's products, services and performance in meeting customers' requirements. Consider, for example, whether being a customer of your organisation is easy. Many organisations are internally focused and think negatively of their customers – but ultimately customers pay the bills.

Try to drag yourself outside your organisation and take a look in – outside-in thinking. Think about what your customers see and consider whether they're happy.

Understanding what your customers measure is helpful. Ask yourself whether your customers measure the same things as you – and then think about how their data compare with yours. Consider why differences may be evident. Then think about what your customers do with the output from your processes: where it fits in their processes. Here's a real-life example:

Airlines make money when their planes are in the air. When a plane is out of commission, perhaps for servicing, the airline makes no money – the company needs the plane up and flying again as quickly as possible.

TRUE STORIES

Staff in General Electric's (GE) aircraft engines division discovered the value of outside-in thinking when they realised their customers were measuring GE's performance a little differently from the way the organisation did. GE would receive an engine into their servicing process – and their clock would start. When the service was complete, their clock stopped and they reported that this service had taken x hours to complete.

What they were forgetting was the fact that their customers were counting the time from when the engine came off the plane to the time when it was put back on – the *wing-to-wing time*. The phrase and the thinking caught on. Then-chief executive officer, Jack Welch, deployed this concept throughout the GE operations and divisions, worldwide.

Think about how your measures measure up. Is there scope for wing-to-wing thinking in your processes?

Chapter 5

Determining the Chain of Events

In This Chapter

▶ Following a chain of events from start to finish using process stapling

▶ Drawing a spaghetti diagram to see how the work gets done

▶ Creating a map of the process

As a manager, your role is to work on the processes that you manage with improvement in mind. You therefore need to know precisely how these processes work. Having an up-to-date picture of how things are done makes DMAIC (Define, Measure, Analyse, Improve and Control) improvement projects far easier to undertake (dive into Chapter 2 for more on doing the DMAIC).

The Measure phase of DMAIC is about understanding how and how well the work gets done. We look at the 'how well' aspect in Part III; our focus here is to understand how the work currently gets done. Only after you understand how the process works *now* can you see the opportunities for improvement in your process and manage performance better.

Finding Out How the Work Gets Done

How to draw a process map is the main focus of this chapter. We look at two types: the deployment flowchart and the value stream map. These maps build on the high-level SIPOC diagram explained in Chapter 3, and provide really helpful pictures of how the work gets done.

Before you draw any kind of process map, visit the workplace and see for yourself what's really happening. The Japanese refer to this observation as 'going to the Gemba'.

Genning up on the Gemba

The Gemba is a Japanese term for the *actual place* – that is, where the action is. Only in the Gemba can you truly see how things are done and it's the only place where real improvement can occur. You may be able to draw up new ways of doing the work in some central management location, or in an engineering office, but the reality is the Gemba. That's where things are defined, and refined, to produce genuine and effective change.

You're likely to find surprises waiting for you in the Gemba. Very often you'll find the process is being carried out differently to how you thought it was happening, especially when more than one team is involved. We cover techniques such as *process stapling* and *spaghetti diagrams* in this chapter. These techniques help you to see the reality of your workplace and enable you to identify unnecessary steps and eliminate waste. (We wade through waste in detail in Chapter 9.)

Practising process stapling

Process stapling offers one way to really understand the process and the chain of events. For example, *process stapling* means taking a customer order and literally walking it through the entire process step by step as though you were the order.

No matter where the order goes, you go too. By following the order you start to see what really happens, who does what and why, how, where and when they do it.

Carrying out a process stapling exercise with a small team of people can be an ideal first step. Sometimes, there can be advantages in beginning the exercise from the end of the process and working backwards. People will be less familiar with this 'reverse flow', helping them think more carefully about things.

The nearby sidebar 'Process stapling in action' demonstrates the power of this technique. You begin to understand all the steps in the process and how much time and movement is involved in carrying out the work. Process stapling helps you identify a number of improvement opportunities, even if you don't use the exercise to create a spaghetti diagram or process map.

Process stapling in action

This example reflects our experience of process stapling in at least one of our client organisations. Ann receives a customer order – she needs to input some information to the system, print out an internal form, add some additional information to it and then send it to Brian.

You now need to 'staple' this form to yourself and take it over to Brian (imagine attaching it to your clothing, for example). Brian is some distance away. Immediately, you have a sense of how much transport is involved.

When you get to Brian, you find that his first action is to correct all of Ann's mistakes. You ask Ann whether she's aware that she'd got things wrong. She's not happy about this, as she thinks she'd been doing what Brian needed, and had always done it this way. Ann tells you that Brian has never mentioned anything about her mistakes. You find that Brian never bothers

to tell Ann about the errors, which had been caused by misunderstanding, because he finds it easier to correct the mistakes himself.

After Brian corrects the errors, he sends the papers to Clare. You're dismayed to find that Clare sits next to Ann – shame the papers didn't go straight to Clare in the first place!

Clare tells you that this step is a complete waste of time. She's told her manager this, but her manager says the step is an important element of Clare's work. Clare just checks that the system is updated, that certain information is in the right box on the form and that Brian has put his signature on the form. She finds this task boring and has never yet found a case that needs correction, so she simply puts these items to one side, lets the work build up and then clears them all on a Friday afternoon before going home.

You might, for example, spot scope for tidying up the workplace, making it easier and safer to find things. (We shine a light on neatness in Chapter 10.) The process stapling exercise helps you spot the frustrations in the process, such as inconsistencies and 'why-on-earth-do-we-do-this?' activities. You can then see the steps that add value and those that don't. (We unveil value in Chapter 9.)

It's not uncommon for only 10–15 per cent of the steps in a process to add value, and more often than not, the 'thing' going through the process spends as little as 1 per cent of the total process time in these steps.

When introducing the idea of process stapling, you may find some people telling you that this is what they already do. But what they actually do is get a group of people in a room and use sticky notes to help draw up the process. They're missing the point! The picture they draw will be what they think is happening. Process stapling enables you to see what's really happening.

Try taking photos of each step in the process. Apart from providing an ideal record of what you've seen, photos enable you to make an effective presentation to management of what you've found. Be prepared for them to be surprised. You can have fun taking the pictures (but not of the managers falling off their chairs in shock, however!), especially if you act the role of the thing going through the process.

As your understanding of the process increases, you're likely to find real value in working with your customers to extend the process stapling concept to incorporate their activities with yours. In this way, you can work out how your process and its output link to your customer's process, what your customer's process looks like and how your customer uses your process outputs.

Extending process stapling provides great insight into how you can generate improvements in your process that really add value to your customer's experience and make an impact that delights him. The technique can also lead to joint improvement activity with a DMAIC project being carried out in concert with your customer.

Drawing spaghetti diagrams

A spaghetti diagram provides a picture of what's happening in the process in terms of movement. The diagram tracks the movement of the thing or things going through the process, including the flow of information and the people carrying out the work.

In Figure 5-1 we show a pretty confused series of movements in a garage as an example. You can apply the technique to any working area, including your office or even your home. You could even use a screen shot of an order entry application, for example, as the "map" and then trace the path of the computer cursor as the agent fills out a form. Spaghetti diagrams aren't restricted to operations that are physically spread out.

Think about the movements you make and the distance you travel when undertaking tasks such as making photocopies, picking up your printing or making a cup of tea.

The spaghetti diagram may throw up some real surprises about how much movement happens in your organisation, including how often things go back and forth. This technique helps you identify waste and provides a visual catalyst to stimulate change in your workplace.

You may already have used this technique at home! If you've installed a new kitchen, you'll know the importance of the triangle formed by the sink, cooker and fridge.

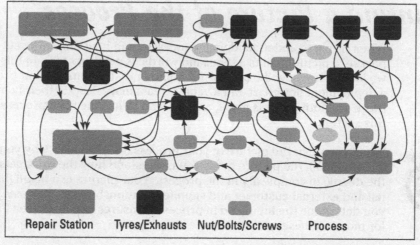

Figure 5-1:
A spaghetti
diagram.

Repair Station   Tyres/Exhausts   Nut/Bolts/Screws   Process

TIP

The different shades used in Figure 5-1 have no special significance, but you do need to distinguish between the movement of people, materials and information. When you create a spaghetti diagram, you may want to use a current office plan, for example showing where the furniture, equipment and power points are located. Make sure the plan really is current and that it includes all additional items, including those boxes in the corner that seem to have appeared from nowhere.

In developing a spaghetti diagram you can measure how far and why people are moving. You may be able to make some simple changes to your office layout to reduce the distance moved, or even to avoid it completely. You could even use a long ball of string or a pedometer to help you develop a more accurate diagram and better understand the movement involved. Recording the total distance travelled on the baseline of the diagram and then doing the same for the new and improved method is good practice. You then have a measure of the extent of improvement made.

When you use process stapling and spaghetti diagrams together, you may see the opportunity for a significant reduction in wasted movement and in other non-value-added steps too. So, in the process stapling example described in the nearby sidebar, is Brian's step necessary? If it were, would sitting Ann, Brian and Clare more closely together make sense?

Unnecessary travelling and movement waste so much time. Siting the relevant people and equipment together is often a relatively simple way of reducing waste and processing time. We look at waste in more detail in Chapter 9.

Painting a Picture of the Process

When trying to understand your processes and how the work gets done, the phrase 'a picture paints a thousand words' is certainly true. In this section we look at two specific options for painting that picture of your process – a deployment flowchart and a value stream map. Despite their names, these are both process maps, and we tend to use the term process map in this section.

When you paint the picture of your process, keep in mind why you're doing it. Developing the picture helps you understand how the work gets done and the degree of complexity in the process. Your picture can highlight the internal and external customer and supplier relationships or *interfaces,* and help you determine the input and in-process measures you need (see Chapter 8 for more on these).

You're not painting this particular picture as the specification for a computer system change, so keep things simple. This picture is for you and will help you manage and improve the process. You're drawing a 'current state' picture to see how things are done *now*.

A 'future state' map shows how the process could be undertaken to achieve a higher level of performance at some future point. Achieving that performance may be harder and could result in the need for a DMAIC project (see Chapter 2 for a detailed overview of DMAIC). When you've drawn and implemented your picture of a future state map, it becomes the current state map. With continuous improvement in mind, you now need to develop a new future state picture.

Your picture can provide a useful framework that prompts a whole range of questions:

- ✔ Who are the customers that have expectations of the process?

- ✔ Why is the process done? What is its purpose? Does everyone involved understand the purpose?

- ✔ What are the value-added and non-value-added steps?

- ✔ How can you carry out essential non-value-added steps using minimal resources?

- ✔ What are the critical success factors – that is, the things you must do well?

- ✔ Why is the process done when it is done?

- ✔ Why are tasks in the process carried out in that order? Are all the steps involved in the process necessary? Do all the steps add value for the customer?

✔ Why is the process carried out by a particular person or people?

✔ What measurement is in place to assess performance and identify possible improvement opportunities? Think in particular of how you might identify and measure those parts of the process that are repetitive and important to ensuring the process conforms to requirements.

✔ What is the cycle time involved in the process? Why is the cycle time longer than the unit time?

✔ What are the barriers that prevent the supplier from producing a quality output?

✔ If decisions need to be made as part of the process, are the criteria that will be used to make the decisions understood by everyone involved? Are the decisions communicated adequately? Are the authority limits appropriate?

✔ How do you and others deal with problems that occur in the process?

✔ What are the most common mistakes that occur in the process? What impact do these mistakes have on customers?

✔ Where have improvements already been tried in the process? What were the outcomes?

Whichever questions you ask, don't forget to keep asking 'Why?'

Keeping things simple

Process mapping uses lots of different symbols, or *conventions;* try to use as few as possible. To create a deployment flowchart, which we talk about in the next section, just two or three conventions are usually enough: the circle, the square box and the diamond, as shown in Figure 5-2:

Figure 5-2: Keeping it simple with process mapping symbols.

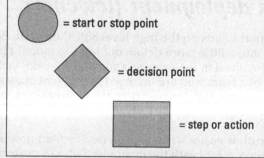

= start or stop point

= decision point

= step or action

© John Morgan and Martin Brenig-Jones

✔ The circle indicates the start and stop points in your process.

✔ The square box signifies a step or action.

✔ The diamond poses a question, where the answer determines which route the process follows next.

Take a bank underwriting a loan application as an example. The process steps may be different depending on the amount of money being requested as a loan. In the case of underwriting the request, it may be that large cases need to go to a senior underwriter or require key documents from the client, whereas a small loan might be processed at a more junior level or need less documentation. So, the diamond indicates a decision point with a question about the size of the loan, as shown in Figure 5-3.

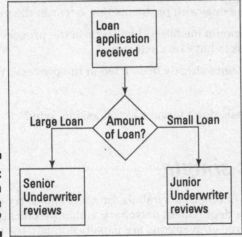

Figure 5-3: Which route do we follow?

© John Morgan and Martin Brenig-Jones

Developing a deployment flowchart

The deployment flowchart builds on the high-level SIPOC diagram described in Chapter 3, and goes into a little more detail, but not too much. This flowchart identifies who's involved in the process and what they do, including the different members of a team who are involved in different stages of the process, and also other teams and departments, the internal customers and suppliers.

Spotting moments of truth is easier when using a deployment flowchart. *Moments of truth* are touch points with the customer (when a customer comes into contact with a company), which we consider in the later section 'Identifying moments of truth'.

Before you begin working on a deployment flowchart, make sure you have an objective for the process that reflects the CTQs (we cover Critical To Quality elements in Chapter 4). And make sure you can answer the question, 'Why are you doing this process?'

Involve the people who work in the process when you develop a deployment flowchart. Because different perceptions exist of how the process works, use a sticky note for each step in the process so that you can move things around simply. You may well discover that the process is more complex than you think it is, which is why carrying out a process stapling exercise first can be so useful.

When you've used your sticky notes to create a flowchart, consider using process mapping software to formally document the process. Many packages are available on the Internet, some offering free 30-day trials, so you can try things out and judge their suitability.

In the sidebar 'Process stapling in action' earlier in this chapter, we introduce Ann, Brian and Clare. If you haven't read this sidebar, have a quick flick through it – we use the same example, beginning with Figure 5-4, when we develop our map. Each time a different person or another area in the workplace is involved, the chart moves horizontally and down. Operations that occur simultaneously are shown on the same level.

These charts usually have vertical lines between the different people and are often referred to as 'swim lane' charts. Every time a flow arrow crosses a dividing line, you should consider taking a measurement.

In Figure 5-4, we focus on Ann, Brian and Clare, but in practice you need to include the customer in the picture to help you identify the moments of truth (see the 'Identifying moments of truth' section, later in this chapter). Computer systems can also be included in your cast of characters. Work might be input to the computer system, for example, with the output coming out somewhere else. Seeing the whole picture is vital.

We cover measurement in more detail in Chapters 6, 7 and 8, but here we highlight some of the opportunities to put measurement in place. So, for example, when the chart moves horizontally and down, a customer and supplier relationship exists, as highlighted in Figure 5-5.

Most problems occur at the interfaces between two people or two departments, for example between Ann and Brian. Measures are almost certainly necessary here to help monitor performance and identify if problems exist, perhaps caused by misunderstanding the requirements.

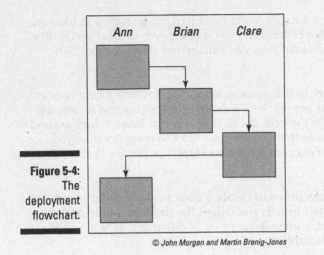

Figure 5-4: The deployment flowchart.

© John Morgan and Martin Brenig-Jones

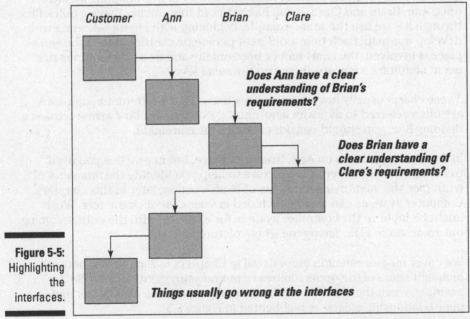

Does Ann have a clear understanding of Brian's requirements?

Does Brian have a clear understanding of Clare's requirements?

Figure 5-5: Highlighting the interfaces.

Things usually go wrong at the interfaces

© John Morgan and Martin Brenig-Jones

Chapter 7 looks at the need to collect good data and develop a data collection plan, and Chapter 8 considers the importance of 'in-process' measures. Your results here, especially the level of rework, will have a major impact on your performance for the customer, so gathering good data and knowing what's happening is essential. In Figure 5-4, for example, you'd want to know whether Ann's output to Brian and Brian's output to Clare is always correct, and so on. If it isn't, you'd then want to find out what type of errors were occurring so that you could begin the process of improving the situation.

Measuring time can highlight other improvement opportunities, as shown in Figure 5-6. For example, you may ask how long each step takes and why.

In Figure 5-6 you're simply measuring *unit time* – the time it takes to complete this step. While this measurement could prompt some interesting questions, viewing the bigger picture is more helpful as it also includes the *elapsed* or *cycle time*. This measurement is the time it takes to complete the entire process, as shown in Figure 5-7. (Elapsed or cycle time is sometimes referred to as *lead time*.)

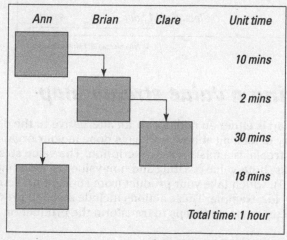

Ann	Brian	Clare	Unit time
			10 mins
			2 mins
			30 mins
			18 mins
			Total time: 1 hour

Figure 5-6: Measuring time.

© John Morgan and Martin Brenig-Jones

Building in the cycle time helps you identify bottlenecks and *dead time* – so-called because from the customer's perspective nothing's happening. In Figure 5-7, step number two is causing a bottleneck. If Brian's step can possibly be removed from the process, and Ann or Clare takes up Brian's work, you may be able to halve the cycle time. Possibly Brian's step is a non-value-adding step (explained in Chapter 9) and isn't needed at all.

Clear links are evident between measuring time and the theory of constraints, which we cover in Chapter 11. In your processes, try to identify and manage bottlenecks, to ask questions that clarify your understanding and to always look for improvement opportunities. Earlier in this section, we listed some typical questions that your process picture may prompt.

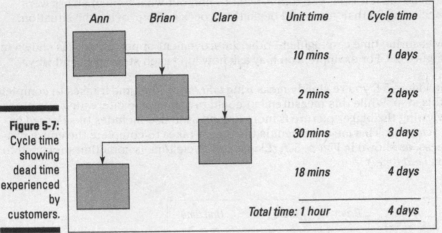

	Ann	Brian	Clare	Unit time	Cycle time
				10 mins	1 days
				2 mins	2 days
				30 mins	3 days
				18 mins	4 days
				Total time: 1 hour	4 days

Figure 5-7: Cycle time showing dead time experienced by customers.

© John Morgan and Martin Brenig-Jones

Constructing a value stream map

A value stream map is either an addition or an alternative to the deployment flowchart as a way of looking at how work gets done in your organisation. The term 'value stream' is a misleading description. The value stream map shows all the tasks, both value-creating and non-value-creating (more on value in Chapter 9), which take your product from concept to launch or from order to delivery, for example. These actions include steps to process information from the customer, and steps to transform the product on its way to the customer.

Toyota's Taiichi Ohno summarised the value stream nicely in 1978, when he said:

> All we are doing is looking at a timeline from the moment the customer gives us an order to the point when we collect the cash. And we are reducing that timeline by removing the Non-Value-Added wastes.

Value stream maps follow a product's path from order to delivery to determine current conditions, but they can also include a picture of the actual working layout in the office or factory to highlight the impact of transport time, for example. You can create and use your value stream map in a way that works for you.

Ideally, your process map includes the external customer. You need to recognise and understand the whole process or system and to spot the moments of truth.

TIP

Process stapling is an ideal first step to help you create a value stream map – and you really do need to go to the Gemba to see what's happening. For the low-down on these concepts, check out the 'Genning up on the Gemba' sidebar and the 'Practising process stapling' section, earlier in this chapter.

The value stream map is similar to the format of a SIPOC diagram, which we talk about in Chapter 3. Ideally, your value stream map includes a picture of where the various activities happen and shows the flow of both materials and information, as shown in Figure 5-8.

Figure 5-8:
Part of
a value
stream map.

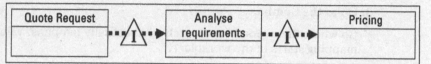

© John Morgan and Martin Brenig-Jones

Figure 5-8 keeps things very simple, and looks very much like a SIPOC diagram. It includes some extra information; in this case, a triangle that identifies work in progress (the 'i' is for inventory) – work waiting to be actioned. Where the 'work in progress' is people in a queue, the 'inventory triangle' shows a 'q' rather than an 'i'. In practice, value stream maps are straightforward, but they'll be a little more detailed than this example (see Figures 5-10 and 5-11) and will use more conventions than you use in a deployment flowchart (see the 'Developing a deployment flowchart' section, earlier in this chapter). A selection of the more commonly used conventions is shown in Figure 5-9.

Figure 5-9:
Value
stream map
conven-
tions.

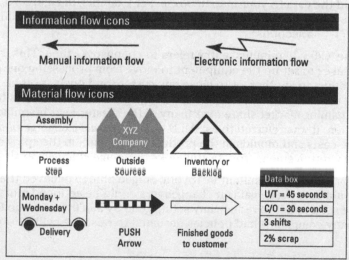

© John Morgan and Martin Brenig-Jones

To draw your value stream map, work through the following steps:

1. **Identify the process you want to look at, agreeing the start and stop points.**

   Describing the product or service this process is supporting is also helpful.

2. **Set up a small team to do the analysis.**

   The team should have knowledge of all the steps involved, from supplier input to external customer, so it must include people working in the process.

3. **Go to the Gemba.**

   Go where the action is and watch what actually happens. Value stream mapping starts in the workplace.

4. **Working at a reasonably high level, draw a process map of the material/product flow in the whole value stream.**

   Some people prefer to do this exercise starting at the customer end and working backwards – rather like process stapling in reverse. Write down the steps as you go, rather than trying to remember everything. As well as material and product flow, remember to capture the information flow that causes product or material to move through the process.

5. **Identify the performance data you'd like to know.**

   Useful information often includes activity or unit time, cycle time, scrap or rework rates, the number of staff/resources, batch sizes, machine uptime, changeover time, working time, inventory and backlog.

6. **Collect the data you need for each step in the process.**

   Add the data to your map in boxes. For example, in Figure 5-9, you can see a data box capturing a range of information, including unit time (U/T = 45 seconds).

   The 'C/0 = 30 minutes' entry refers to changeover time. This is the time it takes to set up the equipment to move from processing one type of product to another, or to close one system and open another. A focus on reducing changeover time was one of the keys to success for Toyota in gaining market share over many of the Western car manufacturers, where it was referred to as SMED – *single minute exchange of die* (die are the casts and moulds in the production system). In the spirit of continuous improvement, Toyota still looks to reduce changeover times.

   Working as a consultant in Toyota, Shigeo Shingo believed the company could make huge gains if changeovers could be actioned more quickly. He set a target to reduce any set-up time by 59/60ths. Shingo felt that many companies had policies designed to raise the skill level of their workers but few had implemented strategies to lower the skill level required by the set-up itself.

Changeovers and set-ups aren't relevant only to manufacturing companies and processes – they're just as relevant to service organisations.

7. **Add arrows to show information flows.**

The value stream map shows information flow as well as material flow, separately identifying whether the information is sent manually or electronically (see the different symbols in Figure 5-9). The value stream map shows the information flow in the top half of the map, with the material flow below.

8. **Add an overall timeline to show the average cycle time for an item.**

This timeline shows how long the item spends in the whole process. The example in Figure 5-10 identifies the process steps A to I and indicates the unit and cycle time. The figure shows a process with a unit time of only four hours, but taking 187 days to complete! You need to look at the bottlenecks highlighted by the difference between the unit and cycle times, as well as the levels of work in progress or inventory identified in the triangles between the steps.

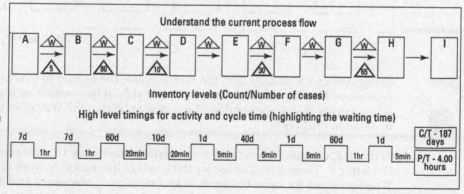

Figure 5-10: Identifying the delays.

© John Morgan and Martin Brenig-Jones

As an example of a value stream map, consider ABC Company's order process. The process begins with customer service receiving an email or telephone order. The product price is checked using the product price database.

Availability is checked in terms of stock inventory using the stock management system. If inventory cannot be allocated, the order is passed to the manufacturing team through the manufacturing order system and scheduled for production the next day.

The delivery date is determined, the customer is advised and the order entry records are completed through the customer service order management system. The 'current state' picture of the value stream will resemble that shown in Figure 5-11.

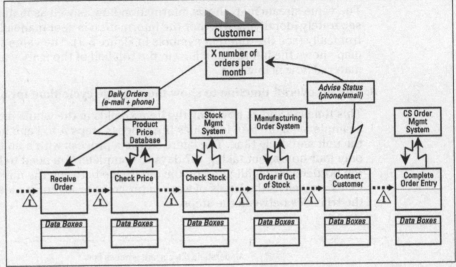

Figure 5-11:
The ABC order process as a value stream map.

© John Morgan and Martin Brenig-Jones

Using averages is usually fine, but do recognise the danger of averages and remember that the actual times vary either side of the mean – known in the scary worlds of statistics and mathematics as 'variation'. We cover variation in detail in Chapter 8.

In the ABC example, the current state map includes some triangles containing the letter 'i'. These triangles are for the levels of inventory, or work in progress. When you create a value stream map for one of your processes, you need to remember that the map describes the current state of your organisation – a snapshot in time. Whether people in the organisation feel the inventory isn't usually that high or low isn't relevant; for whatever reason, the inventory is what it is *right now*.

In order to have a complete view of things, you need to incorporate data such as activity time and cycle time (just as in the deployment flowchart, described earlier in this chapter), and changeover time.

The following example of a value stream map in a service organisation demonstrates how valuable the addition of data becomes. It enables you to not only see how the work gets done, but also how well it gets done.

The next few pages focus on a bank example, and the creation of the value stream map for the loans application process. This example demonstrates the steps in creating the map and then shows how problem areas within the process can be identified, flagged and prioritised for improvement action.

The loans team had already developed a SIPOC diagram (explained in Chapter 3), but they weren't sure that it was entirely accurate. So, the first step in this instance was for them to understand how the work gets done by carrying out a process stapling exercise. In doing so, they took note of the work-in-progress levels (the 'i' in the triangles; see Figure 5-9), and they created a current state map step by step, as shown in Figures 5-12 to 5-18.

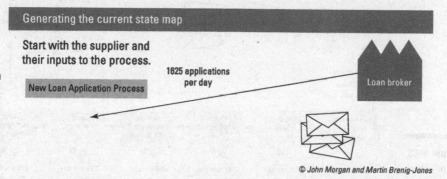

Figure 5-12: Building up the value stream map.

The loan applications are sent into the company by loan brokers acting on behalf of individuals. In Figure 5-13, you can see that 1,625 applications have been received on this particular day.

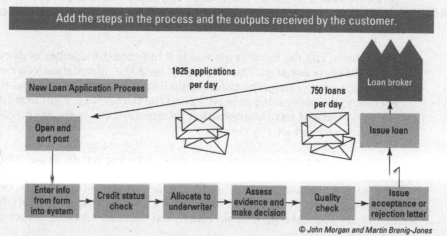

Figure 5-13: Developing the picture.

In many ways, this picture is similar to the SIPOC, but it lacks information about who all the different customers and suppliers are (both internal and external), and the associated inputs and outputs. Having created this picture, it's time to add in some data, as shown in Figure 5-14.

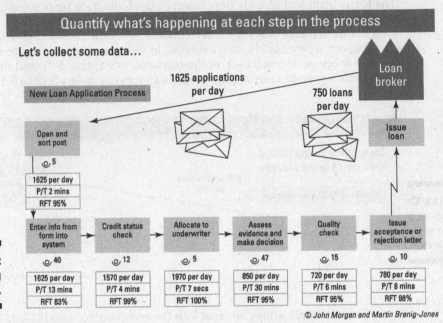

Figure 5-14: Collecting data.

© John Morgan and Martin Brenig-Jones

We're beginning to create a detailed picture of what's happening in this process. The data shows the number of people working on each step, work volumes and the levels of accuracy. Already we can see opportunities for improvement through the reduction of errors.

The symbol and the number alongside it indicate the number of people working at that process step. The data boxes hold the information you decide is important. In this case, the bank has included the number of items received each day, the processing time (P/T) and the percentage 'right first time' (RFT). You might have wanted other information, for example the change-over time or productivity details.

Either way, you can see there's scope for reducing errors, especially in the 'enter info from form into system' step, where the error rate is 17 per cent. This high error rate would be a problem anywhere in the process, but at such an early stage is likely to lead to delays for the customer, particularly if the errors aren't picked up straight away. And think about the cost, too.

By building in the work in progress information, we're getting clues about the backlogs and bottlenecks, and the dangers inherent in a 'push' system are becoming obvious.

In Figure 5-15, the work-in-progress figures – the numbers alongside the triangle – confirm the delays in the process and help highlight the areas that need addressing. The bottlenecks need to be managed, or you'll find that they manage you and your process.

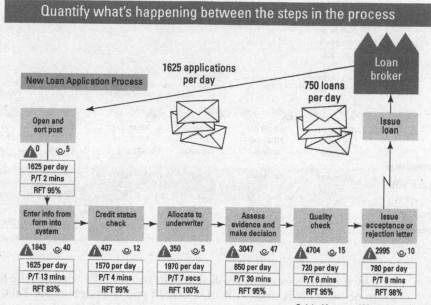

Figure 5-15: Looking at the interfaces.

You can see that for 4,704 items the 'quality check' step is seriously behind, but issues are evident throughout the process, something the addition of a timeline will further confirm.

The timeline shown in Figure 5-16 enables us to focus on the bottlenecks – the difference between the processing time and the cycle time is dead time, and we can see some significant issues that could be addressed by applying the theory of constraints. As you can see, the overall process is taking almost 30 days to complete, but an individual case could be processed in just over an hour.

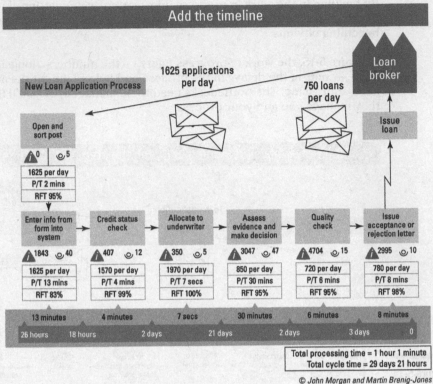

Figure 5-16:
So, what's
the time?

The timeline information will also help you identify whether the line needs to be better balanced. And, of course, if you then determine Takt time (see Chapter 1 for more on this), you can assess the staffing levels needed to deal with the customer volumes.

Clearly, improvement opportunities exist and the next step is to highlight these on the value stream map.

A selection of the opportunities and observations are included in Figure 5-17. This continues the process of bringing the picture to life and creates the basis to discuss the opportunities for improvement action. Apart from tackling the bottlenecks, non-value-adding steps may exist that can be removed, or perhaps people and equipment could be relocated into a more efficiently laid out workspace. Some activities could be combined, too, and, if there are different types of loan application, an option may exist to set up a process team for the relevant product family, using the concept of cell manufacturing.

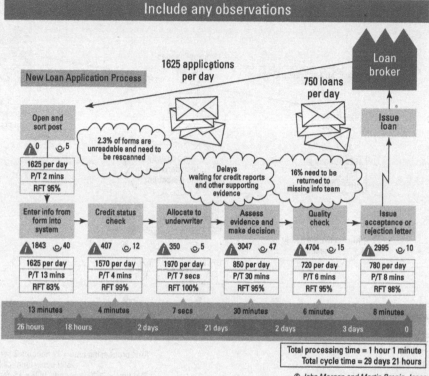

Figure 5-17: Process mapping and data may help highlight the opportunities for analysis.

The improvement ideas or objectives could be added to the map for further review and prioritisation and this could help you develop a future state map in line with that shown in Figure 5-18.

Developing a picture of your process, using a deployment flowchart and/or a value stream map will also help you identify the moments of truth.

Identifying moments of truth

Jan Carlzon, one-time chief executive of Scandinavian Air Services (SAS), developed and popularised the concept of moments of truth in his book of the same name. A moment of truth occurs every time a customer comes into contact with a company, whether in person, on the telephone, by post, when reading company literature or seeing a company advert. Each customer touch point provides an opportunity to make or break the organisation, since the customer is either pleased or displeased with the outcome. Everyone in your organisation is responsible for the outcome of customer touch points and for delivering a great customer experience.

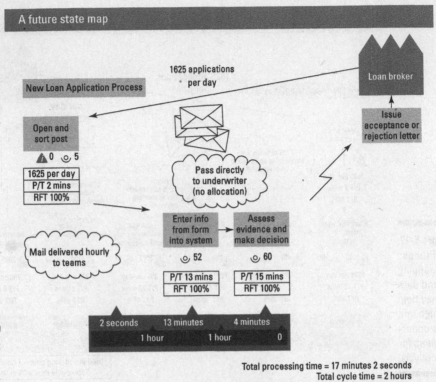

Figure 5-18:
A future
state map.

TRUE STORIES

Carlzon informed all SAS staff that the organisation needed to improve by 1,000 per cent! He asked his staff to improve 1,000 things by 1 per cent and then to keep doing it. He wanted them to focus on customer contacts – the moments of truth – such as booking a ticket, checking in or boarding a plane. Carlzon used an example of a passenger pulling down the meal tray. If the tray was dirty, what would the customer think? What might that tell the customer about the maintenance of the plane?

To achieve what your customers want, you need to understand the many moments of truth opportunities that exist and find ways of enhancing the customer's experience. Process stapling, deployment flowcharts and value stream maps can help you identify both internal and external customer touch points.

Part III
Assessing Performance

Getting the balance of measures and understanding how they interrelate:

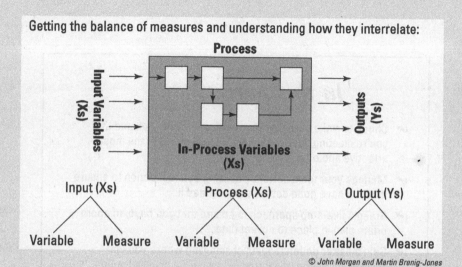

© John Morgan and Martin Brenig-Jones

Visit www.dummies.com/extras/leansixsigma for a bonus article on why projects miss budget and schedule projections and how you can avoid these problems.

In this part . . .

✔ Check to make sure that your work gets done well and that you're meeting your customers' requirements in the most effective and efficient way.

✔ Manage your team better by utilising data collection to ensure that you have good data when you need it.

✔ Grasp a five-step approach to ensure that you have an appropriate plan in place to collect data.

✔ Gain a better understanding of sampling where you can achieve good analysis by using comparatively small amounts of representative data.

✔ Decide how to best present and interpret your data after you have it with control charts that can help you identify process variation so that you know when to take action and when not to.

✔ Develop an appropriately balanced set of measures to help you understand what influences and affects your results. In doing so, we reference a number of traditionally Lean measures, including Takt time.

Chapter 6

Gathering Information

In This Chapter

▶ Understanding the difference between good and bad data

▶ Deciding how to collect your data

▶ Recognising that data collection is an ongoing process

Managing by fact is one of the key Lean Six Sigma principles. You need accurate, consistent and valid data to manage in this way. This chapter focuses on developing a data collection process to ensure the data you collect meets these criteria.

You need to view data collection as a process that needs managing and improving just like all your other processes.

Managing by Fact

Whether you manage a day-to-day process or lead an improvement project, you need accurate data to help you make the right decisions. The following quote summarises the importance of facts:

> *Unless one can obtain facts and accurate data about the workplace, there can be no control or improvement. It is the task of the middle management and managers below them to ensure the accuracy of their data which enables the company to know the true facts.*

> Kaoru Ishikawa, *What is Total Quality Control? The Japanese Way*

The following sections highlight the importance of good data, focus on the need to review your existing measures and develop an effective data collection plan to help you manage your processes.

Realising the importance of good data

Good data may prompt you to implement an improvement project by high-lighting poor performance against the CTQs (see Chapter 3) or show you opportunities to tackle waste (see Chapter 9). It enables you to understand the current performance levels of a process and provides you with the means to benchmark that performance and prioritise improvement actions.

When you undertake an improvement project, you need to analyse the causes of the problem you're tackling – good data helps you quantify and verify those possible causes. In developing solutions to address root causes, you need good data to help you determine the most effective approach.

You're probably aware of the phrase 'rubbish in, rubbish out', which is often applied to data. You need to ensure you have good data going into your various management information reports and analyses. For that, you must have a sound data collection plan, and we describe the key elements you'll need a little later in this chapter. First, you need to consider what you're measuring.

Reviewing what you currently measure

Many organisations have data coming out of their ears! Unfortunately, that data isn't always the right data. Sometimes organisations measure things because they *can* measure them – but those things aren't necessarily the right things to be measured and the resulting data doesn't help you manage your business and its processes.

Sometimes data isn't accurate – intentionally or not – and even if the data is accurate, it may be presented in a way that makes interpretation difficult. Managers often present data as a page full of numbers to encourage comparisons with last week's results or even the results for this week last year. This situation is compounded further if the results show only averages or percentages and you can't understand the range of performance or the variation in your process performance. This range and variation in performance is what your customers will be experiencing (see Chapters 4 and 7).

In Chapter 7 we explain the importance of variation and how to use control charts to help you understand when and when not to take action. Without this understanding, a tendency exists to take inappropriate actions because managers are making the wrong decisions.

Figure 6-1 provides an effective format to help you review your measures.

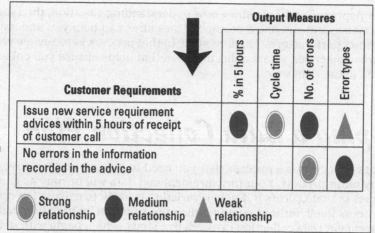

	Output Measures			
Customer Requirements	**% in 5 hours**	**Cycle time**	**No. of errors**	**Error types**
Issue new service requirement advices within 5 hours of receipt of customer call	⬤	⬤	⬤	▲
No errors in the information recorded in the advice			⬤	⬤

⬤ Strong relationship   ⬤ Medium relationship   ▲ Weak relationship

© John Morgan and Martin Brenig-Jones

Figure 6-1: Getting the measure of the CTQs.

Deciding what to measure

You probably know that choosing what to measure and how to present your data are important. But so too is deciding what *not* to measure. Lean Six Sigma requires you to manage by fact and have good data – but that doesn't mean you need more data than you currently produce. It means you have the right data.

You need to review the data you currently have and decide whether it really is helping you manage your process. Does the data add value or is it a waste? Who uses the data? How and why is the data used? The CTQs provide the basis for your process measures and you need to consider whether your current measures help you understand your performance in meeting them. Figure 6-1 uses symbols to identify the strength of your performance measures in relation to the CTQs.

If you look at the CTQ for delivery within five hours, you can see that the first measure in the matrix, the percentage issued within five hours, is rated only as a 'medium strength'. That measure tells you how many cases are processed within the CTQ service standard, but it doesn't tell you anything about the actual results, and the range of performance. Some cases will have been actioned in one hour and some in ten hours, for example. This really important information is provided by the second measure, the 'cycle time', where you're recording the results of each and every case, or at least a representative sample. With this information, you can determine the average performance, the range of performance, and, of course, you can extract the 'percentage within five hours' information because you can see how many cases took five hours or less.

In Chapters 7 and 8 we show how understanding variation, the range of performance and creating a balance of measures can help you understand and predict performance. The first stage in that process is to review your measures and create a data collection plan that helps ensure you collect the right data in the right way.

Developing a Data Collection Plan

Data collection is a process that you need to manage and improve, just like any other process. Your measurement and data will be only as good as the process that collects it. Enough variation is likely to exist in the operational process itself, without compounding the situation by variation in the measurement. Data collection involves five steps, which begin with determining the output measures for your processes:

1. **Agree the objectives and goals linking to the key outputs from your processes that seek to meet the CTQs.**

2. **Develop operational definitions and procedures that help ensure everyone is clear about what's being measured and why.**

3. **Agree ground rules to ensure that you collect valid and consistent data.**

4. **Collect the data.**

5. **Carry on collecting the data and identify ways to improve your approach.**

Beginning with output measures

In this first step, we begin with the end in mind by considering the output measures. By agreeing on the end goals for data collection, and linking the data to your key outputs, everyone in the team understands why they're measuring what they're measuring. After the output measures have been agreed, you need to develop some additional measures to help you understand how the inputs to your process and the various activities in the process are influencing the output results. Chapter 8 covers this issue and looks at the importance of getting a balance of input, in-process and output measures to help manage your process.

Agreeing on goals and outputs is usually straightforward if you've described the CTQ customer requirements in a clearly measurable way (we explain how to do so in Chapter 4). Use our suggested symbols in Figure 6-1 to check whether you have an appropriate set of measures. You need at least one strong measure for each CTQ.

When you have a collection of output measures, use Figure 6-1 to review whether your output measures are appropriate – this may be particularly relevant if you've only recently determined the CTQs. After using Figure 6-1 in this way, you may consider abandoning some measures and creating other, more appropriate ones.

Cycle time (sometimes referred to as lead time) is the most important data. If you simply measure whether or not each item meets the service standard, you don't know the range of performance being delivered. For example, you may see that the organisation processes 80 per cent of orders within the service standard of five hours, but you may not be able to see that some orders take one hour, some take two or three hours, and the 20 per cent that fail take at least ten hours. With the cycle time data you can understand fully what happens.

In Figure 6-2 we show a process trying to meet the customer's requirements. The feedback from the customer and the process highlights a gap that you need to close – that is, you need an improvement action.

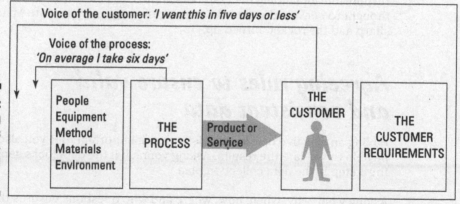

Figure 6-2: Matching the voices of the customer and the process.

© John Morgan and Martin Brenig-Jones

In this example, we use average cycle times to represent the 'voice of the process'. Doing so isn't actually a good idea, as average cycle times can be misleading. The average process performance in Figure 6-2 is six days, so the process doesn't meet the customer's requirement of 'five days or less'. But even if the *average* performance had been five days, the process probably wouldn't have been good enough. The customer sees every cycle time, not just the average.

Creating clear definitions

Describing your measures in a way that removes any ambiguity about what's being measured is the second step in your data collection plan. This description is called an *operational definition*.

When you know what you plan to measure, you need to provide clear, unambiguous operational definitions. These operational definitions help everyone in the team to understand the who, what, where, when and how of the measurement process, which in turn helps you produce consistent data. For example, if you measure cycle time, you define when the clock starts and finishes; which clock you use; whether you measure in seconds, minutes or hours; and whether you round up or down.

The 1999 launch of NASA's Mars Lander is a famous example of murky definitions. This $125 million rocket was designed to investigate if water had existed on the red planet. Unfortunately, the rocket disappeared, never to be seen again. The cause was rather embarrassing: the team that built the spacecraft and managed its launch worked in feet and inches . . . but the team responsible for landing the craft on Mars worked in metric – and no one had thought to convert the data. As a result, the angle of entry into Mars was too sharp and the rocket burned up.

Agreeing rules to ensure valid and consistent data

Having an effective operational definition is important, but you also need to be able to validate the results. Asking yourself if the data looks sensible is the third step in the data collection plan.

Asking what, why, when, how, where and who questions ensures that your data is both valid and consistent. In addition, Lean Six Sigma provides a statistical way to check things out. There will be 'enough' variation in the process itself, without adding additional variation through the measurement system.

Measurement System Analysis (MSA) describes the overall approach to ensuring the validity of your measures. Gauge R and R and Attribute Agreement Analysis are the techniques used for assessing continuous and discrete data, respectively. *Gauge R and R* is a technique for assessing the repeatability and reproducibility of the measuring system – it confirms how much the measurement system contributes to process variation (see Chapter 7 for more on process variation).

Repeatability is a measure of the variation seen when one operator uses the same system to measure the same thing. So, imagine you've asked someone to measure a batch of items to determine the time it took to process them. You'd then ask her to measure the same batch again to see whether she gets the same results. If she doesn't get the same results, you need to decide whether the difference is important.

Reproducibility is a measure of the variation seen when different operators use the same system to measure the same thing.

To check reproducibility, you ask someone else to measure the same batch of items and see if his results are different from those of the first person. The person doing the measuring must *not* know the previous results. Again, if a difference does exist, you need to decide whether it's important and if action is needed to improve the measurement system. We offer some broad guidelines to help you make that judgement in a moment.

In our example in Figure 6-3, two people – Timekeeper A and Timekeeper B – check the same batch of products in a random sequence. By averaging the difference of the two readings over the number of products in the batch, we can determine the gauge R and R.

Measure	Timekeeper A	Timekeeper B	Tolerance
Vet form	45	41	9.30%
Add info. to form	90	89	1.12%
Update records	175	177	1.14%
Print agreement	100	95	5.13%
Issue to customer	66	72	8.70%
Total Time	**476**	**474**	**0.42%**

Figure 6-3: Checking out the measurement system.

© John Morgan and Martin Brenig-Jones

In Figure 6-3, gauge R and R is good for total time at 0.42 per cent, but is less accurate for the sub-processes. Overall these results are very good, but we could try to improve 'Vet form' if we really had nothing else to do.

The calculations from the table have been made as follows: take the difference between the two 'times', and divide this by the mean average of the two times, expressing the result as a percentage. So, for example, if we look at 'Vet form', the difference between Timekeepers A and B is 4 seconds, the mean average is 43 seconds, and the resulting tolerance is 9.30% (4/43 × 100%).

Determining what's good in gauge R and R terms is somewhat subjective and no truly right answers exist. We can offer some broad guidelines but when you decide whether to take action, much depends on the process and the consequences of inaccurate data. Generally, if gauge R and R exceeds 10 per cent you should look to improve the measurement system, perhaps focusing on a better operational definition, for example, or using more accurate measuring equipment. If gauge R and R exceeds 25 per cent – change the measurement system!

When health and safety, regulatory or important financial issues are involved, the gauge R and R guidelines need to be a lot tighter. You want very accurate and consistent data if you're making a decision that affects braking distances in the testing of a new car design, for example. Lives could be at stake if the gauge R and R is more than a fraction different. Measuring how long a telephone call takes in a call centre, in contrast, isn't so important.

Figure 6-3 covers *continuous data* – that which can be measured on a continuous scale, such as processing time. *Attribute data* includes whether or not something is present, or is right or wrong, and categories of items, such as types of compensation claim, complaint and financial standing.

To check the accuracy and consistency of attribute data, we use attribute agreement analysis. So, for example, you ask a number of people in the process team to classify the items in a batch into the various categories. You can then compare their assessments both with one another and with an expert's assessments. Doing so ensures consistent classification by the process team and sometimes highlights training needs, too.

In Figure 6-4, you can see how assessors Ann and Brian classify claims consistently between them, but aren't in line with the expert's assessment. The claims need to be coded by category as either AA, AB, AC or BB. This finding indicates a need to improve the quality of the training given to the assessors so that their classification is in line with the expert's view.

Figure 6-4: Attribute data in action.

Claim Number	Expert's Classification	Ann	Brian
1	AA	AA	AA
2	AB	AA	AA
3	AA	AB	AB
4	AC	AC	AC
5	BB	BB	BB

© John Morgan and Martin Brenig-Jones

Collecting the data

Step four of the data collection process covers how you actually collect the data. You'll almost certainly collect some of it manually. Data collection sheets make the process straightforward and ensure consistency. A data collection sheet can be as simple as a check sheet that you use to record the number of times something occurs.

The check sheet is best completed in time sequence, as shown in Figure 6-5. This real example shows data from the new business team of an insurance company processing personal pension applications from individual clients. It captures the main reasons why applications can't be processed immediately; daily recording the number of times these different issues occur. On a daily basis, you can see the number of 'errors' and the number of application forms, and in Figure 6-5 we've recorded the proportion of errors to forms. By adding stratification (day of the week) in this way, we may be able to gain some additional insights about the potential causes of the issues.

Ref	Characteristic	M	T	W	T	F	M	T	W	T	F	Total	%
A	form not signed	2	1	0	1	0	1	1	0	0	1	7	8.3
B	no part number	1	0	2	1	1	2	0	0	0	0	7	8.3
C	address missing	5	2	3	2	3	4	3	5	3	3	33	39.4
D	no cheque	1	0	1	1	1	0	1	1	1	1	8	9.5
E	wrong amount	3	4	1	3	1	2	3	3	4	5	29	34.5
Total errors		12	7	7	8	6	9	8	9	8	10	84	100
Total forms		24	20	21	18	18	24	16	20	14	22	197	
Proportion		.5	.35	.33	.44	.33	.37	.5	.45	.57	.45	.43	

Figure 6-5: Checking out the check sheet.

© John Morgan and Martin Brenig-Jones

Looking across the check sheet from left to right, you can see that we've recorded the total errors by type and have determined their percentage in relation to the whole. This check sheet links neatly to a Pareto analysis, which we show in Figure 6-6. Here, the 80:20 Pareto rule means that generally 80 per cent of the errors are caused by 20 per cent of the error types. Your analysis won't always result in precisely 80:20 and, in our example, the main causes of the problem, C and E, account for almost 75 per cent of the errors.

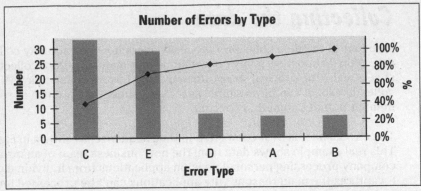

© John Morgan and Martin Brenig-Jones

Figure 6-6: Looking at the vital few with Pareto.

The Pareto chart in Figure 6-6 highlights this fact. The cumulative percentage line helps you decide which errors to focus on. If you tackle type C errors, you'll address 39.4 per cent of the problem, but if you also address type E errors, you'll cover 73.9 per cent. You can tackle the smaller errors, A, B and D, later on. That said, check to see whether any of the error types cost more to resolve than others. For example, you might find that type C and E errors are quite cheap to resolve, whereas type A errors may prove to be very expensive. Recasting the Pareto diagram by cost may give you a different picture.

Even if you use a computer system to automatically measure and generate your data, design the data collection form on paper first. Doing so helps you think through all the details you may need, such as whether and to what extent to take account of segmentation factors (see Chapter 3), which could include different customer or product types, for example.

A *concentration diagram* is another form of data collection sheet. This technique is good for identifying damage to goods in transit, for example by recording where on the product or packaging marks and holes occur. Car hire companies often ask customers to complete concentration diagrams. On a picture of the car, customers have to highlight existing damage, such as dents and scratches. Upon return of the vehicle, the leasing company then checks to see if any further damage has occurred. See Figure 6-7.

An American colleague recently rented a car and, when filling out the form identifying existing damage, inquired about a small indentation. The agent replied 'Buck and a quarter'. When we asked what that meant, she explained that if the indentation was larger than a quarter, it was a dent; otherwise it didn't matter. It wasn't considered a scratch unless it was longer than a one-dollar bill. So, here we see operational definitions in practice, with readily available references for both the customer and the agent.

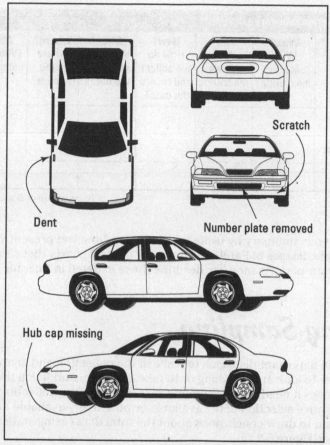

Figure 6-7: Coming up to scratch with the concentration diagram.

Labels within figure: Dent, Scratch, Number plate removed, Hub cap missing

Identifying ways to improve your approach

The fifth step in the data collection process reminds you that data collection is a process and needs to be managed and improved just like any other. Even after you find your initial data, carry on collecting more to identify ways in which to improve your approach. You've determined the data showing your output performance. Now identify and measure the *upstream variables* that influence the output performance of your process. We cover upstream variables in detail in Chapter 8, but typical variables include volumes of work, supplier accuracy, supplier timelines, available resources and in-process cycle times. Measure these upstream variables on a daily basis.

Figure 6-8 provides a data collection summary. Use it to ensure you've covered all aspects of your data collection plan; doing so should lead you to collecting data that is accurate, consistent and valid.

Data Collection summary						
Type of measure	What? What are we measuring?	Why? Why are we measuring this?	How? How do we collect and record the data?	When? When do we collect the data?	Where? Where in the process?	Who? Who will collect it?
Output						
In-process						
Input						

Figure 6-8: Pulling the data collection plan together.

© John Morgan and Martin Brenig-Jones

Enhance your summary by using icons to show how you present your data; for example, images of Pareto diagrams, or control charts that show the variation in your performance (we describe these in detail in Chapter 7).

Introducing Sampling

One of the important decisions to make in the collection and analysis of data is whether to look at everything or to take a sample. And if you take a sample, how big does it need to be? Sampling means that you're collecting only a representative selection of the available or potentially available data, before analysing it to draw conclusions about the total data (using statistical inference) – see Figure 6-9.

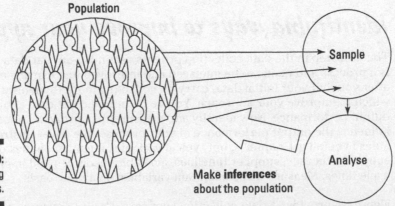

Population

Sample

Analyse

Make **inferences** about the population

Figure 6-9: Making inferences.

© John Morgan and Martin Brenig-Jones

Sampling is used when collecting and analysing all the available data is too difficult or expensive. And sometimes collecting the data destroys it, as with wine tasting or the testing of sutures, for example. Importantly, valid conclusions can often be drawn from a comparatively small amount of data. For conclusions to be valid, the samples must be representative, so that the data you collect fairly represents all of the data. No systematic differences should exist between the data you collect and the data you don't collect.

In other words, every item stands an equal chance of being included. Apart from anything else, that means if you don't understand the segmentation factors involved, you could take an inappropriate sample (see Figure 6-10). Bias can creep into your sample in a whole host of ways without adding this mistake. You need to think carefully about how to formulate your sample.

Figure 6-10: Understanding the segmentation factors is vital.

If you don't understand the segmentation factors of the population, you could take an inappropriate sample.

© John Morgan and Martin Brenig-Jones

Here, we look at two types of sampling: process and population.

Process sampling

The purpose of process sampling is to measure, analyse or control the process. Examples include establishing the baseline performance, identifying opportunities for improvement and ensuring ongoing monitoring and control.

Two broad approaches to process sampling exist. The first involves taking a regular sample, for example every third or tenth item, or taking a sample every 45 minutes, say. Known as systematic sampling (see Figure 6-11), this approach is often used for comparatively low-volume administrative processes.

Process sampling can be relatively easy to do, but may introduce bias; maybe every third or tenth item is somehow significant, for example. The data links into the X moving R control chart, described in Chapter 7. This chart presents data in time sequence enabling you to identify any trends and helping you determine whether any action is needed; to address deterioration in performance, for example.

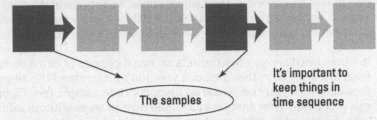

Systematic sampling from a process

Taking a regular sample, for example every third or tenth item or so on. This can be relatively easy to do, but may introduce bias.

Figure 6-11: Using a systematic approach.

The samples

It's important to keep things in time sequence

© John Morgan and Martin Brenig-Jones

Subgroup sampling (see Figure 6-12) involves taking a regular and random sample of, for example, five items, perhaps every day. This type of sampling is used with comparatively high-volume processes where looking at each and every item, or even every tenth item or so, isn't practical. The data also links neatly with the X bar R control chart, described in Chapter 7.

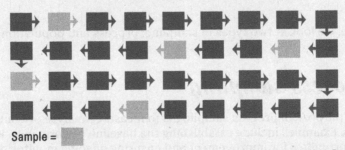

Subgroup sampling from a process

Take a regular and random sample of five items, every hour or two, or every day, for example.

Items processed in time sequence on Monday

Figure 6-12: Subgroup sampling from a process.

Sample =

© John Morgan and Martin Brenig-Jones

Population sampling

Population sampling, as the name suggests, looks at populations. This could mean a customer base, or a population of something that's already been processed, for example loan applications. Other examples include voting intentions of particular groups, the buying patterns of potential customers or the reasons for defaulting on mortgage payments.

So, how do you go about determining the sample size? How large need it be? The flippant answer is, how large can you afford it to be? Broadly speaking, the larger the sample size, the more accurate the sampling results from the data will be. But much will be determined by what you want the data for, how accurate it needs to be and how much variation exists within the population. If the population was comprised of clones, for example, you'd need to sample only one of them!

Start by looking at how accurate you need the results to be, which is determined by precision. *Precision* is how narrow you want the range to be for your estimate. So, for example, estimate the cycle time within two days or estimate the *percentage defective* within 3 per cent. Either the letter 'd' or the symbol Δ for 'delta' is used to represent precision in the sample size formulae.

Understanding the confidence interval is important in that it shows the range of results that are possible from the analysis of your sample, as you can see from the example that follows. Assume that you have selected a precision of plus or minus two days.

Precision is equal to half the width of the confidence interval. So, if your sample of data shows a mean average of 50 days, you are 95 per cent confident that the interval from 48 to 52 days contains the average cycle time. In this example, the width of the confidence interval is four days, and the estimate is within +/– two days.

The 95% confidence figure is the generally accepted norm in sampling. In the formula shown in Figures 6-13 and 6-15, the '2' links to plus and minus 2 standard deviations (95.40 per cent of the population – see Figure 1.2 in Chapter 1). Strictly speaking, this gives you 95.40 per cent confidence and the correct figure should be 1.96 rather than 2; however, we felt that if you were trying these calculations manually, it would be easier to use 2 and the answers would be close enough!

The level of precision will vary according to your requirements. Why do you want the data? What decisions will you be making as a result? So, for example, imagine your mortgage service team has processed 15,000 e-loan enquiries and you want to determine the average processing time. Depending on why you need the information, does your estimate have to be within five minutes – or five seconds? If you're determining staffing and budget requirements, you're likely to want the estimate to be pretty accurate.

You may be surprised to see how the sample size changes according to this requirement. The formula needed to estimate the average cycle time is shown in Figure 6-13.

Figure 6-13:
The formula.

Estimate average cycle time $n = \left(\dfrac{2s}{d}\right)^2$

For example, you want to estimate the average processing time within one minute. To estimate the sample size, you need to know the standard deviation. You need to have some idea of the amount of variation in the data because, as the variability increases, the necessary sample size increases.

But if you haven't sampled anything yet, how can you know the standard deviation? It may be that you already have some relevant historical data or you could use control chart data from a similar process (see Chapter 7 for a description of control charts). If not, you may need to collect a small sample, perhaps as few as 25 to 30 items, and calculate the standard deviation first.

In this example, let's assume you've calculated that the standard deviation is three minutes. So, plugging the various numbers into the formula, the sample size needed is 36. See Figure 6-14.

$$n = \left(\frac{2 \times 3}{1}\right)^2 = 6^2 = 36$$

$$n = \left(\frac{2 \times 3}{0.5}\right)^2 = 12^2 = 144$$

Figure 6-14:
The formula
in practice.

$$n = \left(\frac{2 \times 3}{0.125}\right)^2 = 48^2 = 2304$$

That number increases to 144 if the precision is 30 seconds (0.5 minutes). And to 2,304 if the precision changes to 7.5 seconds (0.125 minutes). As you can see, the more precise you want the result to be, the larger the sample size. Incidentally, we'll come back to this particular calculation (2,304) a little later on, in Figure 6-18.

The formula changes to estimate proportions, as shown in Figure 6-15.

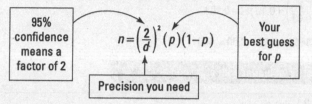

Figure 6-15: Minding your Ps but not the Qs.

Estimating proportions

It's important to realise that sample sizes change signifigantly according to the _p_ value.

95% confidence means a factor of 2

$$n = \left(\frac{2}{d}\right)^2 (p)(1-p)$$

Your best guess for _p_

Precision you need

As before, the usual convention is to work with a 95 per cent confidence level, but there's nothing sacred about this value. Based on the cost of making an error, your project may require a higher or lower degree of confidence.

In this formula, the tricky bit is determining your best guess for _p_, though this may not really be as hard as it seems. Similar processes may already be in place, or you may feel you have a pretty good idea of the 'proportion defective'.

The largest sample size occurs when _p_ = 0.5, or 50 per cent, so if you have no idea what _p_ might be, assume it's 0.5. The worst outcome is simply a larger than necessary sample. Incidentally, the proportion defective is a phrase that doesn't simply describe defects! It may relate to the proportion of customers who are likely to purchase a new product or service, for example.

Again, let's work through an example (see Figure 6-16). What sample size is required to estimate the defect rate in a process, with 95 per cent confidence, when you expect it to be around '10% defective', and where you want the estimate to be within 3 per cent?

The sample size changes to 3,600 if you want the estimate to be within +/– 1 per cent. The sample size formulas assume the sample size (n) is small relative to the population (N). If you're sampling more than 5 per cent of the population (n/N is greater than 0.05), this may be more than you need, and you can adjust the sample size with the 'finite population' formula shown in Figure 6-17.

See how this reduces the sample size of 2,304 that we calculated at the beginning of this section. Remember the population size in this example was 15,000. As you can see, we can reduce the sample to just under 2,000, as shown in Figure 6-18.

The answer with a 3% precision

$$n = \left(\frac{2}{d}\right)^2 (p)(1-p)$$

$$n = \left(\frac{2}{0.03}\right)^2 (0.10)(1-0.10)$$

$$n = 4444.4 \times 0.10 \times 0.90 = 400$$

The answer gets a lot bigger with precision at 1%

Figure 6-16: Precision is a key factor in the sample size.

$$n = \left(\frac{2}{d}\right)^2 (p)(1-p)$$

$$n = \left(\frac{2}{0.01}\right)^2 (0.10)(1-0.10)$$

$$n = 40000 \times 0.10 \times 0.90 = 3600$$

© John Morgan and Martin Brenig-Jones

Sampling from a limited (finite) population

Figure 6-17: It's finite.

$$n\text{ finite} = \frac{n}{1+\frac{n}{N}}$$

© John Morgan and Martin Brenig-Jones

Figure 6-18: Bringing the sample size down.

$$n\text{ finite} = \frac{2304}{1+\frac{2304}{15,000}} = \frac{2304}{1.1536} = 1997$$

© John Morgan and Martin Brenig-Jones

Calculating precision from the affordable sample size

Figure 6-19:
Precisely
what can
we afford?

◆ For an average within ± d units

$$d = \frac{2s}{\sqrt{n}}$$

◆ A proportion within ± d%

$$d = 2\sqrt{\frac{(p)(1-p)}{n}}$$

© John Morgan and Martin Brenig-Jones

You may have worked out the sample size needed for the precision you'd like, but how big a sample can you afford to look at? If it's less than the sample size should be, what will the affordable sample provide in terms of precision? And, will that be precise enough? By moving our formula around, as shown in Figure 6-19, we can calculate the precision provided by the sample size and make a business decision as to whether it will be sufficient.

This section has provided an overview of sampling and the formulae needed to determine sample sizes for populations, either of people or things that have been processed or produced. Hopefully, it's enabled you to appreciate that valid conclusions can be drawn from comparatively small samples, but that, in order for your sample to avoid bias, it must be representative.

Collecting data takes time and energy, and it costs money, too. Make sure you collect data that's useful – and accurate! If you're going to do it, do it properly.

Chapter 7

Presenting Your Data

- -

In This Chapter

▶ Investigating variation

▶ Using control charts

▶ Looking at different ways to display data

- -

This chapter introduces the importance of understanding and identifying variation. If you can identify what type of variation you're seeing in your process results, you can determine whether action is needed or not, and avoid taking inappropriate action and wasting effort.

Control charts can be used to identify types of variation in your process and in the various materials, goods and parts coming into your process, for example. This chapter covers how to use these powerful data displays. We focus on the most commonly used type, the X moving R, or individuals and range, control chart.

Later in the chapter we refer to some other data displays and ways to assess variation, looking at histograms and hypothesis tests.

Delving into Different Types of Variation

Things are seldom exactly the same, even if at first glance they appear to be so. Variation exists in people's heights, in the many shades of the colour green, in the number of words in each sentence of this book and in the time different people take to read this book.

Variation comes in two types – common cause and special cause:

✔ **Common cause or natural variation** is just that – natural. You should expect it, you shouldn't be surprised by it and you shouldn't react to individual examples of it.

✔ **Special cause variation** isn't normally what you expect to see – in the context of your processes, something unusual has happened that's influencing the results. But it can result from a process change you've made to improve performance. In this instance, it will be the evidence you're looking for to confirm that the improvement has had an impact on performance.

You can use statistical process control (SPC) and control charts to identify and define variation in your business processes, and we explain just what these are and how to use them in the later section, 'Recognising the Importance of Control Charts'.

Defining the type of variation is important as it ensures you take action only when you need to. Confusing one type of variation with the other creates problems.

Understanding natural variation

Natural variation is what you expect to see as a result of how you design and manage your processes. When a process exhibits only natural variation, it's in *statistical control and stable*. Being in statistical control doesn't necessarily mean that the results from the process meet your customer CTQs (Critical To Quality elements of your offering – see Chapter 4) but it does mean that the results are stable and predictable. If the results don't meet your CTQs, you can improve the process using DMAIC (Define, Measure, Analyse, Improve and Control – see Chapter 2).

To determine whether the variation is natural or special, try the following simple experiment with some colleagues.

First, write down the letter 'a' five times. This in itself forms the basis for an interesting discussion on giving clear instructions so that everyone understands the requirement. You may find that some people write their 'a's across the page, and others down the page. Some use capital letters, and others lower-case. One or two may even write 'the letter "a" five times'!

Now look at your own letters and ask whether they're all the same. Each 'a' is probably slightly different, but generally they're likely to be pretty similar and at least each one can clearly be identified as a letter 'a'.

The difference between your letters is natural variation, and your process for producing the letters is stable and predictable. If you repeat the exercise, you're likely to see the same sort of variation. To reduce the variation, you need to improve the process, perhaps by automating your writing or introducing a template. We continue this exercise in the 'Avoiding tampering' section later in this chapter.

Spotlighting special cause variation

Special cause variation is the variation you don't expect. Something unusual is happening and affecting the results. Special cause variation may occur if you don't identify an important 'X variable', which influences your process results, or if you don't manage the variable appropriately. The Xs will include a range of variables – for example, the accuracy and timeliness of the inputs to your process that you receive from suppliers, or the level of rework within your process (for more on X variables, see Chapter 8).

When a special cause exists, the process is no longer stable and its performance becomes unpredictable. You need to take action to identify the root cause of the special cause, and then either prevent the cause from occurring again if it degrades performance, or build the cause into the process if it improves it.

Not all special causes are bad. Sometimes they provide evidence that an improvement has worked. We describe how you can identify special causes later in this chapter, but first we need to stress why doing so is so important.

Distinguishing between variation types

You need to be able to tell the difference between the two types of variation. If you think something is special cause variation when in fact it's natural, you may inadvertently tamper with the process and actually increase the amount of variation. Likewise, if you think something is natural variation when it's really special cause, you may miss or delay taking an opportunity to improve the process.

Avoiding tampering

In the 'Understanding natural variation' section earlier in this chapter, we ask you to write down the letter 'a' five times as an example of natural variation. We suggest that, to reduce the amount of variation, you need to review and improve the process. In this section we show what happens if you tamper with the process by reacting to an individual example of common cause variation.

As an example, imagine that your manager doesn't understand the importance of distinguishing between natural and special cause variation. He wanders through your work area to see the output being produced. He feels that your letter 'a's show too much variation and asks you to show how you produce them. As you begin to demonstrate, your manager asks you to stop writing and points out that using your other hand is much better – after all, this is the hand he uses!

If you try writing with your other hand, your results probably show increased variation, and chances are you take longer to produce the output. Now imagine the output goes through an optical scanner – depending on the quality of your letters when you write using your other hand, you might see further problems. Your manager then provides some unhelpful ideas to solve this problem, too.

Unfortunately, tampering happens all the time in many organisations. Managers often feel their role is to tamper.

Another example of tampering is pointless discussion. You may often see reports comprising pages of numbers that somebody expects you to understand and perhaps base decisions on. In Figure 7-1 we show a typical set of information that is practically meaningless to all but the person who created it.

Figure 7-1:
A typical
dataset
providing
little useful
information.

	Sales Performance - **May**									
	Location A					Location B				
PRODUCT	Previous month	Target	Current month	Target	% change from last year	Previous month	Target	Current month	Target	% change from last year
1	34	30	37	30	-5.4	59	50	56	55	-7.6
2	260	250	230	250	3.3	226	250	267	250	12.8
3	75	75	65	70	0.4	125	130	133	135	5.9
4	3	2	4	2	2.7	16	15	18	15	-6.7
5	4678	4750	4978	5000	10.6	1657	1600	1753	1700	5.9
6	930	950	1006	975	2.9	975	1000	952	1000	-1.5
7	950	975	1100	1050	-3.9		975	950	975	-6.2
8	43	45	48	45	-2.8	75	75	78	85	8.4

© John Morgan and Martin Brenig-Jones

Figures relating to sales activity often provide good examples of pointless data. You may hear statements such as, 'This week's figures were better than last week's, but not as good as those of the week before that' or 'It rained last Thursday, but the team did a great job this week' – almost certainly the differences in the weekly figures are a measure of the natural variation in the process and not due to a special cause.

Using control charts can help you make sense of the figures by enabling you to distinguish between natural and special variation – but you may need to change the way you think. The different thinking needed is described as you work your way through the data from Figure 7-1, eventually using it to create a control chart in Figure 7-3.

Displaying data differently

The data in Figure 7-1 don't tell you much. But if you present the data in a more visual form, you may begin to understand them. Figure 7-1 shows a typical set of row-by-column data, highlighting the sales performance for two different locations in the month of May. The figure refers to eight different products. You can see the number of actual sales, along with some targets.

Instead of giving the figures for only one month, a more useful method is to plot a graph, called a *run chart*, using figures for a series of months. A run chart plots the data in time order – it is a time series plot that makes it easier to spot any trends. A run chart doesn't tell you whether the variation is natural or special – to know that, you use a control chart to see whether any changes are part of the natural variation of the process or whether they're unusual and need a second look.

In Figure 7-2 we use the figures for Location A and Product 3 to create a run chart that presents data through to the following March.

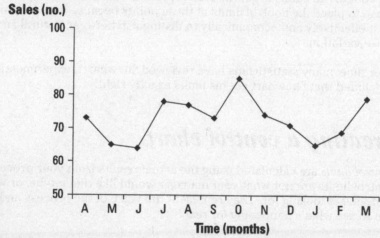

Figure 7-2: Presenting data as a run chart.

© John Morgan and Martin Brenig-Jones

Recognising the Importance of Control Charts

Control charts provide the only way to identify and understand variation.

Walter Shewhart, who felt that businesses wasted too much time confusing the types of variation and taking inappropriate action, developed control charts in the 1920s. Shewhart envisaged the control chart as a way to simplify identification of variation. He knew his control chart should be a run chart showing the mean average, and also the upper and lower control limits

(UCL and LCL). These upper and lower control limits show the natural range of the process results – but he was uncertain where to place these control limits.

Shewhart conducted thousands of experiments to determine the most appropriate position for the control limits. Using the data from the sub-group or sample taken, he discovered that the best positions were at plus and minus three standard deviations from the mean. We explain standard deviations in Chapter 1, but essentially, one standard deviation tells you the average difference between any one-process result and the overall average of all the process results. It's a measure of variation and at plus one and minus one standard deviation from the mean average, you're likely to incorporate almost two-thirds of your total results. At plus and minus two standard deviations, you cover approximately 95 per cent of the results and setting the control limits at plus and minus three standard deviations includes 99.73 per cent of the data. Forget the statistics for the moment, though. Shewhart chose to place the control limits at these points because here they work most effectively and economically to distinguish between natural and special cause variation.

Over time, many statisticians have reviewed Shewhart's experiments and concluded that Shewhart got his limits exactly right.

Creating a control chart

Control limits are calculated using the actual results from your processes. The control limits are not what your manager would like them to be, or what the customer is looking for. They represent the voice of the process and enable you to see what's happening for real.

Using the results from a process, you can calculate the mean of the first 20 points, represented by a central line on the control chart, together with the control limits, denoted by UCL and LCL. These control limits represent the natural variation of the readings. We show the details for calculating the control limits in Figure 7-7 later in this chapter. Right now, we need to look at the control chart in Figure 7-3. If you feel apprehensive about calculations, don't worry too much about the maths: the calculations are relatively straightforward, and you can use software to do them for you.

Building on our example from Figures 7-1 and 7-2, we've built in some more data for Location A and Product 3. The control chart for the sales figures appears in Figure 7-3. The chart shows that the sales process exhibits variation, and that it is natural. We use the rules of statistical process control (SPC) to distinguish the type of variation. We cover SPC rules in the 'Unearthing unusual features' section later in this chapter, but for now work on the fact that, because all the data fall within the control limits, the

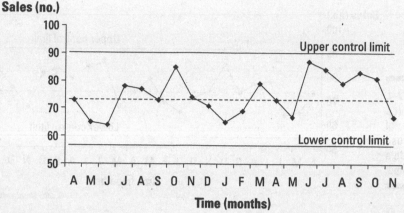

Figure 7-3:
Control chart for a process exhibiting natural variation.

© John Morgan and Martin Brenig-Jones

readings reflect natural variation. This won't always be the case and you'll need to look out for unusual patterns in the data. These patterns are part of the rules we describe in the 'Unearthing unusual features' section.

If a process exhibits only natural variation, then it is in statistical control and is *stable*. Being stable means that the process results are predictable and you'll continue to get results that display variation within the control limits. Not reacting to individual data items is the key.

Just because all your readings reflect a process that's under control, stable and predictable, doesn't mean your results are necessarily good. For example, you may find a large gap between the voice of the process and the voice of the customer (see Chapter 4 for more on these voices). You might not realise it, but your processes are trying to talk to you and you need to listen! Control charts provide an effective way to understand the voice of the process.

Because the process is stable, you can at least review the whole process to find improvement opportunities.

When you take action to improve the process, you must update your control chart to show the changes. Charts should provide a 'live' record of what happens – a 'clean' control chart probably isn't being used properly.

Unearthing unusual features

You can identify special causes of variation in a number of ways. Noticing when a data item appears outside the control limits is an obvious one, as we show in Figure 7-4.

Figure 7-4:
Occurrence
of a special
cause
outside a
control limit.

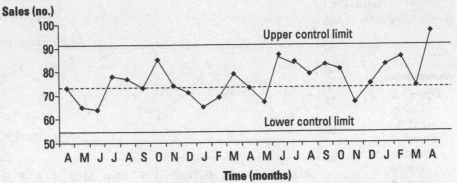

© John Morgan and Martin Brenig-Jones

You also have some special causes to contend with if you spot a run of seven consecutive points that are all:

- ✔ Going up
- ✔ Going down
- ✔ Above the mean
- ✔ Below the mean

Also watch for two other anomalies:

- ✔ The middle third rule, which is based on the assumption that approximately two-thirds of the data will appear in the middle third of your control chart. This brings us back to standard deviations. The middle third of the control chart covers plus and minus one standard deviation, approximately two-thirds of your population data. If the spread of the data is out of line with this pattern, a special cause may be responsible. We aren't great fans of this rule because it can be applied too rigorously and lead to confusion – we tend to focus on the point outside the control limits and the run of seven rules.

- ✔ Unusual patterns or trends, where, for example, something cyclical is occurring or data is drifting upwards or downwards over time, but isn't by itself offending any of the other rules.

This chapter concentrates on the most important signal – a data point outside the upper or lower control limits. You need to find the root cause and then either prevent the special cause from occurring again (if the result is bad) or build the special cause into the process (if the result is good).

TIP

Statistical process control is a broad subject, and in this chapter we provide only the key points. For more detail, grab one of our companion editions – *Six Sigma For Dummies* or *Six Sigma Workbook For Dummies* (John Wiley & Sons, Inc.).

In Figure 7-4, you can see a point outside the control limits. This probably indicates a special cause and you need to investigate it, but be aware that very occasionally you'll find a point outside the control limits that is a natural part of the process and lies in the small proportion of data outside the 99.73 per cent covered by the control limits. This is known as a false alarm, though you won't know that, of course, until you've investigated.

Maybe you know why the April sales figure is unusually high. Perhaps you ran a special promotion, coupled with the provision of a range of extra resources, resulting in a sales figure out of line with the previously expected values – and therefore outside the control limit. In SPC terms, the sales value for April is outside the system. This represents a good special cause – you need to see if you can build it into the process.

Sometimes you find a reason for an out-of-control signal that you can integrate into your improvement programme. As with this example, if you have a very high sales figure, and you know why, you can integrate this reason into the system and use it as part of an improvement strategy (of course, if it's the result of a special promotion, doing so may not be practical).

A special cause that most people are pleased to see is the proof that a change in the process has been successful. Figure 7-5 shows a situation where a process review has been carried out and an improvement action taken. The numbers on the vertical axis refer to the number of errors produced in sequential documents – perhaps the sales order forms.

Figure 7-5:
New control limits set after a process review and improvement action.

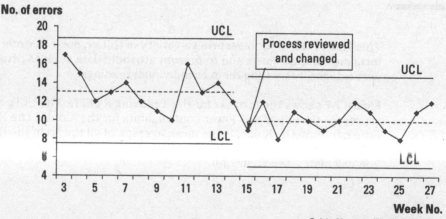

© *John Morgan and Martin Brenig-Jones*

The results that follow the change to the process are all below the original mean (the dotted line), reflecting an improvement in the process. The control chart gives us evidence of a change for the better – in this case, seven consecutive points below the original mean. You can now recalculate the control limits and head down a track that may highlight new special causes to be actioned. Reducing variation is one of the key principles of Lean Six Sigma – and that's exactly what you're seeing in Figure 7-5.

Choosing the right control chart

You can use a number of different SPC charts, but broadly they all follow the same concepts and rules. *Variable charts* display data that's been measured on a continuous scale, such as time, volumes or amounts of money, while *attribute charts* track data that's counted, or whether a particular characteristic is present, or right or wrong. Each type of chart has its own standard formula for calculating control limits, but generally the same rules for interpreting the results, and the presence of a centre line, the mean, apply to all.

Of the available control charts, the *X moving R*, or *individuals*, chart is the most versatile. In the X moving R chart, the 'X' represents each of the data points recorded – perhaps a series of sales volumes or the time taken to process each order. 'Moving R' describes the *moving range* – the absolute difference between each consecutive pair of Xs, as shown in Figure 7-6.

Figure 7-6:
Determining the moving range.

X	47	38	7	57	45	59
Moving R		9	31	50	12	14

© John Morgan and Martin Brenig-Jones

This chart is ideal for measuring a variety of things, such as cycle time performance and volumes, and to present attribute data such as proportions or percentages by treating them as individual readings.

Figure 7-7 shows the formula for the X moving R chart. The UCL$_X$ and LCL$_X$ represent the upper and lower control limits for the X data. The X with the little bar above it (X bar) is the mean average of all the Xs in the data you're using to construct your chart. R bar is the mean of the moving range values you calculate – see Figure 7-6.

In addition to the control chart for the X values, you can also create a chart for the moving range values. The formulae make use of 'standard constant' values, in this case represented by A_2, D_3 and D_4. These have been calculated using statistics to provide shortcuts in the calculations.

The X moving R chart

$$UCL_X = \bar{X} + (A_2\bar{R}) \qquad LCL_X = \bar{X} - (A_2\bar{R})$$

A_2 is one of a number of constant values used in calculating control limits. If the moving range is determined by looking at each pair of Xs, then A_2 will always be 2.66.

Figure 7-7: Looking at the formula for the X moving R chart.

The formula for the Moving Range part of the chart is:

$$UCL_R = D_4\bar{R} \qquad LCL_R = D_3\bar{R}$$

D_4 is another of the constants used. Its value for the X moving R chart is 3.267. D_3 has no value for this chart, and the LCL_R will always be 0.

© John Morgan and Martin Brenig-Jones

REMEMBER

Control charts are a key technique in the analysis, control and improvement of processes. Be aware that top-level management should initiate control charts, not those working with the processes. Managers should understand variation and then demonstrate that understanding through their behaviour if their teams are to appreciate the benefits of control charts and SPC. This means that if the data is natural variation, managers shouldn't be tampering.

Examining the state of your processes

You can demonstrate your understanding of variation by using control charts to review performance in regular management meetings. Doing so can show you a number of important things that enable you to make more effective decisions. In particular, control charts help you to determine the state of your organisation's processes and potentially to transform the operational meetings. This would be the case where the main thrust of current meetings is asking why this week's results are worse than last week's, and using the data to blame people for poor performance. Similarly, where the results are better than the previous week, people are praised for higher performance. No understanding of natural or special cause variation exists and tampering is rife. This type of meeting and behaviour tends to lead to the distortion of data and process, and a failure to manage by fact.

A process can be in one of four states, which provide the basis for more effective discussion and action, as shown in Figure 7-8:

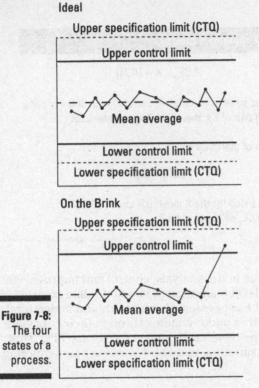

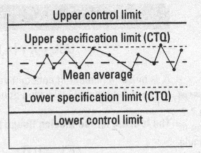

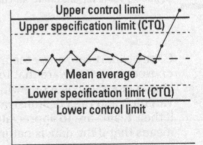

Figure 7-8: The four states of a process.

© John Morgan and Martin Brenig-Jones

- In an **ideal state**, the process is in statistical control and meets the customer's requirements. If you use a traffic-light system at your operations meetings, you can think of this state as a 'green light' – you need no discussion about why this week's numbers differ from last week's. Knowing whether the process is in statistical control and meets the CTQs is what's important. By continuing to use the control chart, you can monitor the process and make sure it remains ideal. You may also want to improve on ideal – perhaps by delighting the customer or reducing the costs associated with the process – but to do that you need to implement an improvement project that looks at the whole process.

- A **threshold state** – or 'amber light' – describes a process that's in statistical control but doesn't meet the customer specifications. Your discussion then focuses on the action that you need to take to bring the process into an ideal state. Again, you don't need to discuss the variation between this week's and last week's numbers, because the process is predictable. Assuming a DMAIC improvement project is initiated (see Chapter 2), your ongoing discussions will concern the progress you make. By continuing to use the control chart, you can monitor the effectiveness of your improvement efforts and, in due course, provide evidence that they're working, perhaps with the identification of a special cause, similar to that in Figure 7-5.

✔ When a process is in the **on the brink state**, it meets the customer's requirements but is not in statistical control. The process has special causes and is unpredictable. This is a red light situation – at any moment the process may slip into chaos.

✔ Chaos – the serious **red light state** – describes a process that's not in statistical control and doesn't meet the customer's specifications. By continuing to use the control chart, you can monitor the removal of special causes and the eventual improvement and stability of the process. Removing these special causes from the process before you begin to change is important; if you don't, it's highly likely they'll impede your efforts to improve.

In a culture of continuous improvement, moving to an ideal state via a threshold performance is fine. Improvement efforts should always focus on bringing the process into a state of statistical control first – special causes can confuse your improvement efforts if you don't understand the interactions they are causing.

Take a bite-sized approach to improvement, monitoring as you go.

As your use and understanding of control charts increases, you may wish to incorporate additional information concerning the capability of your processes. Capability indices help you understand more about how well your processes are doing in terms of meeting the CTQs.

Considering the capability of your processes

A process in statistical control is not necessarily a good process. The process is predictable, but it still may not meet your customers' CTQs. Two *capability indices* can be used to help assess your performance.

The capability indices compare the process performance and variation to the CTQs and provide both a theoretical and actual measure to demonstrate the relationship. They tell you precisely how capable the process is of meeting the CTQs.

These indices are relevant only when your process is in control and the process is predictable. The first capability index – the C_p *index* – looks at the variation in the process compared with the specification limits of the CTQs.

Using the C_p index is like gauging whether or not you can get your car through a gap. Imagine that the width of the control limits in your control chart is represented by the width of the car in Figure 7-9, and the arch represents the width of your customer's specification limits, his CTQ. Consider whether you can drive through the arch.

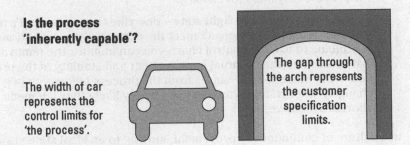

Is the process 'inherently capable'?

The width of car represents the control limits for 'the process'.

The gap through the arch represents the customer specification limits.

Figure 7-9: Taking your driving theory test.

The process is 'Inherently Capable' but only if it's 'centred'.

In Figure 7-9, you can see that driving through the gap is possible – but only just. You need to drive very carefully and 'centre' the car. In other words, you need to line up the mean of the control chart with the mid-point of the customer's specification. The C_p index tells us how many times the car can, in theory, fit inside the arch. In our example, the car fits inside the arch just once, so the C_p value is 1.0.

C_{pk} is the second capability index and it describes the 'location'. C_{pk} tells you how well you're 'driving' – that is, how well you manage your process. The location describes the position of your process performance as presented by your control limits when compared to the CTQ specification.

In Figure 7-10, the driving needs some improvement. Here, the C_{pk} value is less than the C_p value. If C_{pk} is less than 1.0, it doesn't meet the CTQ. In process terms, you need to shift the mean by improving this threshold process. Reducing the variation also makes the 'fit' of the car in the arch that little bit easier.

How well is it being driven?
If the process is off centre,
it isn't capable.

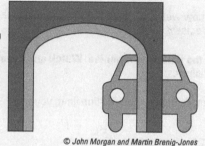

Figure 7-10:
The driving
needs
improve-
ment.

© John Morgan and Martin Brenig-Jones

To fully assess a process you need both the C_p and the C_{pk} values. You also need to be in control of the process for these indices to be meaningful. The C_{pk} value is never greater than the C_p value. When the process mean is running on the 'nominal' – the mid-point of the customer specification – C_{pk} and C_p are the same value. This involves good management of the process, or, continuing our car analogy, some careful driving.

Figure 7-11 shows the formula for calculating the C_p and C_{pk} values for the X moving R chart (see the 'Choosing the right control chart' section earlier in this chapter). The difference between the control limits, the UCL and the LCL, on your control chart covers six standard deviations. The difference between the upper and lower customer specification (USL–LSL) is usually referred to as the *tolerance*. The USL and LSL represent the range of the customer's CTQ. For example, he may want a product delivered within five days, but describe his requirement as an upper specification of five days and a lower specification of one day. Three days would be the nominal value of this specification, the mid-point, and the tolerance, the difference between the specification limits, would be four days.

Dividing the tolerance by the distance between your control limits (six standard deviations), you have the C_p value – the theoretical number of times you can fit the car within the arch. Your C_p value must be at least 1.0 if you are to meet the CTQ, though this really is the minimum. Some organisations set their suppliers a minimum target of 1.33 or higher for the goods or parts they provide to them.

Figure 7-11 describes how the formula for working out your C_{pk} depends on the position of the mean on your control chart.

The Cp Index

$$Cp = \frac{USL - LSL}{UCL - LCL} = \frac{Tolerance}{6\ standard\ deviations}$$

- For the process to be inherently capable, the Cp index needs to be at least 1.0.

- It may be inherently capable, but how well is it located? You need to use the other capability index, Cpk to find out precisely.

You need to use one or the other of the following formulae: Which one depends on the position of the mean on the control chart.

- If the mean is closer to the customer's upper specification limit, you use

$$Cpk = \frac{USL - \overline{X}}{3\ standard\ deviations}$$

- If the mean is closer to the lower specification limit, you use

$$Cpk = \frac{\overline{X} - LSL}{3\ standard\ deviations}$$

- 3 standard deviations is the distance from the mean of the control chart to the upper control limit; 6 standard deviations is the distance between the upper and lower control limits.

Figure 7-11: The capability formula.

© John Morgan and Martin Brenig-Jones

To put the capability indices into context, think location, location, location! You need to manage your processes in a way that tightly controls variation and *locates* the mean of your control chart on the nominal of the customer specification. Figure 7-12 shows the effects of doing so.

In Figure 7-12, the process has a C_p value of 2.0 – in theory, it can fit inside the arch twice. If the C_{pk} is also 2.0, the process is very capable of meeting the customer specification and does fit inside the arch twice. On the other hand, if your driving isn't so good – that is, you don't manage your process well enough – you can see the effect as the C_{pk} value reduces, moving from left to right in the figure. When C_{pk} is below 1.0, you're unable to consistently meet the customer's specification.

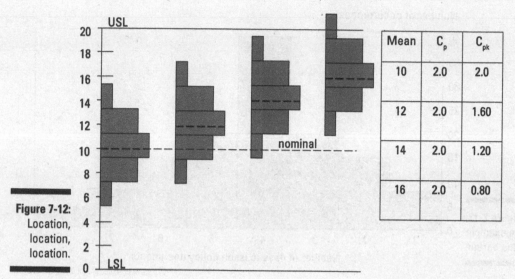

Figure 7-12: Location, location, location.

The capability indices help give you a complete picture of performance. They can help you prioritise improvement action, too. By comparing the C_p and C_{pk} values of different processes, you can decide where to focus your improvement efforts, perhaps concentrating on those processes for which the values are less than 1.0.

Additional ways to present and analyse your data

As we explain in this chapter, process data may be presented in control charts, enabling you to determine the state of the process and its capability of meeting CTQs. This information provides you with a clear picture of the action needed, if any.

Once the control chart indicates that the process is stable, we can use other charts to examine the data. The histogram, shown in Figure 7-13, is a chart frequently used to look at large (>50) samples.

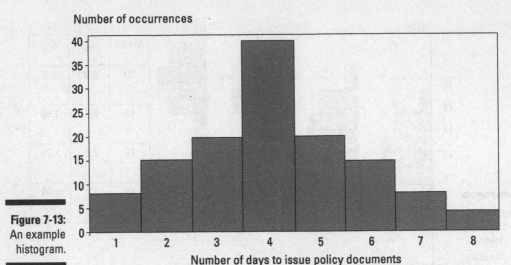

Number of occurrences

Figure 7-13:
An example
histogram.

Number of days to issue policy documents

© John Morgan and Martin Brenig-Jones

Histograms can be helpful in providing a picture of the mean and range of performance, and indeed the distribution of the data; they don't help you determine the *type* of variation that you're seeing, however, which is why we use a control chart. In Figure 7-13, the data appear to be distributed normally, but this isn't always the case.

Sometimes you might see examples of skewed data, where, perhaps, a lot of items are processed quickly but a long tail of data reflects items that are delayed for some reason – see the chart in Figure 7-14. These delayed items may be creating customer complaints or increasing your processing costs in some way – or both! With a skewed distribution, the mean is pulled to the right or left of centre and the broadly even spread of data we see in the 'bell-shaped curve' of a normal distribution is shaped accordingly.

You need to understand the reasons for the delay, perhaps using a check sheet and Pareto diagram to present your results (see Chapter 6 for more on these). The histogram can also help you identify the need to segment your data, as shown in Figure 7-15.

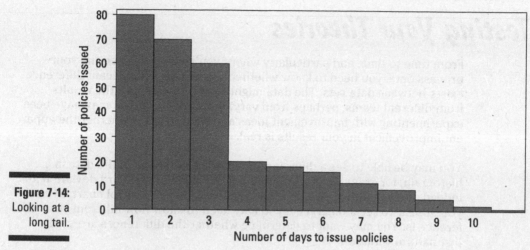

Figure 7-14: Looking at a long tail.

© John Morgan and Martin Brenig-Jones

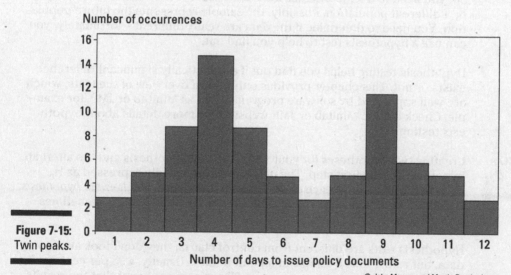

Figure 7-15: Twin peaks.

© John Morgan and Martin Brenig-Jones

Looking like a camel with two humps, this *bimodal distribution* (two peaks) contains two 'populations', and to fully understand what the results are showing you need to separate them. The two populations could well be two different product lines, where one takes longer to process because of its increased complexity, for example, or the results might be from different locations dealing with different processes.

Testing Your Theories

From time to time, and particularly where you've been segmenting your process data, you need to know whether a statistically significant difference exists between data sets. The data might show, for example, the results from different teams, perhaps from varying locations. Or you may have been experimenting with improvement ideas and want to know whether the apparent improvement in your results is real.

You may be able to see a difference by viewing the shape of the data in a histogram, for example, or by comparing the mean or standard deviation, or indeed, the amount of variation that's showing up in a control chart. Even if you appear to see a difference, you may need to know how different your difference is. You may want to determine whether the differences are 'real' or just natural variation.

So, you need to decide whether the data has come from the same population or a different population. Possibly, the sample represents the future population. You need to determine if the data are really different – fortunately, you can use a hypothesis test to help you find out.

Hypothesis testing helps you find out if a statistically significant difference exists or not. This chapter provides only a brief overview of the tests, which are well supported by software programs such as Minitab or JMP, for example. Check out the Minitab or JMP websites for more details about hypothesis testing.

 Creating two hypotheses for your tests, the null hypothesis and the alternate hypothesis, is the first step. The *null hypothesis*, usually expressed as H_0, proposes that no difference exists between the data. The *alternate hypothesis*, H_A, states a difference is evident. The alternative hypothesis is sometimes presented as H_1.

Hypothesis tests are different from control charts; they don't look at ongoing data, but rather take a sample at a point in time. Usually, a 95 per cent confidence level is used; that is, you can be 95 per cent confident that the results display either a statistical difference or they don't.

Two hypothesis tests may be especially useful: the T-test and the ANOVA. The *T-test* looks at two sets of data (as shown in Figure 7-16), and the *ANOVA* considers three or more sets of data.

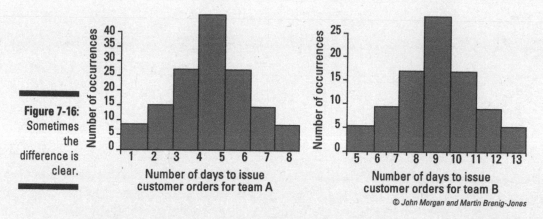

Figure 7-16: Sometimes the difference is clear.

An example of using a T-test is determining whether a process change has really improved performance: you look at the before and after results, perhaps following a DMAIC project. An example of using ANOVA is comparing the results from several teams in order to identify whether one team is performing better than others, which perhaps provides an example of best practice to follow. A *p value* determines whether a real difference exists in your data. Using the usual confidence level of 95 per cent, if p is less than 5 per cent ($p < 0.05$), you can be 95 per cent confident that a difference exists – a 5 per cent chance of spuriously seeing a difference when one isn't there still exists, but the odds are overwhelmingly (19 to 1) against this being the case. If p is equal to or greater than 5 per cent ($p >$ or $= 0.05$), you can conclude that insufficient evidence exists to reject the null hypothesis. You can interpret this conclusion in one of three ways:

✔ The samples come from the same original population.

✔ You have too much variation.

✔ Your samples are too small to detect any real difference.

Where a difference is evident, in the performance of teams at different branches, for example, don't jump to conclusions about why. The difference could be related to the way the data is collected, the size of the branch, the number of staff, their experience, the market segmentation, and so on. Through discussion and analysis of the process, you need to find the reasons, so you can build in best practice or find ways to eliminate the root causes of problems.

Chapter 8

Analysing What's Affecting Performance

In This Chapter

▶ Finding out what's at fault

▶ Using data to prove the point

▶ Introducing the maths of Lean Six Sigma

Whether you manage a day-to-day operation or are involved in a DMAIC (Define, Measure, Analyse, Improve and Control) improvement project, you need to understand what factors can affect performance, especially if you encounter problems in meeting your customers' requirements. In this chapter, we introduce a selection of tools and techniques to help you identify the 'guilty parties'. We focus on how and how well the work gets done – the process and the data.

Unearthing the Usual Suspects

If you've seen the Oscar-winning film *The Usual Suspects*, you may remember its false trails and red herrings. Not until the closing scenes do you find out just who the guilty person is. Many of the usual suspects are innocent – just like in real life and in your search for the root causes of problems in your process.

People often jump to conclusions about the possible causes of problems; in many organisations, managers seem to 'know' for sure what the causes are. Usually, however, a whole range of suspects influence performance and affect your ability to meet customers' CTQs (Critical To Quality requirements) – but chances are only a vital few are actually 'guilty'. Consider the following fishy tale.

A shortage of oysters off the eastern seaboard of the US has occurred in recent years. Clearly, this is a symptom of global warming or pollution. But perhaps not: research carried out by a Canadian university shows how the functional elimination of large sharks from the east coast, especially the scalloped hammerhead, has inadvertently resulted in dwindling supplies of shellfish as the result of an increased population of the rays who eat them – see Figure 8-1.

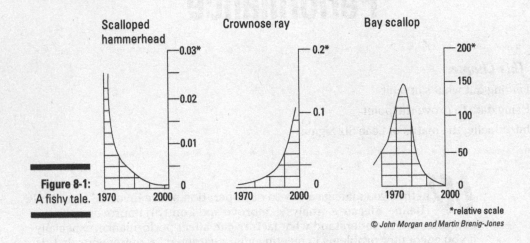

Figure 8-1: A fishy tale.

*relative scale

© John Morgan and Martin Brenig-Jones

Generating your list of suspects

To find the guilty party, you generate a list of possible causes, check out each possible cause and gradually narrow down the list. In this section we look at the methods available to help you root out the suspects.

Creating a cause and effect diagram

The fishbone, or cause and effect, diagram (see Figure 8-2) was developed by Dr Ishikawa and provides a useful way of grouping and presenting ideas arising from a brainstorming session.

The head of the fish contains a question that describes the effect you are investigating (make sure you choose a narrowly focused question or you'll end up with a whalebone!). For example, you might ask, 'What are the possible causes of delays in delivering customer orders?' or 'Why are there so many errors in our invoices?' You can group the possible brainstormed causes under whatever headings you choose. In Figure 8-2 we use the traditional headings of People, Equipment, Method, Materials and Environment. You may find these headings useful in prompting ideas during the brainstorming session, but be aware that they can also inhibit more lateral thinking.

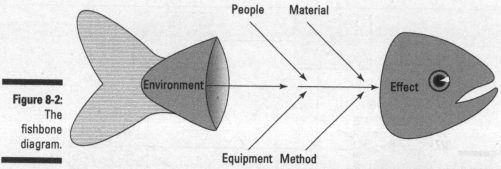

© John Morgan and Martin Brenig-Jones

Figure 8-2: The fishbone diagram.

The team comes up with their ideas on the possible causes, writing the ideas on sticky notes so that you can move them around easily during the subsequent sorting process.

Place your major cause headings on the left-hand side of the diagram, forming the main 'bones' of the fish. The brainstormed ideas (the potential main causes) form the smaller bones. For each possible cause, ask the question 'Why do we think this is a possible cause?' and list the responses as smaller bones coming off the main cause. You may have to ask 'Why?' several times to identify the probable reason, though you might still need to validate this with data.

Use an interrelationship diagram next, to help you focus on the right Xs (or input variables – see the following section for an explanation), as shown in Figure 8-3. Remember, the numbers next to the boxes represent arrows out over arrows in.

Instigating an interrelationship diagram

Using an interrelationship diagram helps you identify the key drivers behind the effect you're investigating in your fishbone diagram. We cover the interrelationship diagram in Chapter 2, where we show how you can use it with an affinity diagram – a really useful way of helping you get to the root cause, the key driver of the problem you're addressing.

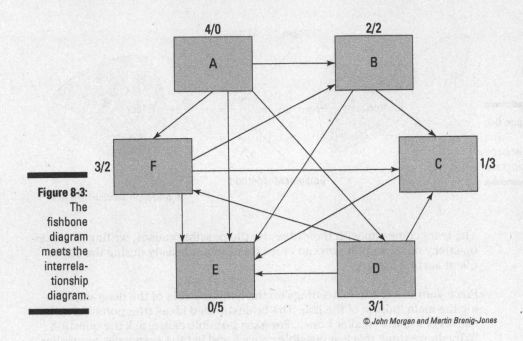

Figure 8-3: The fishbone diagram meets the interrelationship diagram.

Investigating the suspects and getting the facts

Managing by fact is vital, so validating the possible causes highlighted by your interrelationship diagram (see previous section) is the next step. All those possible causes are innocent until proven guilty. To validate your causes, you may need to observe the process and go to the Gemba (the place where the work gets done – see Chapter 2), or check out the data to see whether they confirm your suspicions. You'll probably need to collect some additional data to do this. Chapter 4 covers the development of measurable CTQs, which provide the basis for the measurement set of your process, and Chapters 6 and 7 introduce the importance of a data collection process, beginning with the need to measure the outputs of your process.

In Lean Six Sigma speak, the output measures are Y data, and the results here are influenced by the upstream X variables. Xs and Ys are actually just cause and effect. Individually and collectively, the various Xs influence your performance in meeting the customer CTQs, the Y variables. Sometimes, Xs are referred to as 'independent variables' and Ys as 'dependent variables'. Clearly, the Y results depend on you managing the Xs very carefully.

A SIPOC diagram (see Chapter 3 for the details) provides an ideal framework to help you think about all your process measures and now you need to pull together a set of X measures, if you don't already have them. A range of X variables will be coming into your process – the input variables. These input variables affect the performance of the Ys, and may include the volume of activities, for example the number and type of new orders. The input variables may well concern the performance of your suppliers, too, perhaps in terms of the level of accuracy, completeness and timeliness of the various items being sent to you. The inputs might be from customers or suppliers, but either way, they'll impact on how you perform. How often do you need to go back for missing information or clearer instructions, for example?

A range of X variables will exist in the process itself – the in-process variables. Here, your deployment flowchart or value stream map (see Chapter 5 for details) can help you highlight the potential Xs, including activity and cycle times, levels of rework, the availability of people or machine downtime, for example. Again, these Xs will affect your performance. As you identify the X measures you need, so you're building a balance of measures to help you manage your process. You're likely to find that the SIPOC and deployment flowchart are especially helpful here.

Getting a Balance of Measures

To fully understand the performance of your process, you need a balance of input, in-process and output measures, as shown in Figure 8-4, with perhaps one to three measures for each. You also need to recognise that the input and in-process variables will influence the results in your output variables, so your measures should clearly link together.

Figure 8-4: Getting the balance of measures and understanding how they interrelate. The different variables will all need corresponding measures to hep you assess performance.

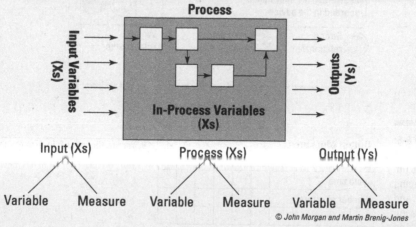

Getting the balance of measures and understanding how they interrelate:

© John Morgan and Martin Brenig-Jones

Connecting things up

Figure 8-5 provides a reminder of how the CTQs are pulled together and incorporates Figure 6-1 from Chapter 6. Figure 6-1 shows how you need to put the measurable CTQs into a matrix, determine the output measures and assess the output measures as strong, medium or weak.

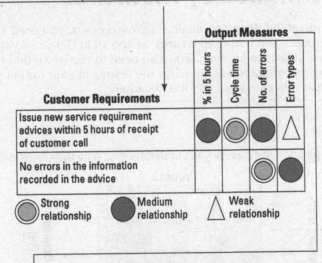

Voice of the customer	Key issues	Measurable CTQ
To meet timescales we need to know about new service requirements asap	Speed is key as the service must be completed within agreed timeframes	Issue new service advices within 5 hours of receipt
We must have the right details and information	Accuracy is vital to avoid wasted activity and lost time	No errors in the documentation

The Fishbone may have highlighted some gaps.

Do we have the right measures and an appropriate balance? Perhaps we need to segment the data in some way.

Output Measures

Customer Requirements	% in 5 hours	Cycle time	No. of errors	Error types
Issue new service requirement advices within 5 hours of receipt of customer call	●	●	●	△
No errors in the information recorded in the advice			●	●

○ Strong relationship   ● Medium relationship   △ Weak relationship

What are the input & in-process X variables?

Output Measures — What are the input & in-process measures?

Output Measures						
% in five hours						
Cycle time						
Number of errors						
Type of errors						

○ Strong relationship   ● Medium relationship   △ Weak relationship

Figure 8-5: Linking things up: developing and reviewing the measures.

© John Morgan and Martin Brenig-Jones

Now you put the output measures into the Y to X matrix, as shown in Figure 8-5, identifying the X variables and the corresponding measures for them. You also need to assess how these X measures link to the outputs, ensuring you have at least one strong X measure linking to each output measure, the Ys.

Ideally, you can determine precisely how the variables interrelate, considering the X measures as *leading indicators* and the Y measures as *lagging indicators* – that is, a clear cause and effect correlation is in place. To do this, you need to use a scatter diagram to help prove your point.

Proving your point

When you think you know the cause of the problem in your process, you may need to provide some evidence to back it up. For example, your boss may think she knows the answer, but you may find something different as the result of your careful analysis of the facts.

Figure 8-6 presents a simple matrix to show how the various snippets of evidence match against the suspects:

✔ Remember that correlation may not mean causation.

✔ One hundred per cent certainty is impossible.

✔ More analysis is almost always possible.

✔ Fear of being wrong.

✔ Beware of analysis paralysis.

Evidence	Suspect A	Suspect B	Suspect C
Branch performance data	√	×	√
Complaint analysis	√	×	×
Pareto analysis	√	×	×
Correlation co efficient	√	√	√

Figure 8-6: Being logical.

© John Morgan and Martin Brenig-Jones

This matrix is sometimes referred to as *logical cause testing*, where you summarise the possible causes of the problem, and show whether the various evidence you've gathered from your process and data analysis logically matches the suspects. This process is similar to the way in which a legal trial proves or disproves the guilt of the accused: all the evidence is assembled and tested against the (suspected) final causes.

It's almost always possible to carry out further analysis, but these two questions can help you decide if doing so is sensible:

- ✔ Do you feel that you understand enough about the process, problem and cause(s) to be able to develop effective solutions?

- ✔ Is the value of additional data worth the extra cost in time, resources and momentum?

Using a *scatter diagram* (sometimes referred to as a scatter plot) can help you strengthen your case. A scatter diagram helps you identify whether a potential relationship or correlation exists between two variables and enables you to give a value to and quantify that relationship. The variables are the cause and effect – X and Y. You can use this method to verify potential root causes of a problem or, for example, to validate the relationship between your input and in-process measures against your output measures. If your suspected cause (X) is real, then any changes in X produce a change in the effect (Y). Do be careful, however, as correlation does not always imply causation, and you need to use common sense to draw your conclusions.

The dependent Y variable is always plotted on the vertical axis; the independent X variable is plotted on the horizontal axis. The data is plotted in pairs, so when X = 'this value', Y = 'that value'. We show four such pairs in the first example in Figure 8-7. In this example, a relationship seems to exist between speed and error rate – the faster we do it, the more errors we get. This correlation is positive because the values of Y increase as the values of X increase.

Figure 8-7: Demonstrating correlation with a scattergram.

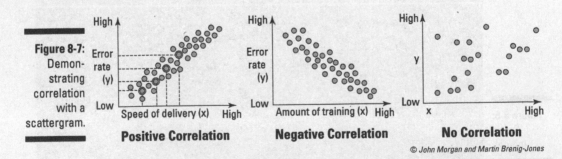

© John Morgan and Martin Brenig-Jones

The second example in Figure 8-7 shows a negative correlation – the values of Y decrease as the values of X increase and, in doing do, appear to confirm our theory that investment in training leads to reduced error rates.

In the third example in Figure 8-7 no correlation exists, so our theory doesn't hold. Whatever the X is, it doesn't influence the Y results; do make sure, though, that the data has been segmented, otherwise a pattern might be hidden from view. Chapter 3 covers segmentation.

Seeing the point

Simply seeing the picture may be enough to demonstrate that you have or haven't found the root cause of your problem, but to strengthen your case you can put a value on the relationship between the variables by calculating the *correlation coefficient*, or r value. This value quantifies the relationship between the X and the Y – it tells you the strength of the relationship, be it positive or negative, in terms of the amount of variation the X is causing in the Y results.

In a perfectly positive correlation, r = +1. In a perfectly negative correlation, r = –1. Usually the correlation coefficient is less than one, as the possibility of only one X affecting the performance of the Y is unlikely; generally, several will be evident and it's likely you will have determined the correlation coefficient value for each of these. Almost certainly, however, one X will be causing the most variation.

The correlation coefficient becomes clearer with a little bit more maths (don't worry – software such as Excel, JMP or Minitab can do it for you). The value R^2 (the coefficient of determination) shows the percentage of variation in Y explained by the effect of X. For example, if r = 0.7, the variable is causing 49 per cent of the variation in Y; if r = 0.8, the value increases to 64 per cent. In either of these circumstances, you seem to have found the important root cause of the problem as these values are particularly high, especially considering that a number of other Xs are also influencing the Y results. With a lower value, for example where r = 0.2 or 0.3, the impact is relatively small, accounting for 4 per cent and 9 per cent, respectively.

Figure 8-8 shows the line of best fit, which can help you see the likely values for data that you don't currently have. Drawing a line through highly cor-related data such as that in the first two examples in Figure 8-8 is easy – you can do it with a ruler and pencil. You can calculate the line precisely using the regression equation, $Y = b_0 + b_1x$, where b_0 = the intercept (where the line crosses the vertical axis, X = 0) and b_1 = the slope (the change in Y per unit change in X).

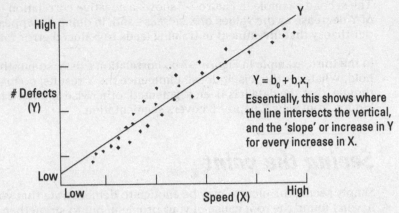

$Y = b_0 + b_1 x_1$

Essentially, this shows where the line intersects the vertical, and the 'slope' or increase in Y for every increase in X.

Figure 8-8:
Working out
the line of
best fit.

Here you can use the data to help you predict things, but remember the potential for a threshold point that changes the picture.

© John Morgan and Martin Brenig-Jones

You'll see this equation presented in a number of ways but, whichever letters you use, the slope will look the same! Figure 8-9 identifies the need to be aware of a threshold point – the straight line of best fit might not always continue into the future as circumstances change.

When just one X is involved, this calculation is known as *simple linear regression. Multiple regression* extends the technique to cover several Xs, as does *design of experiments*, but these more involved statistical techniques are outside the scope of this book (take a look at *Six Sigma For Dummies* by Craig Gygi, Neil DeCarlo and Bruce Williams and *Six Sigma Workbook For Dummies* by Craig Gygi, Bruce Williams and Terry Gustafson, both published by John Wiley & Sons, Inc.).

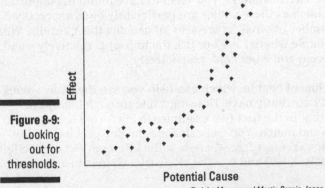

Figure 8-9:
Looking
out for
thresholds.

© John Morgan and Martin Brenig-Jones

Linear regression enables you to make predictions for the value of Y with different values of X, though remember that the straight line might not continue forever. As indicated earlier, a threshold may exist where things change dramatically, as we show in Figure 8-9.

Abandon rate in a call centre is a good example of a threshold point existing where callers might be prepared to hang on the line for a reasonable time, but at a certain point they become irate and slam the phone down.

Scatter diagrams are easy to produce using programs such as JMP, Excel or Minitab. However, be aware of some of the common errors and pitfalls associated with them, such as mixing up the X and Y variables and axes or making the assumption that correlation implies causation. Correlation does not always imply causation, and you need to use common sense to draw your conclusions.

The example in Figure 8-10 shows data from the German village of Oldenberg, for the years 1930 to 1936. As you can see, the figure shows that Walt Disney's *Dumbo* got it right: storks really do bring babies! A relationship does exist in these data – but the X and Y axes are the wrong way round. The village expanded in this period, people built new houses and the increase in the number of tall chimneys proved to be an attraction for nesting storks. More usefully, we could plot the number of houses on the X axis and the number of storks on the Y axis.

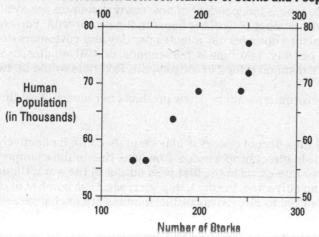

Figure 8-10:
Bringing home the baby.

Source: Box, Hunter, Hunter. *Statistics For experimenters.* New York, NY: John Wiley & Sons. 1978.

Understanding the various Xs affecting the performance of your process is crucial. Once you've identified your Xs, you can ensure the right measures are in place and can work towards creating stable and predictable performance.

Assessing your effectiveness

Several Lean measures are available to help you understand performance and the scale of improvement needed, including Takt time and overall process effectiveness and overall equipment effectiveness.

Taking Takt time into account

Takt time tells you how quickly you need to action things in relation to customer demand. Takt is German for a precise interval of time such as a musical meter. It serves as the rhythm or beat of the process – the frequency at which a product or service must be completed in order to meet customer needs.

The Takt time formula is the available production time divided by customer demand:

$$\frac{\text{The available work time per shift}}{\text{The number of customer orders per shift}}$$

The available time is independent of how many resources are available. It represents the number of working hours in the day or shift. For example, if a widget factory operates 480 minutes per day and customers demand 100 widgets per day, Takt time is 288 seconds, or 4.80 minutes, as shown in Figure 8-11. If demand is for 240 widgets, the Takt time would be two minutes.

Similarly, if customers want two new products per month, Takt time is two weeks.

Recognising the effect of rework is important, because it effectively reduces the Takt time in direct proportion. So, imagine that in the example, a 10 per cent error rate exists in the first-pass output of the work, though this is picked up and corrected. In effect, this 'increases' the number of customer requests from 100 to 110, the 'available' minutes are unchanged at 480, but the impact on Takt time is to effectively make it shorter, at 4.36 minutes. Takt time will effectively be shorter still if we have second-pass corrections to deal with! So, the actual Takt time might be 480, but the rework means you have less time than that in practice.

For example, using the formula:

$$\frac{\text{The available work time per shift}}{\text{The number of customer orders per shift}}$$

- You have 100 customer requests each working day, where you have an eight-hour shift for 10 people

- The number of people isn't a factor in calculating Takt time, so:

  - 8 (hours) x 60 (minutes) = 480 available minutes

  - 480 divided by 100 (customer requests) = 4.80 Takt time

- Even if there were 20 people, the Takt time would still be 4.80.

- It's the production rate needed to meet the demand.

© John Morgan and Martin Brenig-Jones

Figure 8-11:
Calculating
Takt time.

Incidentally, Toyota typically reviews the Takt time for a process every month, with a tweaking review every ten days. Within a service organisation, the use of control charts (see Chapter 7), to understand the likely variation in customer orders for example, can be a helpful way of reviewing Takt time.

Clearly, an important relationship exists between Takt time, cycle time and activity time. If the Takt time is less than the cycle time you have a problem, which must be tackled immediately, ideally using DMAIC. Removing waste may well be part of the solution; preventing it in the first place might be another.

When Takt time equals cycle time 'perfect flow' exists, but too often the flow isn't balanced. This situation can cause bottlenecks that disrupt your ability to meet customer demand. Figure 8-12 shows the dilemma faced by a line experiencing bottlenecks.

In order to meet the Takt time, the level of non-value-added (NVA) activities will need to be addressed, but a better balance will be required, too, as shown in Figure 8-13.

Chapter 9 covers NVA activity in detail, but essentially this relates to unnecessary work that adds no value to the customer.

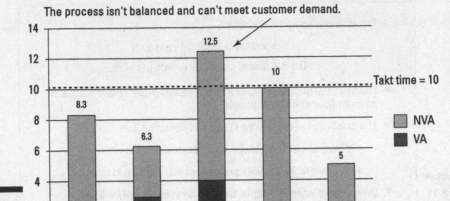

The process isn't balanced and can't meet customer demand.

Figure 8-12:
Visualising
cycle time
versus Takt
time.

Total Cycle Time = 42.1 mins

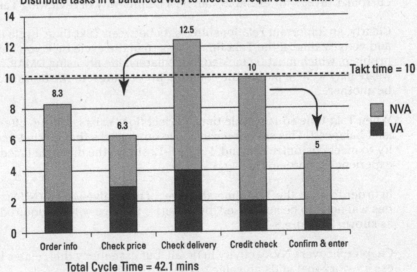

Distribute tasks in a balanced way to meet the required Takt time.

Figure 8-13:
Balancing
the flow.

Total Cycle Time = 42.1 mins

Combine tasks, reduce NVA and simplify things where possible.

Considering overall process and equipment effectiveness

In analysing your performance, you may also want to put in place some additional measures, such as *overall process effectiveness* (OPE) in transactional processes and *overall equipment effectiveness* (OEE) in manufacturing. We use OPE and OEE to measure and understand the performance and effectiveness of equipment or processes. Each of these summary measures has three components: availability, performance and quality.

- **The availability rate** measures downtime losses from equipment failures and adjustments as a percentage of the defined and scheduled time.

- **The performance rate** measures operating speed losses – running at speeds lower than design speed and stoppages lasting for brief periods as agreed.

- **The quality rate** expresses losses resulting from scrap and rework as a percentage of total parts run.

These elements are multiplied together, where

$$OEE = Availability \times Performance \times Quality.$$

So, with Availability at 90 per cent, Performance at 95 per cent and Quality at 99 per cent,

$$OEE = 0.90 \times 0.95 \times 0.99 = 84.6 \text{ per cent.}$$

In service organisations, or for transactional processes, OPE tends to be used. Here, you take the following three elements, again multiplying them together to determine the OPE:

A = availability of equipment

P = productivity

Q = quality rate

Take a look at *Lean For Dummies* by Natalie J. Sayer and Bruce Williams (John Wiley & Sons, Inc.) for more detailed information about the OPE and OEE.

Part IV
Improving the Processes

DMAIC/DMADV transition points:

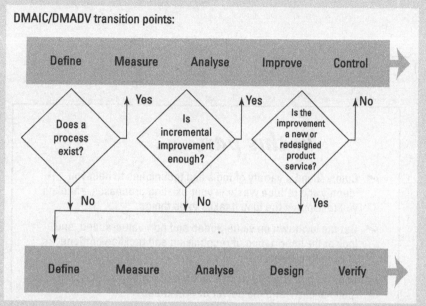

© John Morgan and Martin Brenig-Jones

Head to www.dummies.com/extras/leansixsigma for an example of a suitable use of Failures Modes Effects Analysis (FMEA).

In this part . . .

✔ Comprehend a variety of tools and techniques to help you identify and reduce waste in your existing processes, enabling you to improve the time it takes to do things.

✔ Get the lowdown on value-added and non-value-added, and look at the importance of recognising and tackling bottlenecks in your processes.

✔ Improve process flow with a number of concepts, including 'pull not push' and the power or prevention.

✔ Examine how to design new processes so that they deliver Six Sigma performance from day one with the House of Quality (Quality Function Deployment).

Chapter 9

Identifying Value-Adding Steps and Waste

In This Chapter

▶ Adding value to your organisation

▶ Seeing how most problems result from just a handful of issues

▶ Working waste out of your organisation

▶ Taking a greener approach

'*W*e need to add value.' How often do you hear someone in your organisation say something similar to this? Perhaps you use the phrase yourself. Unfortunately, many organisations don't have an agreed definition of 'value-added' or indeed 'non-value-added' and this leads to confusion and missed opportunity. People place different interpretations on what this commonly used Lean Six Sigma expression means, and the use of the terms to help remove unnecessary steps and actions and to simplify processes can be lost.

This chapter focuses on waste, generally, describing the 'seven wastes' popularised by Toyota's Taiichi Ohno, and a few more that have been added to the list since. These various wastes need to be removed to reduce costs and processing time and to improve service to the customer.

Interpreting Value-Added

Lean Six Sigma focuses on providing value for the customer (see Chapter 2), so knowing what value actually means in your organisation is crucial. Chapter 4 covers the CTQs, those critical to quality customer requirements that your organisation needs to meet. In examining how your processes try to meet those CTQs, you need to assess whether all the steps involved are really necessary, and if they occur in the best sequence. For determining if each step adds value to your process, a standard definition that everyone in your organisation can use and understand is a prerequisite.

Providing a common definition

For a step to be value-adding, it must meet the following three criteria:

- ✔ The customer has to care about the step.
- ✔ The step must either physically change the product or service in some way or be an essential prerequisite for another step.
- ✔ The step must be actioned 'right first time'.

The first criterion in this list is rather subjective. Put yourself in the shoes of the customer: if he knew you were doing this particular step, would he be prepared to pay for it? In providing value for your customer you need to give him the right thing, at the right time and at the right price (see Chapters 2 and 4 on meeting CTQs).

You need to look at your process from your customer's perspective. You may be processing orders in batches, for example, and waiting until you've completed the entire batch before despatching the products. The step putting an individual customer's order to one side while you finish processing others hardly adds value from his perspective.

Consider another example. You have to refer your customer's mortgage application to a senior underwriter to approve the loan. The customer won't be happy to pay for this step, especially if it involves sending his papers to another location – he expects you to be able to approve the loan. If the process involved the client's paperwork for the mortgage going back and forth between underwriters the situation would be even worse.

The second criterion – the step must change the product or service – means that activities such as checking, revising, expediting and chasing are clearly non-value-adding. Challenging your process steps with this criterion seeks to prevent unnecessary checking and the movement of items back and forth between different steps in the process.

Chapter 5 describes a process-stapling exercise for highlighting non-value-adding steps. Some steps in your process may be completely unnecessary – so remove them. Ensure the removal won't cause an unexpected knock-on effect elsewhere in the process, though. If you carry out the process stapling thoroughly, you can see all the vital elements in your process and how they interrelate and can make a simple improvement with no unforeseen adverse effects.

Very often, managers have 'bolted on' these unnecessary steps as a knee-jerk reaction to something going wrong in a process. It was almost certainly the wrong thing to do, but before too long, it became recognised as an important step in the process. As other errors occurred over time, so more 'bolt- on' steps were added, leading now to a prime opportunity for a value-added analysis to help make the process flow more easily. Our experience is that checking work to avoid errors can be a pretty hit-and-miss affair – we always recommend trying to build quality in through prevention and error proofing.

Making sure a step is done right first time is the third criterion in checking value-added. Rework costs time, effort and money and is definitely a non-value-adding activity. Chapter 10 looks at addressing errors using prevention and error proofing.

Carrying out a value-added analysis

After you establish a common definition for value-added, you can review your processes and see if any non-value-adding steps can be removed. This section describes how to go about a value-added analysis, but bear in mind that you're likely to want to keep some of the non-value-adding steps you discover. For example, some regulatory requirements may be in place that the customer may not be interested in, but which you must adhere to. These are usually described as 'essential NVAs'. Some organisations feel it appropriate to add an additional column to Table 9-1, to capture this type of NVA, often under the heading of either 'Essential or Business NVA'.

You need to analyse your process, so looking at Chapter 5 may be helpful. A value-added analysis really is as straightforward as it sounds, though: just look at each step in your process and determine if it's necessary. Use the matrix in Table 9-1 to capture your data. Completing and analysing the detail might create some surprises; typically, very few steps add value.

Table 9-1	A Value-Added Analysis		
Process Step	*Unit or Activity Time*	*Value-Added Time*	*Non-Value-Added Time*
Vet application			
Enter on system			
Run credit check			
Issue offer			
Diary follow up			
Client confirms			
Issue cheque			
Total Time			
Percentage Time	100%		

As part of your analysis, assessing the unit or activity time for each of the process steps is sensible. Unit time is the time it takes to complete a process step (we cover unit time in more detail in Chapter 5). The unit or activity time is the sum of the value-added and non-value added time, including the 'essential or business NVA time' if you chose to show it as a separate column.

If you know how long a step takes to complete and the salary costs associated with the people working in the process, you can work out the approximate cost of that non-value-adding activity, which may well encourage you to improve the step or eliminate it.

Understanding the unit time is relevant for all of the non-value-adding steps, but perhaps especially so in terms of rework activity. Chapter 5 looks at mapping your processes. Very often process maps are produced assuming the work is carried out right first time. Unfortunately, this ideal situation isn't always the case, as you can see in Figure 9-1 (the dotted lines represent rework).

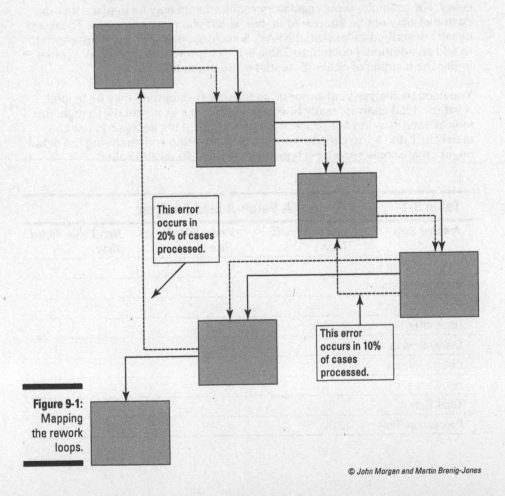

This error occurs in 20% of cases processed.

This error occurs in 10% of cases processed.

Figure 9-1:
Mapping
the rework
loops.

Mapping, perhaps in a different colour, the rework loops in your process and recording how often they're used can be very revealing. In possession of your cost information, you can then start to prioritise your efforts to prevent these expensive errors (see Chapter 10 for more on preventing errors occurring in the first place).

Once identified, many non-value-adding tasks can probably be eliminated. However, some will remain necessary for regulatory, health and safety or environmental reasons. Termed 'essential non-value-adds', these activities need to be carried out as quickly and efficiently as possible. Ensure your process allows this to happen.

Assessing opportunity

Typically, only 10 to 15 per cent of the steps in a process add value and, more often than not, these steps represent as little as 1 per cent of the total process time. These numbers may sound impossible, but just think about what happens in your own processes.

In relation to these figures, the scope for improvement is huge, especially in reducing cycle time – the time it takes to process a customer order. As Taiichi Ohno said:

> All we are doing is looking at a timeline from the moment the customer gives us an order to the point when we collect the cash. And we are reducing that timeline by removing the non-value-added wastes.

Reducing the timeline between a customer's order and receiving payment is your mission and the value-added analysis described in this chapter starts you on that journey.

Looking at the Seven Wastes

Muda is Japanese for waste. In any process, some steps add value and some don't. Some of these non-value-adding steps have to stay, however, perhaps because of limitations in available technology or resources. Others can be eliminated immediately, perhaps through a DMAIC (Define, Measure, Analyse, Improve and Control) project (see Chapter 2).

In waste terms, non-value-adding steps are described as either 'type one' or 'type two' Muda, respectively.

These broad types of waste can be broken down into seven categories:

- ✔ Overproduction
- ✔ Waiting
- ✔ Transportation
- ✔ Processing
- ✔ Inventory
- ✔ Motion
- ✔ Correction

Sometimes, these categories are introduced as 'Tim Wood':

- ✔ **T**ransportation
- ✔ **I**nventory
- ✔ **M**otion
- ✔ **W**aiting
- ✔ **O**verproduction
- ✔ **O**verprocessing
- ✔ **D**efects

In the following sections we look at each of these wastes in turn, using these seven categories.

Owning up to overproduction

Overproduction is producing too many items, or producing items earlier than the next process or customer needs. This type of waste contributes to the other six wastes.

Working in a service organisation, we discovered a classic example of *process suboptimisation*: improvement or inappropriate targets in one part of the process cause problems elsewhere in the process. The manager of Department A was determined to show how good both he and his team were compared with the other departments involved in the downstream process. He set a production target that required overtime on the part of his team, but which showed extremely high levels of productivity that earned praise from senior management. Unfortunately, this increase in output created problems in the immediate downstream process step, leading eventually to the work being stored as a two-week backlog. Even more unfortunately, the manager of Department B received the blame and was pressured by senior management and those working on the process steps even farther downstream. Overproduction had struck again!

A classic example of overproduction involves printed material. When you see how the unit price for leaflets or brochures, for example, dramatically reduces as the volume increases, over-ordering is really tempting. Ordering the higher volume and paying so much less per unit makes sense. Or does it? Do you have a large amount of printed material that's unlikely to be used, taking up valuable storage space or out-of-date? How much is literally thrown away?

Playing the waiting game

Waiting essentially means people are unable to get on and process their work. This delay may be caused by equipment failure, for example, or because people are waiting for the items they need in their part of the process.

Waiting can result from late delivery by external or internal suppliers, or perhaps the incomplete delivery of an order. One of our favourite examples of unnecessary waiting involves photocopiers. Large organisations need top-of-the-range photocopiers but often senior management decides, on the basis of cost, that basic models will suffice. Unfortunately, cheaper models aren't designed to deal with the volume demands of large organisations, and keep breaking down, leaving staff to either wait for them to be repaired or wander round trying to find a photocopier that does work.

Troubling over transportation

Transportation waste involves moving materials and output unnecessarily. Sending partly completed batches of work through the internal mail system because processing teams are located inappropriately is an example. Movement of goods to and from the same place is another. Transportation processes involving non-value-adding steps are even more wasteful.

Transportation waste can also include moving surplus material (see the 'Owning up to overproduction' section, earlier in this chapter). The need to move things around in order to find space for other things, for example, is often the result of overproduction. (Chapter 11 covers pull production systems, whereby items are only requisitioned when they're actually needed.)

Picking on processing

Over-processing waste covers performing unnecessary processing steps, involving, for example, irrelevant information or the completion of too many fields on a form. Putting too many additional information leaflets into a letter being sent to a customer – piggy-backing on the real purpose of the correspondence – is another example.

Processing of unnecessary information is the real crux of processing waste. Consider situations in which customers filling in order forms, and people processing them, have to provide or input more information than is really needed. Eventually, the processing team identify the 'key fields' and, provided they complete those, the application can be progressed. So what was the other information for? Sometimes it can be justified as potentially important marketing information, but so often it isn't needed or even used.

Investigating inventory

Inventory waste links to overproduction resulting in too much work in progress or too many brochures, leaflets or stationery in stock.

Working with a banking client, we reviewed the process for issuing cheque statements to account holders. Large machines are used to sort the statements and stuff the envelopes, but this particular work area didn't have sufficient capacity to deal with the volume of statements. The people who worked in this area needed an additional machine, but had no room for one. Or did they?

In reality, poorly utilised space in their storage room (in part caused by keeping over-ordered and out-of-date literature) had created an overspill of inventory onto the work area floor space. This overspill was preventing the acquisition and location of the additional and much-needed equipment. We used the Five Ss – sort, straighten, scrub, systemise and standardise (see Chapter 10 for more on these) – as a framework to help keep things neat and tidy, with a place for everything and everything in its place. Using the Five Ss, we created space to facilitate the introduction of the extra machine and an accompanying increase in processing output.

Watch out for the overproduction of items simply to meet productivity targets. A demand for costly space to store them is likely to result!

Moving on motion

Time for some ergonomics. Motion waste covers a range of movements, including that of people, perhaps because of the inappropriate siting of process teams or equipment, or the need to find misplaced documents. This type of waste also includes the need to access too many screens, double-handling or seeking unnecessary approvals.

Motion waste certainly includes unnecessary movement caused by a poorly designed workspace: positioning of computer screens or the height of a desk or work bench, for example. Motion waste is a particular focus in assembly plants, where saving even a few seconds in the various stages of assembling a high-volume product can be vital in enabling reduced costs and increased production.

Some years ago, researchers compared the relative positions of the controls on a lathe with the size of an average male worker. They found that the lathe operator had to stoop and move from side to side to operate the controls. The 'ideal' person to fit the lathe would measure 4 feet 6 inches tall, 2 feet across the shoulders and have an arm span of 8 feet!

This example epitomises the shortcoming in design when no account has been taken of the user. People come in all shapes and sizes, and ergonomics takes this variability into account in the design process. Ergonomics is about ensuring a good fit between people, the things they do, the objects they use and the environments in which they work, travel and play. A range of best practice guidelines is available on the Internet, covering areas such as lifting and the ideal design of workstations.

One goal of ergonomics is to design jobs to fit people. Job design in ergonomics recognises that everyone is different. Variability in height, weight, length of arms, size of hands and so on, needs to be taken into account, and study of the human body (anthropometrics) provides data on how these vary across the population.

Applying these principles involves following a logical process:

1. **Analyse the job.**

   What is required to do the job properly and safely?

2. **Identify any stressful elements of the job, focusing on issues related to physical movement.**

   Is machine access too tight for the largest worker? Do short workers have to crane their necks to read displays? Do workers have to reach above their shoulders or below their knees?

3. **Determine the relevant body dimensions linked to the problems identified.**

   Height, weight, arm length or hand size can be issues, for example.

4. **Decide how much variability needs to be accommodated in the design.**

   You can use data from various anthropometric studies (studies of the human body) to help you determine the appropriate specifications in your design. Many of these are available on the Internet or from relevant government departments. You may be able to create the design based on the actual measurements of your existing staff, for example, using the extremes of their height and/or weight information.

5. **Involving the operators and users, redesign the workstation as appropriate.**

   Build in adjustment capability to accommodate size or arm-length differences between members of staff.

Benefits of applying this five-step process are improved efficiency, quality and job satisfaction. Costs of failure include error rates and physical fatigue, or staff absence as a result of injury.

Coping with correction

Correction is the seventh waste and it deals with rework caused by not meeting customer CTQs (critical to quality requirements), providing incomplete replies or simply making errors.

Figure 9-1, in the 'Carrying out a value-added analysis' section earlier in this chapter, is a process map showing levels of rework. You can use unit time information to put a cost on rework. American quality guru Phil Crosby refers to PONC – the *price of non-conformance*. This simple measure puts a price on how much it costs to do things wrong, to not meet customer requirements. He estimates that, in a service organisation, PONC accounts for somewhere between 25 to 40 per cent of annual expenditure!

Errors are a costly waste. Chapter 10 focuses on how to prevent them.

Looking Beyond the Seven Wastes

The Japanese believe seven to be a lucky number, which is why they identify the 'seven wastes' even though they know at least eight exist! This eighth category is failing to use the potential of people.

Wasting people's potential

The 'waste' of human potential can be viewed from two perspectives – misused or untapped.

Misused potential can result from not properly structuring the way work is distributed and described. So, for example, how often do you see misalignment of individual and departmental goals, causing people to work at cross purposes? And how often do you either hear or say the words, 'that's not quite what I meant'? Spending a little more time on properly describing and agreeing the requirements of the task is time well spent – assuming the task is a value-adding one!

Untapped potential is often the result of managers assuming their staff leave their brains behind in reception when they come into work. Think about all the things people do in their spare time, running clubs or societies, acting as treasurer or being a school governor, organising social events and raising funds for charity, being members of teams or choirs, and so on. These activities require skills and talents. Skills and talents that aren't always recognised in the workplace – it's such a waste!

Another form of people waste stems from competition between teams in the same organisation. Co-operation can cut out so much wasted effort. Time will also be well spent on agreeing the 'one best way' of carrying out the various process activities of the organisation – standardisation is covered in Chapter 10.

In looking for opportunities to reduce or eliminate waste, you can find a clue in words that begin with 're'. Although plenty of 're' words are fine – recycle is one of them – many indicate doing things more than once. Look out for rework, reschedule, redesign, re-check and reject!

Going green

Nowadays you also need to consider waste in the context of the environment and the use of energy. The term 'green lean' describes this approach. We could write an entire book on this subject, so here we limit ourselves to just a few examples to get you thinking.

Packaging and the use of inappropriate materials – too much packaging and too much plastic – are obvious targets. Consider the energy and resources used in producing possibly unnecessary packaging.

Supermarket 'two for one' offers simply encourage the purchase of too much food, which may then be thrown away when it passes its sell-by date before it's needed.

Other examples of waste are over-heated buildings, machines left turned on or in standby mode and overnight lighting of empty premises. These are so simple to address and yet so many businesses don't bother to do so.

Considering customer perspectives

The various wastes described in this chapter are all seen from an internal perspective. But, given that one of the key principles of Lean thinking is providing customer value, what do customers see from a waste perspective? How does internal waste affect them?

Certainly, customers will experience delays in waiting; consider queues, late deliveries or slow responses. Waiting and delays will also result when they order products that are currently out of stock or when the wrong product is delivered and a re-order is needed. Also think about the effects of poor communication or inadequate instructions, errors and defective products. They all create waste.

Customers are also likely to feel frustrated with the amount of duplication they experience. Having to re-enter or repeat information and details, whether on forms or in telephone conversations, especially in situations where they're transferred from one person to another, is time-wasting for the customer – and the organisation. The financial services industry, in particular, provides another example of waste: that generated by the abuse of existing customers in favour of securing sales to new customers. This industry often displays too little loyalty to existing customers, who are effectively encouraged to transfer their business elsewhere. Special deals are offered to new customers on terms that aren't available to existing clients. And to add insult to injury, requests for access to these special terms by existing customers are often refused.

Acquiring new business is an expensive process, yet organisations then seem quite prepared to let it walk out of the back door. What a waste. What poor management and business philosophy.

All forms of waste, whether internal or external, are expensive!

Focusing on the Vital Few

Witnessing the scale of waste in your own organisation makes you appreciate the need to tackle things in bite-sized chunks. Quantifying the scale of the waste problem, and breaking things down into manageable pieces, involves measurement. Chapter 6 covers measuring your processes using check sheets and Pareto diagrams.

The various types of waste can be put into a Pareto chart, and though Pareto's 80:20 rule (that, generally, 80 per cent of the problems/errors are caused by 20 per cent of the problem/error types) won't always be exact, it's likely to reveal that a vital few areas are causing most of the problem(s).

The Pareto example shown in Figure 9-2, taken from the Waste and Resource Action Programme (WRAP) data for 2009 and based on diaries kept by 319 households, shows some 1.5 million tonnes of food and drink being wasted in the UK.

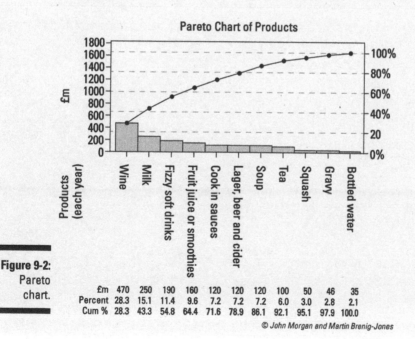

Figure 9-2:
Pareto
chart.

	Wine	Milk	Fizzy soft drinks	Fruit juice or smoothies	Cook in sauces	Lager, beer and cider	Soup	Tea	Squash	Gravy	Bottled water
£m	470	250	190	160	120	120	120	100	50	46	35
Percent	28.3	15.1	11.4	9.6	7.2	7.2	7.2	6.0	3.0	2.8	2.1
Cum %	28.3	43.3	54.8	64.4	71.6	78.9	86.1	92.1	95.1	97.9	100.0

© John Morgan and Martin Brenig-Jones

You need to find your vital few and start to work on them. One way of doing so is to organise regular waste walks. These are rather like process stapling exercises (see Chapter 5), but instead the focus is on spotting examples of waste. Consider arranging a rota for such walks so that everyone working in the organisation gets involved. This approach means you benefit from lots of fresh eyes and also secure people's sense of engagement and willingness to undertake subsequent improvement (Chapter 18 covers the people element in Lean Six Sigma projects).

Chapter 10

Discovering the Opportunity for Prevention

In This Chapter

▶ Applying good housekeeping

▶ Using prevention rather than cure

▶ Undertaking proactive maintenance

▶ Levelling your processes

The concept of prevention has been in existence for a long time – a very long time. Even before our grandmothers told us that prevention is better than cure, and probably even before Laozu had highlighted its importance back in 600 BC:

> Before it moves, hold it,
>
> Before it goes wrong, mould it,
>
> Drain off water in winter before it freezes,
>
> Before weeds grow, sow them to the breezes.
>
> You can deal with what has not happened,
>
> Can foresee
>
> Harmful events and not allow them to be.

Prevention is a good way to tackle waste and delays in your processes (which we cover in Chapters 9 and 11). If you create less waste and fewer delays, you reduce the need for rework and avoid some other non-value-adding activities, too. For example, by providing more information upfront to your customers, you may reduce the volume of customer enquiries.

Keeping Things Neat and Tidy

A simple 'housekeeping checklist' can help you to reduce waste and wasted effort in the workplace. In Lean Six Sigma, you use a system called the *Five Ss* to create this checklist.

In using the Five Ss, you need to run a *red tag exercise*, a tracking process that identifies things in the process that you don't need, whether inventory, stationery or something else.

You may also find that visual management techniques, such as signs, symbols and colour coding help you in your housekeeping.

Introducing the Five Ss

The Five Ss link to the concept of just in time (see Chapter 11 for more on this approach), which aims to provide the tools and materials you need to do the job *only* when you need them. Implementing the Five Ss usually leads to a safer and more pleasant working environment that encourages both self-management and team working. Here are the Five Ss:

✔ **Sort** encourages you to look at the tools, materials, equipment and information you need to do your job, and separate them into those used 'frequently', 'occasionally' and 'never'. You can sort based on your experience, but 'tagging' the items in some way can be helpful (see the 'Carrying out a red-tag exercise' section later in this chapter).

✔ **Straighten** literally means straightening things up and putting everything you use frequently easily to hand. Straightening may include, for example, toolkits, files or email folders, or may involve moving a printer to a more convenient location. Things that you don't use frequently need to be put somewhere else, recycled in some way or thrown away! You need to decide how many items need storing, how they should be stored and where. Naturally, these stored items should be appropriately labelled to facilitate their easy access in the future.

✔ **Scrub** concerns keeping the things you use, and the environment you work in, clean and tidy, and appropriately maintained. Make your workplace shine: get rid of rubbish and dirt, and don't leave scrap lying around. Make sure your tools are current, safe and clean, and that all the information and documents you use are up-to-date and well-presented. Check that equipment and machinery are routinely serviced and maintained.

> ✔ **Systemise** means strengthening your approach. Design a simple way of working so that your tools and information stay sorted, straightened and scrubbed. Essentially, systemise involves regularly re-doing the first three Ss! Doing so helps identify the reasons why the workplace becomes messy and cluttered, and prompts preventive thinking to find ways of stopping the problems recurring.
>
> ✔ **Standardise** the whole approach and keep doing it. Stick to this system every day, train everyone in the application of the Five Ss, regularly review things and tell others about your effective method of working so it becomes a way of life.

Carrying out a red-tag exercise

A *red-tag exercise* is a tracking process to help highlight unneeded items. If you use the Five Ss, which we describe in the previous section, red-tagging can become a useful element of 'Sorting'. You could, for example, tag the various items on your desk on a particular date, see when you use them next and then update the tag with the time and date. If you haven't used them in, say, one month, then move to 'Straighten' so they can be appropriately relocated. Once all the obvious things have been thrown away, or 'relocated', you'll be left with only those things that you regularly use and need to hand. In a culture of 'green lean', unneeded things might well be taken to a secure storage location, where they are reviewed and either used in other internal operations, sold, recycled, given away or finally scrapped.

You can use red-tagging at home, too – for example, to keep your wardrobe from bursting.

You may need to form a team to work on red-tagging your wider working areas, appointing a champion and team members. You identify the areas to tackle, for example inventory, equipment, stationery and supplies, and agree and communicate the criteria and timeframe of the exercise.

The team red-tags items, evaluates the results, and agrees and takes the necessary actions. Working in this way involves organising the needed items regularly so they're easy to locate and use. The team may use the red-tag exercise at the same time as introducing or enhancing visual management (see the next section) to make checking that items are where they should be easier. Visual management helps ensure that items in use can be returned to the right place, and that missing items are easily identified; see the 'shadow board' for tools in Figure 10-1.

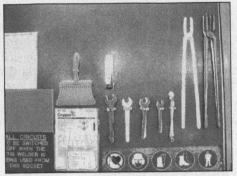

Figure 10-1: A shadow board helps you see at a glance if any tools are missing.

Using visual management

Visual management takes many forms in the workplace and also outside of it; traffic signs are an obvious example! In the workplace, a variety of displays, charts, signs, labels, colour-coded markings and so on can be utilised. Using a visual approach helps everyone see what's going on, understand the process and know that tasks are being carried out or items stored correctly.

Visual management is a complementary approach to support the Five Ss, the control plan (see Chapter 2), health and safety (see Chapter 4), kanban (see Chapter 11) and more.

As well as helping to show if something is out of place or missing, visual management is also used to clearly mark walkways or parking areas, or to identify sites – where a hard hat needs to be worn, for example. A clear link to the Five Ss exists.

Displays and controls could include data or information for the people working in a particular area, keeping them informed of overall performance or focused on specific quality issues. Visual controls could also cover safety, production throughput, material flow or quality metrics, for example.

Essentially, visual management is an important technique for supporting improvement; it ensures the workplace is well-organised and that things can be easily found. It's a very effective way of communicating results and involving people.

Visual management isn't enough by itself, though. It needs to lead to appropriate and timely actions. Process performance review meetings are thus important. These meetings are one of the secret ingredients of success, as shown in Figure 10-2. They might take 5 or 20 minutes; what matters is

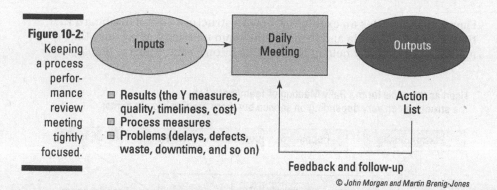

Figure 10-2:
Keeping a process performance review meeting tightly focused.

- Results (the Y measures, quality, timeliness, cost)
- Process measures
- Problems (delays, defects, waste, downtime, and so on)

Feedback and follow-up

Action List

© John Morgan and Martin Brenig-Jones

holding them regularly and making them focused. A clear *IPO* must exist whereby participants know the *Inputs* they need to make, the meeting *Process* is defined and understood and everyone knows what *Outputs* the meeting is intended to produce.

Apart from reviewing performance and the activity for the day ahead, process performance review meetings also provide a forum to discuss improvement opportunities and ideas. This approach follows the After Action Reviews (AARs) used by the US military. An AAR is an assessment conducted after a mission, project or major activity that allows the people involved to review and understand what happened and why. Essentially, the process looks at what you planned to do and achieve, and then analyses what actually happened in practice. Were results better or worse than anticipated? Either way, what lessons emerge and what now needs to be done as a result?

> *The Army's After Action Review (AAR) is arguably one of the most successful organisational learning methods yet devised. Yet, most every corporate effort to graft this truly innovative practice into their culture has failed because, again and again, people reduce the living practice of AARs to a sterile technique.*

> – Peter Senge

Senge's observation is all the more remarkable when you consider that the US Army is such a hierarchical and bureaucratic organisation. But in carrying out these reviews, the Army really is involving all of the participants, from the lowest-ranking soldiers up to commanders. It's an approach that encourages the involvement of all participants in sharing their observations, thoughts and ideas, which ultimately provides the link to continuous improvement by making sure everyone's on board and kept up-to-date.

Include 'use by' dates on the displays to ensure the information remains current and empower everyone to remove and bin an item if they see that it's out-of-date. Place a silhouette behind each item (see the shadow board in Figure 10-1) so that it's immediately obvious that an issue must be updated.

Figure 10-3 provides an example of how to structure an activity board that then forms the agenda and focus for the team meetings. Make sure the meetings are actually held in the same location as the board is displayed!

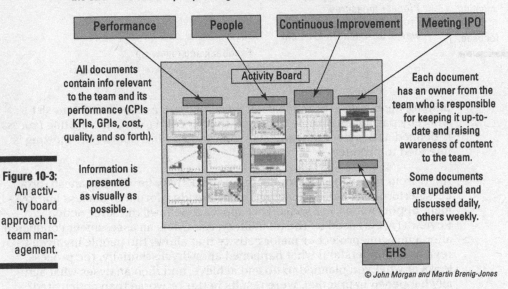

Used as the basis for the Daily Meeting of Team/work cell, the structure can vary depending on service but there are five key elements:

Performance   People   Continuous Improvement   Meeting IPO

Activity Board

All documents contain info relevant to the team and its performance (CPIs KPIs, GPIs, cost, quality, and so forth).

Each document has an owner from the team who is responsible for keeping it up-to-date and raising awareness of content to the team.

Information is presented as visually as possible.

Some documents are updated and discussed daily, others weekly.

EHS

© John Morgan and Martin Brenig-Jones

Figure 10-3: An activity board approach to team management.

In this example, you can see that five key areas are highlighted for discussion. Whatever form your visual display takes, aim to keep the information simple, easy to read and understand, and up-to-date in terms of data. You shouldn't need to spend time interpreting the message. Examples of visual management are everywhere, and most people see them every day, as road signs, traffic signals and written notices. Visual management aims to:

- ✔ Help people know where they are.
- ✔ Highlight important messages and rules about health and safety.
- ✔ Help people know where to find things.
- ✔ Highlight when things aren't where they should be.
- ✔ Identify when things go wrong – and what to do.
- ✔ Communicate information about performance, to both staff and visitors.
- ✔ Help people prevent errors and accidents by using standard colours.
- ✔ Help highlight waste.

Visual management takes many forms, from using standard colours for pipes, cables and wiring, to showing clearly marked out walkways or parking spaces, and designated floor space for equipment and machines. Figure 10-4 provides some examples.

Management attitudes, behaviours that lead to appropriate and timely actions, and use of the other preventive tools and techniques that we describe in this chapter need to support the visual management approach.

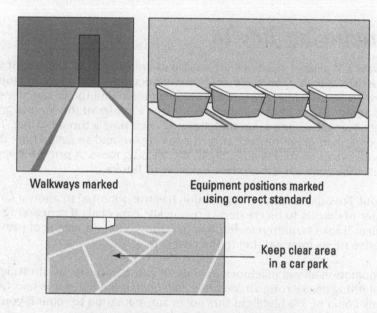

Walkways marked

Equipment positions marked using correct standard

Keep clear area in a car park

Note: Colour of bins matches colour of signs

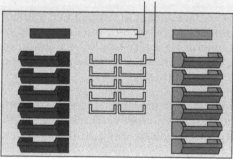

© John Morgan and Martin Brenig-Jones

Figure 10-4: Keeping to the mark.

Looking at Prevention Tools and Techniques

You can prevent or at least reduce the impact of problems by using a whole range of tools and techniques. Sometimes, they'll be all you need to achieve Lean Six Sigma performance.

Introducing Jidoka

Jidoka is a Japanese word describing the prevention of defects and it works on the principle that, once a defect or error occurs, production is stopped to ensure no further defects or errors are produced until the cause of the problem is remedied. In 1902, Sakichi Toyoda, the founder of the Toyota group, invented an automated loom that stopped each time a thread broke. This immediate halt prevented the thread spewing out and so saved time that previously was wasted in sorting out the ensuing mess. A printer stopping when its ink runs out is a modern example of Jidoka.

Without Toyoda's concept, automation has the potential to allow a large number of defects to be created very quickly, especially if processing is in batches. Jidoka is often referred to as *autonomation* – a means of preventing defective items from passing to the next process.

Autonomation allows machines to operate autonomously, by shutting down if something goes wrong. *Automation with human intelligence* is another term for this concept. We highlight the 'no' in autonomation to remind you that *no* defects are allowed to pass to a follow-on process.

Jidoka also embraces the concept of 'Stop at every abnormality', which means a manual process stops whenever an abnormal condition occurs. Sometimes in manufacturing, every employee is empowered to 'stop the line', perhaps following the identification of a special cause on a control chart (see Chapter 7 for more on these).

Forcing everything to stop to immediately focus on a problem may seem painful at first, but is an effective way to quickly get at the root cause of issues. In batch processing, discovering problems immediately is crucial.

Reducing risk with Failure Mode Effects Analysis

Failure Mode Effects Analysis (*FMEA*) is a prevention tool that helps you identify and prioritise potential opportunities for taking preventive action. Identifying the things that might go wrong – the *failure modes* – is the first step.

By looking at what might go wrong (the failure modes), you can assess the impact of what happens (the effects) when it does go wrong, how often it is likely to occur and how likely you are to detect the failure before its effect is realised. For each of these potential events you assign a value, usually on a scale of 1 to 10, to reflect the risk. FMEAs are created for processes, systems and designs. They are also applied to safety concerns.

Table 10-1 provides a typical rating scale for a service organisation.

Table 10-1		Weighing up the risk	
Rating	*Severity of Effect*	*Likelihood of Occurrence*	*Current Detectability*
1	None	Remote	Immediately detected
2	Very minor effect	Very low	Found easily
3	Minor	Low	Usually found
4	Low to moderate	Low to moderate	Probably found
5	Moderate	Moderate	May be found
6	Moderate to high	Moderate to high	Less than 50% chance of detection
7	High	High	Unlikely to be detected
8	Very high	Very high	Very unlikely to be detected
9	Hazardous	Extremely high	Extremely unlikely to be detected
10	Disastrous	Almost certain	Almost impossible to detect

To help you prioritise your actions, you calculate a *risk priority number* (*RPN*). This value is the result of multiplying your ratings for the severity of the risk (from Table 10-1), the frequency of occurrence and the likelihood of detection. You then find ways to reduce the RPN. Figure 10-5 provides an example of an FMEA template. It includes columns that enable you to consider the failure modes and their effects, determine the RPNs, allocate the responsibility for improvement and recalculate the RPN, once the improvement actions have been taken.

Failure Modes and Effects Analysis template

Process: _____ Team: _____ FMEA Date (original): _____ (revised): _____

What?				Why? When? Where?					How?	Who?	Action Results				
Item/process step	Potential failure mode	Potential effect(s) of failure	Severity	Potential cause(s) of failure	Occurrence	Current controls and measures	Detection	RPN	Recommended actions	Responsibility and completion target date	Action taken	Severity	Occurrence	Detection	RPN

© John Morgan and Martin Brenig-Jones

Figure 10-5: Weighing up the risk with FMEA.

In determining ratings for the various failure modes in your processes, working with members of the relevant process team and looking at each step in the process is sensible. To ensure you identify each step, we recommend you use a deployment flowchart rather than a value stream map, as the latter might not have sufficient detail for a process FMEA.

Your ratings against the descriptions in Table 10-1 are based on your experience rather than absolute fact, so when you complete the exercise, step back and make sure the numbers seem sensible. Next, prioritise the failure modes that need to be addressed and determine actions to reduce the RPN scores. Consider a pharmacist as an example. Going back a few decades, many things could go wrong – for example, a child could open a bottle of her parents' tablets, swallow them and become ill. Looking at the ratings in Table 10-1, the severity rating is therefore high. The detection rating is also high and the occurrence rating is probably somewhere in the middle. This failure mode may happen every day, but the pharmacist is unaware until the damage has occurred.

The RPN in this example is high. To address the failure mode, pharmacists now use child-proof containers and print warnings on them about keeping tablets out of the reach of children, create tablets that don't look or taste like sweets and reduce the strength of individual tablets.

Examine your own processes to see if FMEA creates any opportunities for improvement. Consider each step in your process and identify its failure modes. In coming up with your RPN, remember that these numbers are subjective; use common sense in determining the action needed.

In creating your list of possible failure modes, call upon your own experience but also use techniques such as *negative brainstorming* (also called anti-solution brainstorming). This technique turns brainstorming on its head and instead of asking, for example, 'What possible failure modes are evident in the ABC process?' takes a different tack and tries, 'How can we ensure the ABC process goes wrong?'

You may be surprised by the ideas that your team members put forward. Some of the suggestions will be silly, but that doesn't matter – indeed, it helps make the exercise fun.

When you have your list of failure modes, ask the question, 'How many of these things really happen?' Changing your negative statements to positive ones can produce a solution to your problem.

Negative brainstorming not only helps develop your list of potential failure modes, it can also begin the process of identifying ways to reduce the risks and improve the process.

Error proofing your processes

Error proofing – sometimes referred to as *Poka-yoke*, Japanese slang for 'avoiding inadvertent errors' – is key to working out the actions you need to take to improve your process.

Poka-yoke approaches either prevent mistakes from being made or make the mistakes obvious at a glance. Poka-yoke approaches are:

- ✔ Inexpensive
- ✔ Very effective
- ✔ Based on simplicity and ingenuity

Poka-yoke doesn't rely on operators catching mistakes, but it does help to ensure quick feedback 100 per cent of the time, leading to process improvements and reductions in waste.

Consider the 1-10-100 rule, which states that, as a product or service moves through the production system, the cost to your organisation of correcting an error multiplies by 10. Looking at the processing of a customer order, for example:

- ✔ Order entered correctly: £1
- ✔ Error detected in billing: £10
- ✔ Error detected by customer: £100

The 1-10-100 rule fails to pick up the additional costs associated with dissatisfied customers sharing their experience with others, something that can escalate rapidly on social media, for example. Error proofing, all in all, is really worth doing.

Examples of prevention and error proofing are observable in your everyday life. Your car may flash a warning light if you don't use the seat belt. Some high-tech cars even have breath-testing devices that prevent ignition if you exceed the legal alcohol limit. And at home you probably have smoke detectors and electricity trip switches.

Three types of error proofing approaches exist: contact, fixed value and motion step:

- **Contact error proofing** involves products having a physical shape that inhibits mistakes – see Figure 10-6.

  The physical design makes installing parts in any but the correct position impossible. Electronic equipment design, and that of its various attachments and extensions, for example, ensures the right cables can only go into the right sockets. This situation is achieved through a combination of part sizes and shapes, as well as colour codes. Although the latter is an example of visual management and might not prevent you from trying to plug something into the wrong socket or location, nevertheless the concept is trying to prevent you from doing so! Another example is a fixed diameter hole through which all products must fall. Any oversized product is unable to pass through, and the potential defect associated with it is thus prevented.

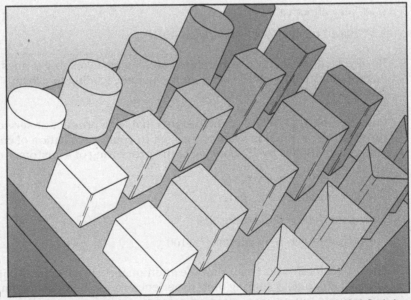

Figure 10-6: Square pegs and round holes: Contact error proofing.

© John Morgan and Martin Brenig-Jones

✔ **Fixed value error proofing** identifies when a part is missing or not used and essentially ensures appropriate quantities. A simple example is the French fry scoop used in a takeaway, which is designed to ensure a consistent number of fries precisely fits the package served to the customer. A further example is 'egg trays' used for the supply of parts – spotting that something's missing is easy as one compartment is empty.

✔ **Motion step error proofing** automatically ensures that the process operator has taken the correct path or number of steps, possibly by breaking a photocell light sensor, or stepping on a pressure sensitive pad during the assembly cycle. A security guard patrolling the outside of a building may have several points in his journey where he has to radio in to confirm all is well. A very different example is how spell-checkers provide automatic warnings when words are incorrectly spelt throughout the completion of a word-processing document – the operator needs to click on the highlighted word to decide whether to change it.

Profiting from Preventive Maintenance

Preventive maintenance means being proactive to prevent equipment failure and system problems. Contrast this approach to diagnostic or corrective maintenance, which is performed to correct an already-existing problem. If you own a car, you may understand the concept of preventive maintenance: you don't change your oil in response to a problem situation – you do it before things go wrong, so your engine lasts longer and you avoid car troubles down the road.

Preventive maintenance is a schedule of planned maintenance actions aimed at the prevention of breakdowns and failures. Preventing the failure of equipment before it actually occurs is the primary goal. Preventive maintenance is designed to preserve and enhance equipment reliability by replacing worn components before they fail and activities include equipment checks, partial or complete overhauls at specified periods, oil changes, lubrication, and so on. In addition, workers can record equipment deterioration so they know to replace or repair worn parts before they cause system failure. Recent technological advances in tools for inspection and diagnosis have enabled even more accurate and effective equipment maintenance.

An ideal preventive maintenance programme prevents all equipment failure before it occurs. For example, in an airport, preventive maintenance may be in place in critical service areas such as escalators, lighting and aircraft bridges.

As with all prevention activity, some people see preventive maintenance as unduly costly. This logic dictates that regular scheduled downtime and maintenance is more costly than operating equipment until repair is absolutely necessary – and may well be true for some components. Long-term benefits and savings associated with preventive maintenance, however, also need to be considered.

Without preventive maintenance, for example, unscheduled equipment breakdown will result in costly lost service time, something that would become apparent through OEE measures (see Chapter 8). Also, preventive maintenance results in savings by increasing the service life of effective systems. Long-term benefits of preventive maintenance include:

✔ Improved system reliability.

✔ Decreased cost of replacement.

✔ Decreased system downtime.

✔ Better spares inventory management.

You can't always prevent things from going wrong or equipment from failing. But when they do, your ability to recover from problems quickly is key.

Avoiding Peaks and Troughs

This section focuses on dealing with work activity to avoid too many peaks and troughs in the volumes and types of work being processed. Levelling the work isn't easy, but it is the foundation of Toyota's celebrated production system. The Japanese refer to the concept as *Heijunka*, extending it to incorporate the need for 'standard work' – the processing of work in a consistent manner.

Introducing Heijunka

Heijunka is the underlying concept of the Toyota Production System (TPS), shown in Figure 1-1 in Chapter 1. The TPS consists of two columns – Jidoka (for more about this concept, see the 'Introducing Jidoka' section earlier in this chapter) and just in time (see Chapter 11) – supported by Heijunka.

Heijunka involves smoothing processing and production using levelling and sequencing. For a process to run smoothly and consistently with many different kinds of output, it has to average, not just in volume, but also in kind. So, you need to process the different types of customer order, for example, based on the date they're received rather than dealing with the more straightforward cases first and allowing the more difficult ones to build up and be delayed.

Heijunka involves the following elements:

✔ **Levelling** involves smoothing the volume of production in order to reduce variation. Amongst other things, this technique seeks to prevent 'end-of-period' peaks, where production is initially slow, but then quickens in the last days of a sale or accounting period, for example.

✔ **Sequencing** involves mixing the kinds of work processed. So, for example, when setting up new loans, the type of loan being processed is mixed to better match customer demand and help ensure applications are actioned in date order. Managing this approach may be easier in manufacturing, where a producer may be able to hold a small buffer of finished goods to respond to the ups and downs in weekly orders. Keeping a small stock of finished goods at the very end of the value stream, near shipping, this producer can level demand to its plant, and to its suppliers, making for more efficient utilisation of assets along the entire value stream while still meeting customer requirements.

✔ **Stability and standardisation** seeks to reduce variation in the way the work is carried out, highlighting the importance of following a standard process and procedure. This technique links well to the concept of process management and the control plan, where the process owner continuously seeks to find and consistently deploy best practice.

Concepts such as Heijunka can't be implemented overnight – for example, Toyota has taken many years to achieve the successful application of levelling and spreading the load but is now a driving force in the growing awareness of lean-thinking principles in the Western world.

Spreading the load

Keeping things balanced and level means your process flows are smoother and your overall processing times faster. But be warned – this situation isn't easy to achieve, either at work or on your way there!

Consider variable speed limits on motorways, which aim to maintain a steady, continuous flow of traffic, enabling us to all keep moving and avoid stops and starts during busy periods. Unfortunately, some drivers always speed up between the speed cameras, only to brake hard when they get to the next one, an approach that creates braking and delay back down the road.

In the workplace, you need to try to avoid peaks and troughs in activity, if you can. The month- or quarter-end cycles in many organisations highlight the difficulties of peaks. Actioning financial reconciliations, for example, on a daily or weekly basis may be possible, thus avoiding the monthly or quarterly peak of activity. You need to determine whether an opportunity to change frequencies exists in your organisation.

In Chapter 9 we talk about waste, or *Muda*. This expression is often used together with two other words, Mura and Muri. *Mura* describes unevenness in an operation; for example, people hurrying then having to wait, as in the motorway scenario. *Muri* means overburdening equipment in some way.

Consider Mura and Muri in the context of maintaining a smooth and level flow at a transport depot. You have several three-tonne trucks, but you need to transport six tonnes of material to your customer. You have four options:

- All six tonnes on one truck = Muri and a probable broken axle.
- Four tonnes on one and two on another truck = Muri, Mura and Muda.
- Two tonnes on three trucks = Muda.
- Three tonnes on two trucks = Muri-, Mura- and Muda-free!

So, this last option is the optimum way of delivering the material to your customer. It uses an evenly distributed approach, no waste occurs and trucks aren't overburdened.

In an office environment, consider the over-use of a photocopier that is not designed for high-volume copying but is being used for just that purpose. Breakdowns are inevitable, leading to waste in the form of people waiting or walking around the office to find a copier that is working.

Carrying out work in a standard way

Sometimes, the first step in preventing problems and rework is agreeing on a standard process. Formulating a standard process gives you real gains easily and leads to stability and predictability in the process. Actually, you can't really begin to improve a process until you standardise it. Following standardisation, you have a genuine chance to stabilise the process and prompt further improvements. In Chapter 5, we look at techniques such as process stapling and process mapping to help you develop both the best approach and a standard approach to the way work is done.

Standardising the one best way of how the work gets done is key, but in a culture of continuous improvement you may find better ways to do the work that become the new 'one best way' until further improvement occurs. Of course, if defects occur, your first question needs to be, 'Has the standard process been followed?' If it has, then the process needs to be improved.

In this evolving culture of continuous improvement, fuelled and supported by Lean Six Sigma, you need to keep improving your process, encouraging ideas from the people working within it. As you grow increasingly confident in applying the Lean Six Sigma principles, so you'll recognise that no end exists to the process of improving processes.

Chapter 11

Detecting and Tackling Bottlenecks

. . . .

In This Chapter

▶ Finding the weak points in your process

▶ Picking pull instead of push production

▶ Rethinking the layout of your organisation

. . . .

In this chapter we focus on those points in the process flow where demand exceeds capacity – bottlenecks. In Lean Six Sigma, some people call bottlenecks *constraints*. Whichever term you use, the effect is the same: the bottleneck, or constraint, sets the pace for your process and determines the speed and volume of your output. Put simply, either you manage the bottlenecks or they manage you.

Applying the Theory of Constraints

You need a framework to help you manage your constraints. This section looks at how to identify the bottlenecks in your process, prioritise them for action, and reduce or eliminate their effect using Eli Goldratt's five-step approach.

Identifying the weakest link

Think of your organisation as a chain like the one in Figure 11-1 – a series of functions or divisions that are dependent on each other, even if the people within the organisation don't recognise and accept that fact. For example, you don't ship parts until they're packaged, and you don't package parts until they're manufactured, and so on. Answering the question 'How strong is the chain?' is easier than you may think: the chain is as strong as its weakest link. Find your bottleneck and you find the weakest link in your chain.

Figure 11-1:
Working on
the chain
gang.

© John Morgan and Martin Brenig-Jones

Conventional wisdom supports the idea that improving any link in the chain improves the chain overall, and 'global' improvement is the sum of the local improvements. But time for some different thinking: this local improvement approach leads to *process sub-optimisation*, where apparent improvements in one part of the process actually make things worse in another part. You need to make your improvements with an understanding of the end-to-end process, or the chain. And you need to take only those local actions that strengthen the chain, by focusing potentially scarce resources on the constraint.

Improving the process flow

Eli Goldratt suggested a *theory of constraints* involving a five-step approach to help improve flow:

1. **Identify the constraint.**

2. **Exploit the constraint.**

3. **Subordinate the other steps to the constraint.**

4. **Elevate the constraint.**

5. **Go back to Step 1 and repeat the process.**

A *constraint* is a bottleneck. A constraint occurs wherever and whenever capacity cannot meet demand. You can *identify* constraints where you have a build-up of people (a queue), material (inventory), units to be processed or work in progress (a backlog).

When you find the bottleneck or constraint, you can then find ways to improve the processing capability at the bottleneck point in the process flow. You need to *exploit* the constraint, that is, maximise its potential, ideally without major expenditure.

For example, if your constraint is a machine, try to keep the machine running during the working day. Don't close it down for servicing; you can do that after hours. If the constraint is a person, then make sure his work is covered during his breaks for lunch, for example. Any time lost at the constraint has a big effect on the whole process, which takes you to Step 3 of the theory.

To *subordinate* the other steps to the constraint, you use the constraint to dictate the pace at which the upstream activities send their output to the constraint, which tells the downstream activities how much they can expect to receive from the constraint.

As an example, consider the deployment flowchart in Figure 11-2, featuring Ann, Brian and Clare.

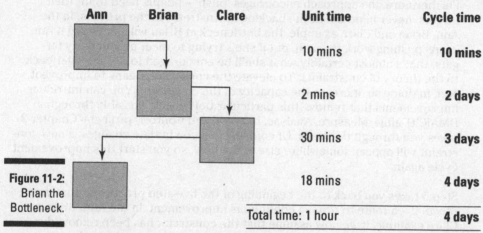

	Ann	Brian	Clare	Unit time	Cycle time
				10 mins	10 mins
				2 mins	2 days
				30 mins	3 days
				18 mins	4 days
				Total time: 1 hour	4 days

Figure 11-2: Brian the Bottleneck.

© John Morgan and Martin Brenig-Jones

Brian is the main bottleneck. Ann producing more than Brian can deal with is pointless, as doing so will simply create an increasing pile of work in progress. Brian is setting the pace for the process and, ideally, is *pulling* the work through accordingly, rather than letting Ann *push* it through at her pace. This situation may mean that Ann can tackle some additional tasks, possibly even helping Brian. Either way, you can improve the constraint, though you may find productivity measures and targets get in the way.

More often than not, productivity measures and targets are a driver of bad behaviour. You get what you measure, and if people are measured on productivity, then you'll get productivity and meet the target! But at what cost?

Too many examples exist of productivity 'credits' being allocated to different types of work without taking the bigger picture into account. This situation seems especially the case in the public sector, but private companies can be just as bad.

People look at the allocation of these credits and, from experience, quickly realise that work type A, for example, is quite simple but nevertheless gains good productivity credits, whereas work type B is a lot harder and the credit seems too low for the tasks involved. No prizes for guessing which type of work gets done first. The type A work is processed first; the type B becomes a lower priority. So tasks aren't done in sequence, and a backlog of the harder and increasingly older type B work builds up – but that situation's okay because the productivity target has been met!

Furthermore, the approach encourages 'push' – people need to hit their targets, never mind about the backlog downstream in the process. In the Ann, Brian and Clare example, the bottleneck at Brian will get worse if Ann keeps pushing work through, but if she's trying to meet productivity targets, that's almost certainly what she'll be encouraged to do. Let's get back to the theory of constraints. To elevate the constraint means to improve it, and, in doing so, increase the capacity of the constraint. You can introduce improvements that remove this particular bottleneck, possibly through a DMAIC (Define, Measure, Analyse, Improve and Control) project – Chapter 2 takes you through the steps. Of course, once you initiate changes, a new constraint will appear somewhere else in the flow, so you start this improvement cycle again.

Step 5 takes you back to the beginning of the five-step process so that you *repeat* it – a route to driving continuous improvement. In the Ann, Brian and Clare example, if we now assume that the constraint has been removed at Brian's step, you'd then need to address the 'new' bottleneck in the process, which appears to be with Clare.

Building a buffer

The constraint sets the pace for the process – subject to the external customer requirements, it tells the upstream process steps the rate of production needed, and the downstream process steps how much work to expect, as well as their production rate. However, imagine if one of the upstream steps wasn't able to produce things on time – a machine could break down, for example. Placing a small buffer in front of the constraint to ensure sufficient work is always available is a good idea, just in case an upstream process step experiences problems, such as machine failure. This upstream step can work faster than the constraint if necessary, so things should soon catch up, but in the meantime the process flow is uninterrupted. This concept is called 'drum, buffer, rope'.

The imaginary 'drum' is the beat of production set by the constraint, rather like the drum beating the pace for the oarsmen on a Roman galley. The buffer provides the contingency that keeps the constraint working even if one of the upstream steps slows or fails temporarily. The 'rope' cordons off, or controls, the flow of work by preventing too much coming through to the constraint – this image also helps you imagine the work being pulled through at the right pace. In Figure 11-3, the drum equates to the production of 40 items each day, even though the process steps both upstream and downstream of the constraint could produce more, their output will each be reduced to 40 items.

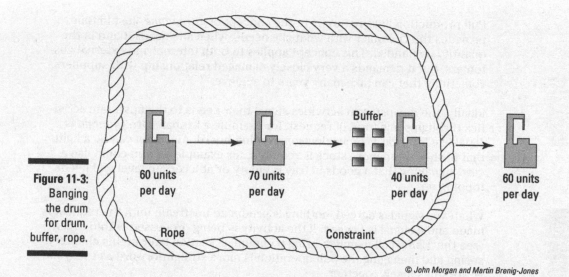

Figure 11-3: Banging the drum for drum, buffer, rope.

60 units per day → 70 units per day → Buffer → 40 units per day → 60 units per day

Rope   Constraint

© John Morgan and Martin Brenig-Jones

Managing the Production Cycle

Whether you work in a manufacturing organisation or a service industry, you need to understand and manage the production process.

Using pull rather than push production

Pull production is a system in which each process takes what it needs from the preceding process exactly when it needs it, and in the exact amount necessary. The customer thus pulls the supply and helps avoid being swamped by items that aren't needed at a particular time. In our example in Figure 11-2 in the preceding section, Brian pulls the work through at his pace when he wants it, not when Ann can send it. Pull production reduces the need for potentially costly storage space. For example, in an environment where pull production isn't in use, overproduction in one process, perhaps to meet local efficiency targets, may result in problems downstream, increasing work in progress and creating bottlenecks. Symptoms of overproduction include the following:

- ✔ **Too many:** Making more items than needed.
- ✔ **Too soon:** Making them earlier than needed.
- ✔ **Too fast:** Making them faster than needed.

Pull production links naturally to the concept of *just in time*. Just in time provides the customer with what she needs, when she needs it and in the quantity demanded. This concept applies to both internal and external customers, but it demands a very closely managed relationship with suppliers, something that can take many years to achieve.

Ideally, the downstream activities signal their needs to the upstream activities through some form of request, for example a kanban card (*kanban* is Japanese for a card) or an electronic andon board. An *andon* can be a light that flashes when more stock is required, for example, or you could use a card signalling that a goods-in tray is empty or at a certain level and needs topping up.

Whatever signal is agreed, nothing is produced upstream until the request is made and a signal is flagged. If the activity is being processed within a 'cell' (see the 'Using cell manufacturing techniques' section later in this chapter), seeing and managing the pull operation is more straightforward as everyone is working closely together.

A simple example of the kanban signal in practice is the stationery cupboard. A re-order card is placed in an appropriate position within the stock and when the card is revealed as someone takes a new memo pad from the remaining pile, for example, a re-order is made to ensure the stock of memo pads doesn't run out. The kanban system is also evident in your chequebook, as a re-order form towards the end of it.

Moving to single piece flow

Single piece flow means each person in the organisation performs an operation and makes a quick quality check before moving their output to the person in the next process. If a defect is detected, Jidoka is enacted (this concept is covered in Chapter 10); that is, the process is stopped, and immediate action taken to correct the situation and take countermeasures to prevent reoccurrence.

Ideally, single piece continuous flow processing is carried out within 'cells', with the relevant people and machinery sited closely together. See the 'Using cell manufacturing techniques' section later in this chapter.

Recognising the problem with batches

Single piece flow is a real change of thinking that moves you away from processing in batches, but it may be difficult to achieve, and organisational logistics may mean you need to continue with batches. If that's the case, you need to be aware of the pitfalls associated with batches.

Traditionally, large batches of individual cases or items are processed at each step of the process and are passed along the process only after an entire batch has been completed. Delays are increased when the batches travel around the organisation, both in terms of the transport time, and the time they sit waiting in the internal mail system – at any given time, most of the cases in a batch are sitting idle, waiting to be processed. In manufacturing, this idleness is seen as costly excess inventory.

In batch processing, errors can be neither picked up nor addressed quickly. If errors occur, they tend to occur in large volume, which further delays identifying the root cause. In single piece flow, the error is picked up immediately. With the trail still warm, you can get to the root cause analysis faster and prevent a common error recurring throughout the process.

Looking at Your Layout

In many organisations, especially in offices, the various people involved in a process often aren't sitting together, and can even be located on different floors or in different buildings. This type of layout inevitably results in delays as people and work travel around the organisation.

Identifying wasted movement

People and materials lose vast amounts of time travelling between different locations (Chapter 9 covers waste and how to eliminate it). Use the spaghetti diagram in Chapter 5 (Figure 5-1) to help you reduce wasted travel time.

Using cell manufacturing techniques

Cellular manufacturing organises the entire process for similar products into a group of team members, with all the necessary equipment. This group and its equipment is a *cell*. A cell shouldn't feel like a prison; rather, it should feel liberating for the team members who have real control over what they produce.

Cells are arranged to easily facilitate all operations, often adopting a horseshoe shape, as shown in Figure 11-4. Outputs or parts are easily passed from operation to operation, often by hand, eliminating set-ups and unnecessary costs, and reducing delays between operations.

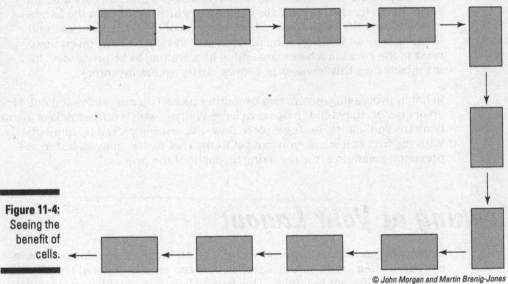

Figure 11-4:
Seeing the
benefit of
cells.

© John Morgan and Martin Brenig-Jones

Working in cells offers the following benefits:

- ✔ The facilitation of single piece flow and a reduction in the use of batches.

- ✔ Faster cycle times and less work in progress, which in turn results in a need for less floor space.

- ✔ Reduction of waste and minimisation of material-handling costs resulting from less movement of people and materials.

- ✔ More efficient and effective utilisation of space.

- ✔ A heightened sense of employee participation.

✔ More efficient and effective use of people in the team, empowering them to take responsibility and control (see Chapter 13). Daily team meetings are easier to arrange, helping to create a culture of continuous improvement, which results in a positive team attitude and an enrichment of job satisfaction.

✔ Elimination of bottlenecks.

✔ Facilitation of visual management (see Chapter 10) – with everyone in the process working closely together in the same area, the team's performance results can be displayed easily for all to see.

Identifying product families

Within cellular arrangements, identifying and processing common *product families* – those products or services involving identical or similar processing steps that previously might have been seen as different activities, each processed by different teams – makes sense. To identify the appropriate product families, you need to create a matrix detailing the process/value stream steps across the page and the different products or services down the page, as shown in Figure 11-5.

	Vet application	Enter on system	Run credit check	Issue offer	Diary follow up	Client confirms	Issue cheque
Bronze plus	X	X	X	X	X	X	X
Silver edge	X	X	X	X	X	X	X
Gold	X	X	X				X
Platinum	X	X					X
Platinum plus		X					X

Figure 11-5: Keeping it in the family.

© John Morgan and Martin Brenig-Jones

This matrix highlights where the process steps are identical or essentially the same for the different products. These steps can then be processed by the same team, increasing your flexibility and processing capability. When we look at the product families and processes, we should be aware of the need to address the three Rs – in this case, the **r**unners, **r**epeaters and **r**arities.

Runners are regular and predictable work activities; the repeaters are also regular work activities, but are fewer in number and frequency than the runners. As their name suggests, rarities are exactly that, occurring every now and then. They need to be addressed as one-off work activities. Some organisations refer to these as *strangers*.

Naturally, the process and value stream maps (see Chapter 5) should take account of these differing activities.

Chapter 12

Introducing Design for Six Sigma

In This Chapter

▶ Designing new processes

▶ Doing the DMADV

▶ Looking at the House of Quality

This chapter provides only an introduction to Design for Six Sigma (DfSS). It is simply an overview because the topic could easily form a standalone book. We look at the DMADV method – Define, Measure, Analyse, Design and Verify – as well as take you on a tour through the House of Quality (otherwise known as quality function deployment). But we stress that it's only a tour and not a full structural survey!

Recognising that a much wider range of concepts, tools and techniques is used in DfSS projects is important, although the House of Quality is certainly a significant part of the toolkit. This book doesn't, for example, cover benchmarking techniques in detail or describe the theory of inventive problem solving (TRIZ), for example.

In the area of innovation, lots of tools are available. Genrich Altshuller categorised more than 2 million patents, classifying them by industry and uncovering the problem-solving process behind the invention. Often the same problems had been solved over and over again using one of only 40 fundamental inventive principles. If later inventors had been aware of the work of earlier ones, solutions could have been discovered more quickly and efficiently.

Introducing DfSS

In Chapter 2, we look at how to improve existing processes using DMAIC: Define, Measure, Analyse, Improve and Control. Sometimes a process doesn't exist and you need to create one, perhaps for new services or products. Or maybe your current process is so poor that scrapping it and starting again makes sense.

In these circumstances you have the opportunity to begin with a blank canvas. You can design products and services, and the processes that support them, that will delight your customers from day one. Imagine processes that aren't plagued with defects. DfSS often concentrates on the 'delighter' curve in the Kano model that we describe in Chapter 4. Think about introducing these new products and services quickly, and to a consistently high standard. You can focus on those organisational processes that create the highest value-adding outcomes.

> *Design is a funny word. Some people think Design means how it looks. But, of course, if you dig deeper, it's really how it works.*
>
> —Steve Jobs

DfSS is a philosophy for designing new products, services and processes, often with high customer involvement from the outset, though that won't always be so – consider inventions by people such as Jobs and Dyson, for example.

When redesigning a process, you focus on the customer. When designing a new service or product, a customer may not exist yet. In this case, you concentrate on the demands of the (potential) marketplace.

Where the customer is involved, we mean both end user customers and internal business stakeholders and users. Customer requirements and the resulting CTQs (Critical To Quality elements – see Chapter 4) are established early on and the DMADV framework rigorously ensures that these requirements are satisfied in the final product, service or process.

Introducing DMADV

The DMADV framework is focused on the customer and her CTQs. Where possible to do so, you have to listen to and understand the voice of the customer, but you may also need to look beyond it in developing your designs.

As with DMAIC (see Chapter 2), managing by fact and not speculation ensures that new designs reflect customer CTQs and provide real value to the customers in line with the principles of Lean Six Sigma.

TIP

DMADV projects are often concerned with introducing radical change within an organisation. A well thought out change management programme is vital to support the change. Our Elements of Change Model described in Chapter 18 provides a framework to address and manage the various people issues that are so important for the successful completion of a project.

Figure 12-1 shows the DMADV phases involved in a DfSS project.

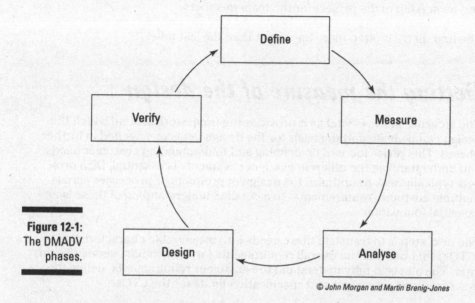

Figure 12-1:
The DMADV
phases.

© John Morgan and Martin Brenig-Jones

Defining What Needs Designing

The Define phase is about scoping, organising and planning the journey for your project. Understanding the purpose, rationale and business case is important, as well as knowing who you might need to help you, and how you will go about managing things. So, understanding the boundaries of the project, including the processes, market(s), customers and stakeholders involved, is vital.

An essential ingredient for success will be ensuring that you and your team have a clear understanding of why the project is being undertaken, and what it's trying to achieve. The Define phase is all about making sure such understanding happens.

You need to bring together the right people at the start, making sure the relevant departments and functions are represented. All too often, this isn't the case and the definition and scope of the project suffers. Using the affinity and interrelationship diagrams (in Chapter 2) can be an especially helpful way of starting a DfSS project. These techniques provide a way of bringing the team of people together and teasing out their various thoughts, issues and agendas, before helping in the identification of the key areas for the project's success. Importantly, the completion of the two techniques creates involvement and ownership of the project for the team members.

The first metre is often more important than the last mile!

Getting the measure of the design

The Measure phase is vital as it provides the framework around which the design can be built, and the basis for the design decisions needed in further phases. This phase focuses on defining and understanding customer needs, and understanding the different customer segments is essential. DfSS projects typically seek to optimise the design of products or processes across multiple customer requirements, so a detailed understanding of these is an essential foundation.

The next step is to translate these needs into measurable characteristics (CTQs) that become the overall requirements for the product, service or process. The aim is to fully understand the customer requirements, define the measures, and set targets and specification limits for the CTQs.

When designing new products or services, you need to make sure the design can be produced with existing processes. If that isn't the case, you'll have to design new processes to accommodate the new design. Considering process capability at this phase, rather than after the design is complete, is a hallmark of DfSS.

Analysing the design

The Analyse phase looks to develop the functional specification, and high-level designs. The Design phase then creates and tests the detailed design.

Analyse begins the process of moving from the what to the how – what the customer needs, to how you might achieve it. This means mapping the CTQs onto the internal functions, and starting to look at alternative design concepts.

Design means how something works, not how it looks – the design should evolve from the function.

—James Dyson

For a service, this analysis means identifying the key functions; for a more tangible product, it means identifying its key part characteristics. Typically, the sub-system characteristics are developed next, followed by the components (parts) of the subsystem.

Functions are what the product, service or process has to do in order to meet the CTQs identified and specified in the design process. In a service environment, functions are best thought of as key high-level processes to be considered. So, for example, the product or service being designed could be a telephone ordering service, with a design goal of an order placement within five minutes. The functions involved could include answer the call, check requirements, check stock and place order, for example. You'll need to carry out an analysis of the functions to understand their performance capability and ensure they're fit for purpose.

The emphasis in a DfSS project is very much on alternative design concepts and the generation, analysis and assessment of a high-level design.

The second part of Analyse involves analysing and selecting the best design concept and beginning to add more details to it. Each element of the design should be considered in turn, and high-level design requirements specified for each. Consideration will also need to be given to how the different components fit and interact with each other. This process usually involves creating several high-level designs, assessing the suitability of each and then selecting the best fit.

You need to assess performance and develop design scorecards to help you analyse the design's capability in terms of delivering the CTQ. Assessments might be carried out through simulations, field tests, or pilots, and, where appropriate, involve the customer so that you can capture her feedback.

Design scorecards provide a systematic method of deploying requirements into the design and predicting the capability of the new design. They capture the critical performance measures at each level and visibly track the measured performance as the design evolves.

In DMADV projects, you need to collect new data for the functional analysis. Given that you're designing something new, the output of this work will probably mean that the resulting input and in-process variables, the Xs (see Chapter 8), will be your choices.

Based on the outputs of the review, the high-level design requirements can be finalised, and a thorough risk assessment undertaken using Failure Mode Effects Analysis (FMEA – see Chapter 10).

Developing the design

The Design phase is also in two parts. It begins by developing the 'how' thinking in more detail. The objective is to add increasing detail to the various elements of the high-level design. The emphasis is on developing designs that will satisfy the CTQ requirements of the process outputs.

The design process is iterative – the high-level design was established in the Analyse phase; now the design is specified at a detailed enough level to develop a pilot and test it. The detailed design activities are similar to those in the high-level design phase but with a significantly lower level of granularity. This step integrates all of the design elements into one overall design.

Finally, the lowest-level specification limits, control points and measures are determined. These will form the basis of the control plan that needs to be in place following implementation (see Chapter 2).

Before implementation, however, you need to pilot the design. Enough detail should now be available to test and evaluate the capability of the design by preparing a pilot in the second part of the Design phase. It's important you plan an effective and realistic pilot.

Verifying that the design works

The design is piloted and assessed in the Verify phase, and, subject to any adjustments that follow the pilot, implementation and deployment follow. As with DMAIC, the final step in the cycle is to assess the achievements made and lessons learned.

The results are verified against the original CTQs, specifications and targets. The project is closed only when the solution has been standardised and transitioned to operations and process management.

You need to ensure that no black holes exist in the handover to the process owner or operational manager. You must work closely with your team to achieve a well-planned and well-documented transition.

Choosing between DMAIC and DMADV

It's possible to start a project using the DMAIC method (see Chapter 2 for a description of all the stages) only to find yourself at some point changing to DMADV. Figure 12-2 provides a picture of the likely decision points in transitioning from one method to the other.

DMAIC/DMADV transition points:

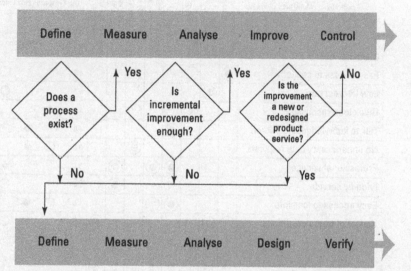

© John Morgan and Martin Brenig-Jones

Figure 12-2: Choosing between DMAIC and DMADV.

DMADV projects call for a range of Lean Six Sigma tools and techniques, including many that you're already familiar with from DMAIC. Perhaps the most important technique, however, is *quality function deployment*, an approach that's often referred to as the House of Quality because of its appearance (see Figure 12-3).

As with DMADV, QFD merits its own book, so here we provide only an overview of this tool.

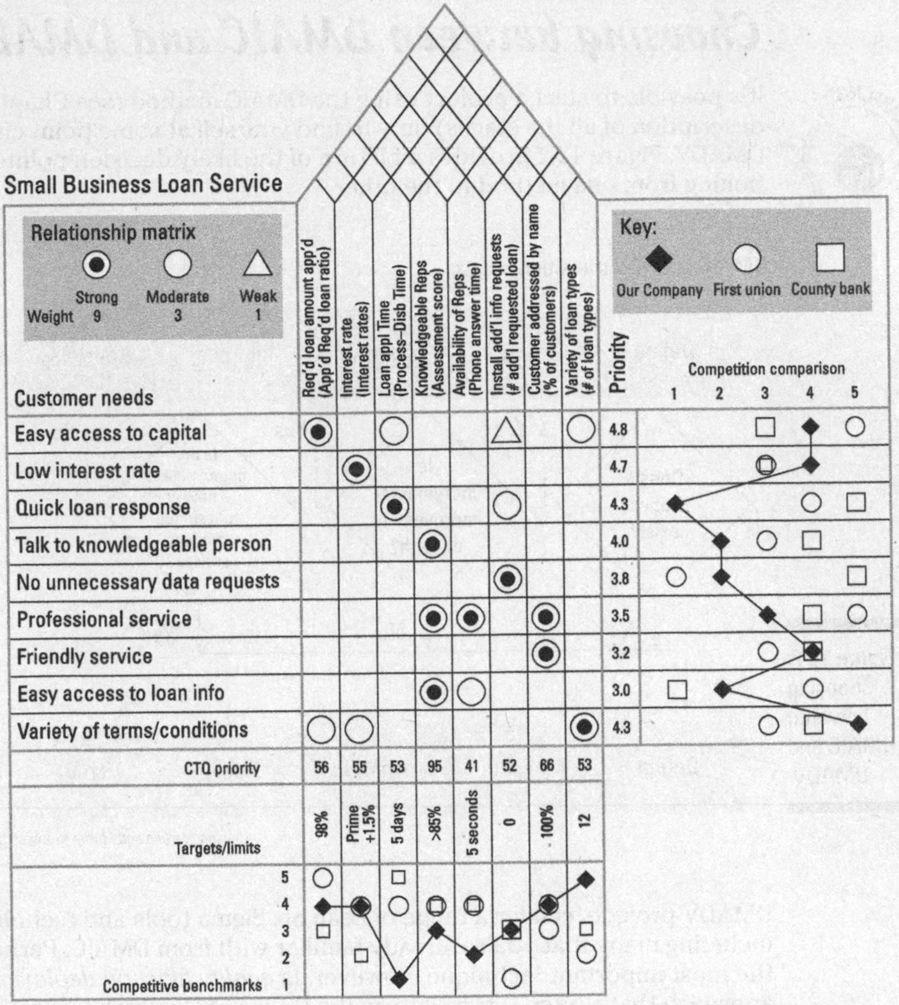

Small Business Loan Service

Figure 12-3: The House of Quality.

Relationship matrix: ● Strong (Weight 9) ○ Moderate (3) △ Weak (1)

Key: ◆ Our Company ○ First union □ County bank

Customer needs	Req'd loan amount app'd (App'd Req'd loan ratio)	Interest rate (Interest rates)	Loan appl Time (Process–Disb Time)	Knowledgeable Reps (Assessment score)	Availability of Reps (Phone answer time)	Install add'l info requests (# add'l requested loan)	Customer addressed by name (% of customers)	Variety of loan types (# of loan types)	Priority
Easy access to capital	●	○			△			○	4.8
Low interest rate		●							4.7
Quick loan response			●		○				4.3
Talk to knowledgeable person				●					4.0
No unnecessary data requests						●			3.8
Professional service				●	●				3.5
Friendly service							●		3.2
Easy access to loan info			●	○					3.0
Variety of terms/conditions	○	○						●	4.3
CTQ priority	56	55	53	95	41	52	66	53	
Targets/limits	98%	Prime +1.5%	5 days	>85%	5 seconds	0	100%	12	

Competition comparison (scale 1–5) and Competitive benchmarks (scale 1–5) shown graphically.

© John Morgan and Martin Brenig-Jones

Considering Quality Function Deployment

Customer research is used to determine the voice of the customer. Competition research helps us hear the voice of the market. Quality function deployment (QFD) helps translate both voices into high-level requirements – the CTQs – and to place measurable definitions, specifications and targets on these requirements.

In the Analyse and Design phases, QFD is further utilised to develop specifications for the lower-level details of the designed product, process or service in order that the high-level customer CTQs can be satisfied.

QFD is a graphical representation of the logic flow, from identifying customer requirements to the detailed development of actions to ensure those requirements are met. A series of interconnected matrices is developed, moving from the requirements, through to design, and eventual implementation and deployment. The 'room numbers' in Figure 12-4 represent the order of the logic flow for completing the QFD.

Clarifying what these houses and rooms are all about

Figure 12-4 shows a house with numbered rooms.

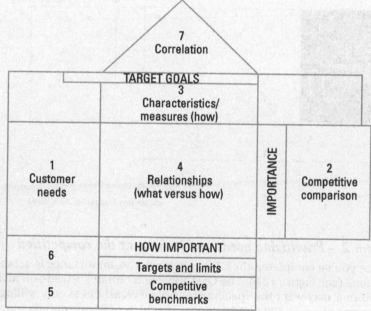

Figure 12-4: 40 Acacia Avenue: seven rooms with a view.

© John Morgan and Martin Brenig-Jones

You'll also discover that QFD doesn't stop at just one House of Quality. In the Analyse and Design phases a second, third and even fourth House of Quality can be built (see the 'Undertaking a QFD drill-down' section later in this chapter).

Room 1 – Customer needs

Before you get to the QFD stage, you'll have identified and segmented your customers, built a data collection plan and conducted your customer research – so what you're left with by this stage is a large amount of voice of customer information.

Room 1 (see Figure 12-5) focuses on organising the information that you've collected and then interpreting and translating that information into a set of CTQ statements.

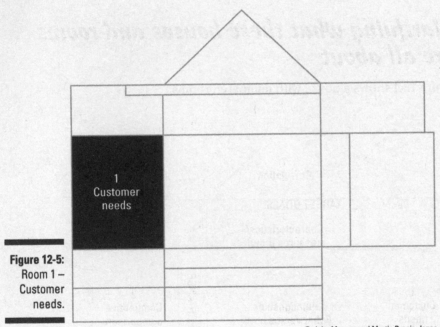

Figure 12-5:
Room 1 –
Customer
needs.

1
Customer
needs

Room 2 – Prioritising needs and looking at the competition

Once you've completed the CTQs, their relative importance is established in Room 2 (see Figure 12-6). The QFD approach initiates a trade-off analysis. The customer may want the specifications of a Ferrari but is only willing to pay the price of a medium-sized saloon – so which of her requirements are the most important? When you enter the design phase, you must understand the priorities from the customer's viewpoint.

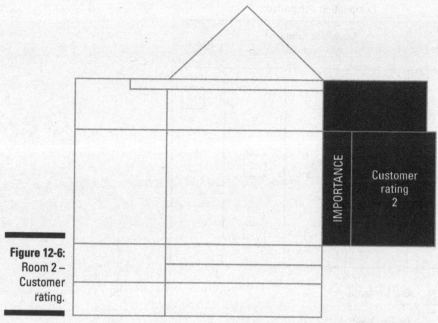

© John Morgan and Martin Brenig-Jones

Figure 12-6:
Room 2 –
Customer
rating.

As part of organising and prioritising customer needs, the customers should also be asked to rate you against the competition. For a redesign effort, the same survey used to determine their satisfaction with your current performance can be applied to determine how the competition satisfies their needs.

Such a comparison can help your team determine the strengths and weaknesses of their current product, service or process. The resulting information is input to the target-setting process for CTQs.

Assign a symbol for your own organisation and one for each of your competitors – these should be market leaders or the most distinguished organisations you directly compete with. For each need in Room 1, ask your customer to assign a rating between 1 (lowest) and 5 (highest) for both your company and your competitors. The highest rating on the scale is typically reserved for how the perfect service performs. A visual comparison can then very quickly be drawn, as shown in Figure 12-7.

In the example, 'our company' isn't doing too well!

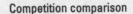

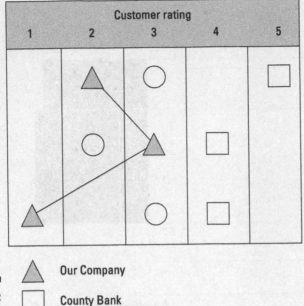

Figure 12-7:
Competition
comparison.

Our Company

County Bank

First Union Lending

© John Morgan and Martin Brenig-Jones

Room 3 – Characteristics and measures

In Room 3 (see Figure 12-8), you start moving from the what to the how of the customer requirements. Until now, you've merely understood what the customer requires; now you need to understand the characteristics and measures that are needed to ensure that the end design meets those requirements.

For each customer attribute, ask what characteristics and measures will indicate how well you're meeting her needs. You need to develop measures for which targets and specification limits can be established. Be aware that measurements can produce two types of data: continuous data, such as time or temperature, and discrete data, such as accuracy – for example, the number of errors that occurred or whether an event happened or not.

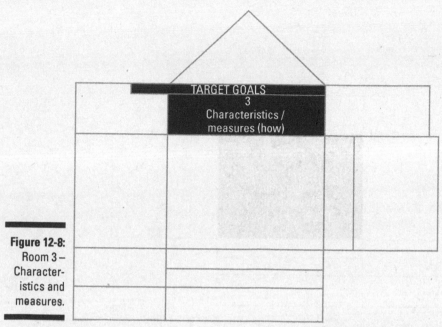

© John Morgan and Martin Brenig-Jones

Room 4 – Relationships

In Room 4 (see Figure 12-9), some analysis starts taking place. You look at the customer CTQs derived from Room 1 and the characteristics and measures described in Room 3, and then start to draw relationships between them. The purpose of this room is to ensure that the requirements of each characteristic and measure are taken into account. Remembering that Room 1 concerns the whats and Room 3 is all about the hows, the key question you're asking when you build Room 4 is, 'Can this "how" achieve that "what"?'

For each relationship between needs in Room 1 and characteristics and measures in Room 3, perform the following steps and complete the relationship matrix shown in Figure 12-10:

✔ Both Figures 12-9 and 12-10 include symbols representing strong, medium and weak. Typically, rating the relationships uses a scale of strong (9), medium (3), weak (1) or none (0).

✔ Calculate the score for each cell by multiplying the priority for the customer need in Room 2 by the (9, 3, 1, 0) value of each related cell.

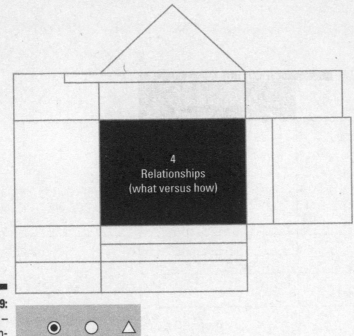

Figure 12-9:
Room 4 –
Relation-
ships.

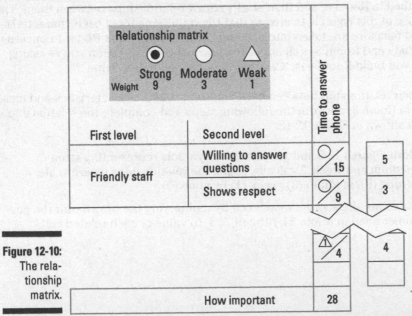

Figure 12-10:
The rela-
tionship
matrix.

Once all of the relationships have been rated, you can add up the individual scores for each measure to determine their importance, carrying out a sanity check and balance at the end to make sure the matrix looks and feels right.

Room 5 – Competitive benchmarking

The term *benchmarking* applies to the process of looking both inside and outside of your own organisation to see both how well others are doing at providing products and services similar to yours (performance benchmarking) and how 'best practice' organisations provide their products and services (process benchmarking).

Technical evaluation (see Figure 12-11) involves using benchmarking to set appropriate goals and targets for the measures identified in Room 3. However, benchmarking also continues to be valid as you move through the Analyse and Design phases – although the focus then is much more on process benchmarking (searching for best practices) than on performance benchmarking (comparing performance measures).

Try to get competitive data for every key measure and analyse it using a 1–5 scale (1 = poor performance, 5 = best-in-class). Use a separate row in Room 5 for each of the 1–5 gradings.

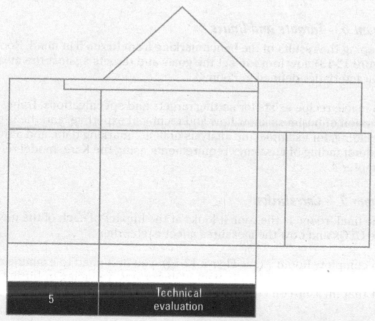

Figure 12-11:
Room 5 –
Technical
evaluation.

Choose one symbol for your organisation and a different symbol for each of your company's competitors. For each measure in Room 3, assign the symbols to the appropriate grading.

Using this exercise, you can gain a very quick visual impression of how your organisation is performing against the competition in all of the key measures, as shown in Figure 12-12.

Figure 12-12:
Grading per-
formance.

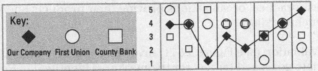

© John Morgan and Martin Brenig-Jones

At this stage it is important to distinguish between qualitative and quantitative benchmarking – the former was done in Room 2, where customer perceptions of your qualitative performance in relation to the CTQs were established. That situation is different to the requirements of Room 5, where you're looking for a comparison of quantitative performance in relation to the measures established in Room 3. Here, you're looking at actual performance as opposed to perceptions about performance.

Room 6 – Targets and limits

Keeping the results of the benchmarking from Room 5 in mind, Room 6 (see Figure 12-13) now looks to set the goals and targets against the measures and characteristics defined in Room 3.

No magic recipe exists for setting targets and specifications. Doing so is a function of business know-how and technical expertise, and the use of tools, including, for example, the analysis of benchmarking data, and a thorough understanding of customer requirements using the Kano model referred to in Chapter 4.

Room 7 – Correlation

The final 'room' is the roof. It looks at the impact of each of the measures on the CTQs and how the measures affect each other.

To complete Room 7 (see Figure 12-14), you first need to examine each measure and assess the likely impact of increasing, reducing or hitting the target for that measure on customer CTQs.

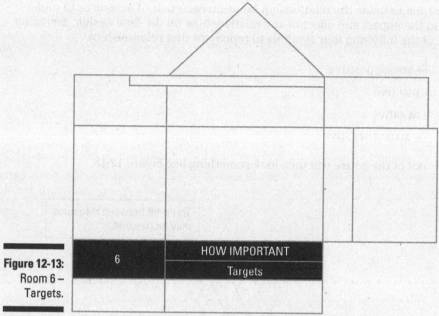

Figure 12-13:
Room 6 –
Targets.

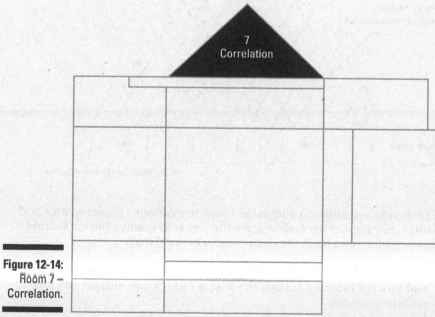

Figure 12-14:
Room 7 –
Correlation.

You then examine the relationship between each pair of measures to understand the impact and effect of any relationships on the final design, assigning one of the following four symbols to represent that relationship:

++ strong positive

+ positive

– negative

– – strong negative

The roof of the house will then look something like Figure 12-15.

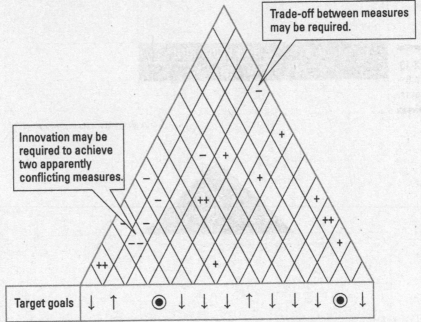

Trade-off between measures may be required.

Innovation may be required to achieve two apparently conflicting measures.

Figure 12-15:
Assessing the impact of measures on customer CTQs.

Target goals

© John Morgan and Martin Brenig-Jones

You're then in a position to understand how the various characteristics and measures may impact the end design – the aim is to resolve the conflicting situations before you build the design. Keep in mind that:

✔ Satisfying negatively correlated measures typically requires a lot of time and forward thinking, though the best solutions and designs will not require trade-offs.

> ✔ Conflict resolution between measures should always focus on meeting the customer needs – not yours!
>
> ✔ Measures with strong positive correlations can become part of the overall design strategy.

Undertaking a QFD drill-down

A QFD drill-down aims to develop further Houses of Quality, gradually refining the level of detail until the design is specified at an implementable level.

As you move from one house to the next, as shown in Figure 12-16, you carry over the corresponding targets and importance measures. The number of houses used in the drill-down may vary but tends to increase with the level of complexity. For a simple service design, the second house may be enough. Generally speaking, product design is more complex and will require more houses than service design.

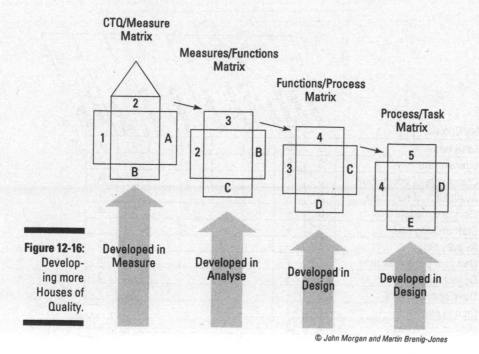

Figure 12-16: Developing more Houses of Quality.

© John Morgan and Martin Brenig-Jones

The second House of Quality is developed in the Analyse phase, where CTQ measures are mapped onto the functions. The CTQ measures and the targets/importance ratings are taken from the first House of Quality. You find the correlations to enter in the cells in Figure 12-16 by asking the following question: 'If I design this particular function correctly, what impact does it have on my ability to meet the CTQ measures/targets?'

The output of the QFD matrix in Figure 12-16 is a prioritisation of functions. It helps to identify where the design effort must be concentrated in order to satisfy the CTQs and thereby the customers.

Making Decisions

TIP

Throughout the DMADV phases and the evolving constructions of the QFD houses, you make decisions about the various design concepts and ideas. The Pugh Matrix shown in Figure 12-17 is often used to help in this process.

Key Criteria	Concept 1 the datum	Concept 2 E-Loan	Concept 3 Phone Loan	Concept 4	Concept 5	Concept 6	Concept 7	Importance rating
Loan term	S	S	–					3
Interest rate	S	S	–					2
Complexity of information	S	S	S					5
Availability of help desk	S	+	+					1
Time to complete form	S	+	–					4
Staff training time	S	+	–					3
Activity time	S	–	–					5
Unit cost per transaction	S	+	–					3
Opportunity for error	S	S	–					3
Development costs	S	–	+					5
Sum of positives	0	4	2					
Sum of negatives	0	2	7					
Sum of sames	10	4	1					
Weighted sum of positives	0	11	6					
Weighted sum of negatives	0	10	23					

Concept selection legend
Better +
Same S
Worse –

Figure 12-17:
The Pugh Matrix.

© John Morgan and Martin Brenig-Jones

Developed in the 1980s by Stuart Pugh, the Pugh Matrix, or *controlled convergence*, provides a simple framework for comparing solutions or concepts against a set of pre-determined criteria. The Pugh Matrix's original intent was to provide a framework to help refine the competing designs by improving the S and – rankings to + and combining the + attributes into a super alternative. It's often used, however, to aid the selection of the best design.

The tool provides a structured way to evaluate alternative or competing concepts, and benefits from being both non-numeric and iterative. It's most often used during 'design projects' and works as described below.

If you face many competing options, try to identify your top five or so favourites. You might find it helpful to represent each concept with a simple sketch and maybe a few words – but ideally not just words alone. The sketches should be produced to the same level of detail and must communicate the key ideas embodied in each option. Finally, give each concept a name.

The list of selection criteria against which the concepts will be evaluated is the crucial part of the matrix. You should already have a detailed understanding of customer needs from your earlier work, and the list of criteria should be straightforward for you to determine. If it isn't, you have some work still to do! Don't forget to include selection criteria that are based upon the needs of the business and internal stakeholders.

The final list of criteria should be unambiguous and must be agreed upon by the full team. Watch out for criteria that are too generic; 'cost', for example, may be more effectively assessed if it's broken down into the various cost drivers.

You don't need to have weighted the criteria at this stage, but doing so is a good idea, perhaps using paired comparisons. Weighting the criteria will certainly help you to focus on the key concepts.

Choose one of the concepts as a 'datum concept' providing a standard reference point. It doesn't really matter which one, but choosing something that already exists can be helpful. Ideally, use a concept from your earlier benchmarking that represents best in class.

In turn, compare each concept with the datum for each of the criteria. If the concept is better or easier, mark it '+'. If it's worse or harder, mark it '–'. Finally, if the concept is similar to or the same as the datum, mark it 'S'. This process is a bit like trying out different strength lenses when having your eyes tested for new glasses!

For each concept, add up the total number of +, – and S scores and take the – total away from the + total. Each concept will now have a score, and ranking them in preferential order is possible.

In discussing the merits of each concept, you may well find a basically good concept that suffers from one poor feature. In this case, a minor modification could improve the overall solution. Finding 'losing' concepts that outscore the others against certain criteria is also possible. In these circumstances, try to combine the best elements into a 'new improved' concept.

As your project unfolds, new concepts may well emerge. If they do, you need to create a new matrix taking one of the stronger concepts as your new datum. If you haven't already done so, weighting the criteria at this stage is sensible.

Naturally, the process is only as good as the team input, the choice of selection criteria and the quality of the basic concepts. Remembering the importance of the 'soft' factors, reflecting on the process is almost certainly worthwhile. Does the team agree on the outcome? Does one solution clearly stand out above the rest? Do the results make sense and do any consistently good or bad features exist? If no outstanding solution emerges, maybe you used ambiguous criteria or perhaps the concepts are too similar.

Although this chapter has provided only an introduction to DMADV and QFD, it does highlight the focus and attention needed to introduce new or redesigned products, services and processes that are defect free.

More often than not, DMADV projects are significantly more resource hungry than DMAIC projects in terms of people, IT involvement and cost, but despite the potentially higher risks, they do, of course, bring higher rewards.

In a large organisation deploying Lean Six Sigma, 20 DMAIC projects will likely be carried out for every one DMADV project.

For most organisations the initial focus of improvement activity will also probably be on bite-sized DMAIC projects and it will be some time before DMADV is used, though market factors may demand otherwise.

As the deployment of Lean Six Sigma takes hold, lots of Lean projects using DMAIC, a moderate number of more 'sigma-based' DMAIC projects and a few DfSS projects will probably be up and running as the organisation gets to grips with reducing rework and waste in general, and improving process flow and reducing cycle times in particular. Where appropriate, rapid improvement projects, again, using DMAIC will also be taking place (see Chapter 15).

Part V
Deploying Lean Six Sigma

Criteria for Success	Rating	
Clear link to a real business need	Yes	No
Measurable cost or performance benefits	Yes	No
Customer requirements well understood or input from the customer can be obtained	Yes	No
Customer satisfaction will be positively impacted	Yes	No
Strong support/sponsorship in place	Yes	No
Scope is clear and reasonably narrow	Yes	No
Historical and current data is accessible	Yes	No
Achievable in 3-6 months	Yes	No
Not capital intensive	Yes	No
Resource is available	Yes	No
Clear ownership for delivery	Yes	No
Project is doable – the problem lies within the organisation's control	Yes	No
Now is the right time to do this project	Yes	No
Process won't be changed by another initiative during the timeframe of the project	Yes	No
Can't afford not to do this project	Yes	No

© John Morgan and Martin Brenig-Jones

web extras

Go to www.dummies.com/extras/leansixsigma for additional information about Kai Sigma, which is the catalyst approach to rapid improvement.

In this part . . .

- ✔ Examine how to use the comprehensive collection of tools and techniques associated with Lean Six Sigma so you can 'make it happen' successfully in your organisation.

- ✔ Understand the key role that leadership plays in creating the right environment for Lean Six Sigma to be effective.

- ✔ Grasp how selecting projects is essential to 'doing the right work.'

- ✔ Identify key issues that you may face when dealing with people in your organisation and how to rally everyone's support.

Chapter 13

Leading the Deployment

In This Chapter

▶ Understanding the importance of leadership

▶ Getting started and considering organisational size

▶ Looking at the role of the deployment programme manager

▶ Appointing a project champion

This chapter is about making Lean Six Sigma happen by leading its deployment from different levels. The key to successful deployment is the organisation's leadership and management. They have to be actively involved and must be seen to be leading and supporting the approach. 'Follow me, I'm right behind you' simply isn't good enough. Having the top-level executives in the organisation fully behind the approach makes it stand a much better chance of success. Leadership doesn't just come from the top, though. In this chapter, we look at the different roles needed to create an effective deployment programme.

Looking at the Key Factors for Successful Deployment

Successful deployment involves:

✔ **Right work:** Ensure your projects are focused on the right issues and linked to your business objectives. Find out what your organisation considers important and then use your organisation's business strategy to drive your Lean Six Sigma projects.

✔ **Work right:** Run your projects effectively, using good-quality people, utilising the right Lean Six Sigma tools and methods, applying sound project management techniques and ensuring rigorous governance through committed sponsorship, project reviews and tollgates reviews.

✔ **Create the right environment:** Lean Six Sigma flourishes as the natural way of working in certain settings. Creating the right environment is about leadership, recognition, training and encouraging people to do the right things effectively, and ensuring the environment supports the team's work.

Figure 13-1 is a simple illustration of a successful deployment model.

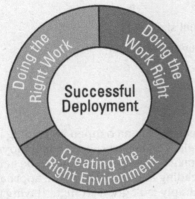

• Doing the right work
  • Strategic alignment
  • Project selection
  • Managing by fact

• Doing the work right
  • Lean Six Sigma tools and methods
  • Programme management
  • Project management
  • Process management

• Creating the right environment
  • Leadership behaviour
  • Effective sponsorship
  • Mentoring, coaching
  • Effective teamwork
  • Resourcing

© John Morgan and Martin Brenig-Jones

Figure 13-1: Successful deployment.

Understanding Executive Sponsorship

Jack Welch, perhaps the world's most famous advocate of Six Sigma when he was chief executive of General Electric, is often cited as the ultimate role model business champion. When Jack Welch was asked by one of the authors of this book how to gain leadership commitment in organisations that don't have a 'Jack Welch at the top', he replied, 'It's no good giving this role to "Harry from Quality".' With all due respect to the excellent Harrys who work in quality departments, commitment has to be actively driven by the leadership at the top of the company. If you haven't got a 'Jack Welch' in your organisation, run a pilot Lean Six Sigma programme and demonstrate the results to the senior executives. You may find you get a convert who becomes the most passionate advocate. Even Jack Welch himself needed a little convincing at the start but once he realised the potential of Six Sigma he was right behind it.

Ideally, the executive sponsor is the most senior person in the organisation, with a real interest in seeing Lean Six Sigma become more than simply a 'quality' initiative. Indeed the reason that the approach has continued to win support from senior executives is because it creates tangible business benefits through delivering improvement and change.

The role of the executive sponsor is to provide strategic direction and support for the overall deployment programme. Effective executive sponsors also recognise that Lean Six Sigma is critical to their own success.

An executive sponsor who really is passionate about Lean Six Sigma shouldn't underestimate the motivational effect he can have on those involved in implementing the approach. If you're a senior executive, here's a quick list of the things you need to do:

- Provide the initial drive and strategic direction for the programme.

- Articulate a clear vision of how you see the future and why this approach is so important.

- Appoint a deployment programme manager.

- Provide the budget and resources for the team as needed.

- Agree on the scope of the programme.

- Make space on your leadership team meeting agenda to review progress and keep yourself informed by getting involved.

- Spread the message – personally through a variety of communication channels and through your behaviour and actions.

- Take part in 'showcases' and recognition events, for example at certification and award ceremonies. Recognition is really key to success.

- Act as a role model – ensure you're not easily diverted off-track.

Active involvement in sponsorship is required, not passive acquiescence. As you understand more about the principles as well as the tools and techniques of Lean Six Sigma, you'll see some great opportunities for their application in and around your own office and in the management processes in your organisation.

Here are four simple Lean Six Sigma techniques that can be encouraged and applied directly by the senior executive team:

- **Avoid jumping to solutions.** When confronted by challenging and complex business problems, do you have a tendency to jump to solutions or expect the team reporting to you to do so? 'Managing by fact' means being informed by intelligent data. Clearly, if the solution really is clear don't hold back but all too often we see situations in which quick-fire (shoot from the lip!) decisions are made at senior level only to be regretted later at great cost to the organisation.

✔ **Beware of the average.** Understand the danger of only seeing averages in regular performance reports and the illusion that targets are being met. Discover the power of variation-based measures, as described in Chapter 7. Control charts provide a visual way to understand the performance of your processes or value streams. Importantly, they enable you to determine when to take action and when not to.

✔ **Encourage the use of visual management.** As described in Chapter 10, although mostly seen at an operational level, simplifying regular reports by using visual management techniques can provide great opportunities for senior management. The approach helps everyone to clearly see what's going on.

✔ **Review one of the management processes that supports the senior executive team.** For example, review the monthly reporting process by carrying out a value-added analysis. In one organisation we worked with, a 70-page monthly progress report was produced, but most of the contents were never read; a cut-down report thus proved to be much more useful and useable.

Considering Size

You may be reading this chapter and thinking that your organisation is too small and that Lean Six Sigma wouldn't work or be relevant. Don't be put off! Stick to the principles. No matter how small your organisation is, it will provide some kind of services or products to customers. In some public service organisations the customers may not have a choice and you might not regard them as normal customers. That's okay. One thing all organisations have in common is that they're driven by processes and Lean Six Sigma will help them manage and improve those processes – as shown in Figure 13-2.

The figure shows how you can start a Lean Six Sigma journey using a straightforward basic toolset. As your continuous improvement maturity develops, process performance improves as you first tame your business processes and then improve them using the more advanced tools from the Lean Six Sigma toolset as you build experience and expertise.

This approach works in all sizes and types of organisation. For example, even the smallest general practitioners' medical practice can apply the principles of Lean Six Sigma. Of course, it won't need to train many or indeed any of its small team to advanced Lean Six Sigma levels. However, having a practice manager trained to Green Belt (see Chapter 2 for a description of how Lean Six Sigma adapts the coloured-belt system from the martial arts) could make all the difference to the effectiveness of the practice.

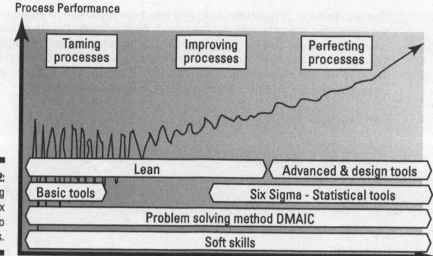

Figure 13-2:
Applying Lean Six Sigma to processes.

© John Morgan and Martin Brenig-Jones

We've worked with many professionals in service organisations who have unquestioning expertise in their chosen field (IT is a good example), but who freely admit that they've never really got to grips with the notion of process excellence. This situation is understandable. A doctor, for example, will receive years of training in his professional area of expertise but wouldn't expect to be an expert in organisational process improvement. The same applies to small departments inside larger organisations – the head of a software development team, for example, may be expected to be an expert in Java but would have little notion of control charts and visual management.

Anyone with a leadership role can start to apply the principles of Lean Six Sigma in his organisation, no matter how small. He won't be able to do it entirely on his own, however. The deployment programme manager is also key to making Lean Six Sigma happen.

Introducing the Deployment Programme Manager

Leadership alone isn't enough to make Lean Six Sigma happen. Good management is also needed and here's where the deployment programme manager comes in.

The deployment programme manager needs to be a respected member of the team who *wants* to take on the role. If your organisation has never undertaken this before, don't worry! The role can be assumed by a good middle manager (in a large organisation) who has the potential to develop further. If you're already developing a 'high potential' group, then look for someone from within it who demonstrates the following characteristics:

- Practical
- Networker
- Resource investigator
- Planner
- Team worker
- Will find the time
- Motivated
- Good communicator
- Open-minded
- Curious
- Has a continuous improvement mindset

We could go on to include a good sense of humour, charisma, dynamism, magician, miracle worker and many other characteristics – but let's be realistic! What is crucial is that the deployment programme manager is capable of not only getting things up and running but also works well with people at all levels (including the senior executive sponsor described earlier in this chapter).

Perhaps controversially we would say that the deployment programme manager doesn't need to be an expert in Lean Six Sigma tools and techniques. At least not at the start of a programme. He does, however, need to have a good project/programme management background and be prepared to learn new skills.

Indeed, the equation we apply to the effectiveness of a solution (as we explain in more detail in Chapter 18) can also be applied to the appointment of a Lean Six Sigma programme manager,

$$E = Q \times A$$

where effectiveness E is a function of Q for technical quality and A for acceptance. In applying this equation to recruitment, you're looking for a balance between technical (hard) and people (change management/soft) skills.

The 'equation' is so simple and yet can be applied when looking to recruit people into the programme at all levels. Even the best Black Belts or even Master Black Belts (see Chapter 2) should offer a balance between hard and soft skills.

The Lean Six Sigma deployment programme manager gets things up and running by:

- Organising senior executive workshop-style training.

- Selecting and working with a suitable training/coaching provider.

- Facilitating the programme start-up through an initial series of improvement projects.

- Ensuring that progress is monitored and that initial projects stay on track and deliver tangible benefits.

- Establishing governance with a light touch.

- Ensuring the message is spread via different channels right across the organisation.

- Putting internal resources in place to support the programme.

- Organising and running a steering group of senior deployment champions from across the organisation.

- Ensuring that employee participation is duly recognised as well as project successes.

- Sharing best practice as it develops across the organisation.

Clearly, no one size fits all, and we're at pains to point out that Lean Six Sigma can drive improvement in organisations of every size and shape, in all sectors. Adapt the role of the deployment programme manager to suit your own situation.

In very small organisations the senior executive sponsor and the deployment programme manager roles can be combined (leadership and management) but, if you can work as a double act, then so much the better.

Starting Your Lean Six Sigma Programme

Investing time in getting the start-up right is well worth it. How you go about launching your Lean Six Sigma programme will affect its success.

Of course, you may be reading this book before you've even floated the idea of running a Lean Six Sigma programme with your team. As a first step, therefore, you may need to think about how you'll win support, especially if people have had negative experiences with other initiatives in the past. Possibly these other initiatives failed because the organisational culture was resistant to change. To make your programme successful, you need to introduce it gradually, in stages.

Consider visiting organisations that have successfully introduced this kind of approach. But bear in mind that it has taken decades for organisations like Toyota or Ricoh to embed this culture into their organisations and they'll be the first to say that they have further to go and more to do. What we find most illuminating about visiting these companies are the leadership and cultural aspects of a genuine continuous improvement culture. The leaders in such organisations often do not realise how good they are, are quite humble and find it hard to describe how this has happened – the approach is so deeply rooted in the values and principles of their organisation, it pervades everything they do. The principles are more important than the tools and in best practice organisations these principles are reflected in the behaviours of the leadership team.

The soft stuff is the key to success! You need to win over the people in your organisation if you want to really embed the approach and obtain sustainable results. Chapter 18 covers the people issues.

Start by engaging the leadership team in a series of 'kick off' events that combine elements of training covering the basics of Lean Six Sigma with how it can best be applied in the particular organisation through a series of targeted improvement initiatives. Most importantly, these sessions need to highlight the role of the senior team and how its members will affect the success of the Lean Six Sigma programme throughout the organisation.

You need to select processes that can be improved by the Lean Six Sigma approach (Chapter 14 has more on project selection). A positive impact early on will smooth the path for integrating the approach throughout the whole organisation.

To ensure the success of your Lean Six Sigma start-up, you need to:

- ✔ Raise awareness and engage senior executives.
- ✔ Identify advocates and champions.
- ✔ Develop a network across the organisation.
- ✔ Develop expertise.

- Deploy Lean Six Sigma tools and techniques through well-developed and important projects.
- Support business unit adoption/roll-out.
- Encourage everyday use of the Lean Six Sigma tools.
- Generate and communicate successes.
- Monitor Lean Six Sigma measures.

Understanding What Project Champions Do

Leadership and management are needed at the overall *deployment* level. At the *project* level, every improvement initiative deserves a champion who's prepared to devote the time and support needed to help the project team overcome any roadblocks on its journey.

The project champion is involved in selecting the project and the team members for it. As the project progresses, the project champion remains involved by:

- Providing strategic direction for the team.
- Developing the improvement charter (see Chapter 2), ensuring the scope of the project is sensible.
- Keeping informed about the project's progress and taking an active involvement in project reviews.
- Providing financial and other resources for the project team.
- Helping to ensure the business benefits are realised in practice.
- Being prepared to stop a project if necessary.
- Helping to get buy-in for the project across the organisation.
- Ensuring appropriate reward and recognition for the project team in the light of its success.

Chapter 14

Selecting the Right Projects

. . . .

In This Chapter

▶ Deploying strategies throughout your organisation

▶ Drawing up a list of improvement ideas

▶ Assessing the suitability of various projects

▶ Prioritising chosen projects

. . . .

The right leadership and management are needed to create the *right environment*, as we describe in Chapter 13, but how do you ensure you're doing the *right work*?

Selecting the right areas in the business to focus on, especially when first starting up a Lean Six Sigma programme ensures early successes and builds confidence.

Driving Strategy Deployment with Lean Six Sigma

In recent years more people have recognised the advantages of using Lean Six Sigma as a method for deploying strategy across their organisations. Strategy deployment is now viewed as such a major area of development that it's covered in our book *Lean Six Sigma Transformation For Dummies* (John Wiley & Sons, Inc.). In a nutshell, strategy deployment looks at how organisations can build on their use of Lean Six Sigma to instigate operational improvements to create a more holistic approach across the entire organisation to drive change and turn strategy into action in a co-ordinated and focused way.

Olympic rowers know only too well that unless team members row in time and in the same direction they'll never achieve gold. Organisations are no different, though often no common purpose exists. Although everyone is working hard, they're not all focused on working on the right things. Getting everyone working well together isn't something that will happen overnight; it takes time and effort and demands clear direction from the top.

The overall goal of Lean Six Sigma transformation is to get the whole organisation moving in the same direction and doing the right things to increase capability and achieve strategic intent. The strategy is broken down into actionable steps and in a way that ensures the scope of the tactical actions is properly agreed and clearly linked to the strategic thinking.

Different approaches to strategy or policy deployment exist, including the application of the Balanced Business Scorecard, and what the Japanese refer to as Hoshin Kanri. The scorecard approach tends to look at the deployment of holistic strategy, whereas Hoshin Kanri is usually more tightly focused on specific strategic objectives.

Strategy deployment is an important subject that's outside the scope of this book but which builds on the foundations set here. For now we limit its scope to the application of Lean Six Sigma to improve operational processes and launching a Lean Six Sigma programme from scratch.

Generating a List of Candidate Improvement Projects

You need to choose a portfolio of projects for launching your Lean Six Sigma programme – but where do you start? As Figure 14-1 demonstrates, so many opportunities seem to be available and so many problems and issues need addressing!

Figure 14-1:
So many options to choose from!

© John Morgan and Martin Brenig-Jones

In fact, selecting the initial projects, along with selecting the right people to work on them, is a practical way of getting the leadership team involved early on in a Lean Six Sigma programme. A well-facilitated project selection workshop is an effective way to kick-start the approach. It gets the senior team working on things that they really care about and using some of the Lean Six Sigma tools in action (for example, a paired comparison, as described in Chapter 4).

We advise running a short (say, two- to three-hour) briefing session a couple of weeks before the project selection workshop to demystify Lean Six Sigma and get everyone considering potential candidates in terms of both processes and people. This way everyone will have had a chance to consult with their own teams, if necessary, and to come armed with their list of candidates before the project selection workshop.

Figure 14-2 describes project selection as a simple three-step process. Once you have a long list of candidates, you then need to assess them and reduce the number to a shortlist of projects that are suited to the approach.

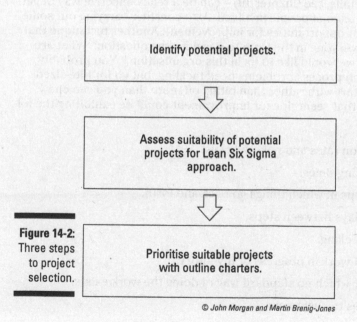

Figure 14-2:
Three steps
to project
selection.

Identify potential projects.

Assess suitability of potential projects for Lean Six Sigma approach.

Prioritise suitable projects with outline charters.

© John Morgan and Martin Brenig-Jones

It may seem obvious, but your first step is to identify your top-level processes, recognise who the customers are and ensure that you understand their requirements.

You could carry out a series of initial process 'health checks' across the organisation reviewing performance measures and using high-level process maps (more on these in Chapter 3). These are likely to be a combination of SIPOC (Suppliers, Inputs, Process, Outputs and Customers) diagrams and value stream maps (see Chapter 3 for more on both of these). These health checks will also help you to start identifying waste and non-value-adding activities. Improvement opportunities may already be obvious, but you may need to collect some data to help quantify and validate them. Typical measures include those to assess activity or unit time, cycle or lead time, error rates and work in progress. You can also start to use control charts to understand the different types of variation in these processes (as described in Chapter 7) as well as looking at process capability. These measures will help you understand how well you're doing in relation to customer requirements, highlight bottlenecks and delays, and enable you to focus on reducing rework activity and bring your processes under better control.

In determining which problem to tackle first, you may want to start simply. The introduction of the Five Ss – sort, straighten, scrub, systemise and standardise (for full details, see Chapter 10) – can be a really effective way of getting everyone in a team of people involved. Also consider carrying out some waste walks to spot opportunities for improvement. Another technique that works well is for everyone in the team to consider the question: 'What are the top ten things we would like to fix in this organisation?' You probably already know which process problems need tackling, but go for bite-sized opportunities to start with rather than biting off more than you can chew. Process activities that seem ripe for improvement could be exhibiting the following symptoms:

- High correction rates and rework levels.
- Long processing times.
- Too many steps in which things go back and forth.
- Excessive delays between steps.
- Excessive checking.
- High levels of work in progress or inventory.
- Processes for which no standard way of doing the work exists.
- Late deliveries to customers.
- High levels of customer complaints.

Potential projects will come from many different sources. Top-down or bottom-up approaches are both fine but as you develop more of a culture of continuous improvement you'll find that more ideas will come from the people who do the work – the process operators (as shown in Figure 14-3).

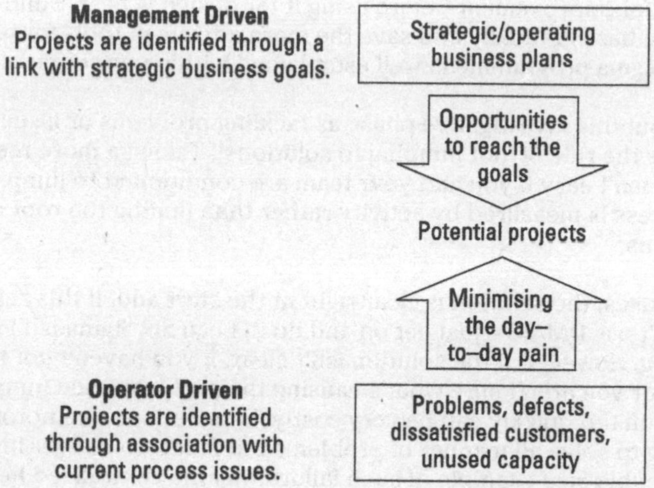

Management Driven
Projects are identified through a
link with strategic business goals.

Strategic/operating
business plans

Opportunities
to reach the
goals

Potential projects

Minimising
the day–
to–day pain

Figure 14-3:
Identifying
where
suggestions
come from.

Operator Driven
Projects are identified
through association with
current process issues.

Problems, defects,
dissatisfied customers,
unused capacity

We recommend that leaders encourage the submission of ideas for improvement and everyone in the organisation responding. Companies such as Ricoh have taken this approach seriously over many years and it's a far cry from the suggestion schemes of old involving an empty box hanging on a wall. Improvement ideas have to be taken seriously within a proper system in which they're evaluated and acted on quickly. Many of these suggestions can be regarded as just-do-it tasks, but some will form good candidates for the Lean Six Sigma approach.

You need to balance strategy and business plans with problems seen in everyday process operations. Generating improvement ideas won't be difficult, but you can't do everything! Each suggestion needs to be assessed to see whether it's suitable for the Lean Six Sigma approach.

Working Out Whether Lean Six Sigma Is the Right Approach

When starting up a Lean Six Sigma programme, we suggest you focus initially on process improvement opportunities using the DMAIC (Define, Measure, Analyse, Improve and Control) approach rather than major process redesign or new product development using DfSS (Design for Six Sigma – see Chapter 12). Although we like DfSS a lot and believe it's a largely undiscovered toolkit, we believe that getting some basic experience from using Lean

Six Sigma for improvement before using it for design is best. Build your knowledge base gradually and save the more advanced tools for when the Lean Six Sigma programme is well established within your organisation.

Think about this investigative phase as tackling problems or issues and remember the rule of 'not jumping to solutions'. Taking a more measured approach isn't easy if you and your team are conditioned to jump into action and progress is measured by activity rather than finding the root causes of problems.

In some cases, the solution *is* clear right at the start and, if this really is the case, don't use DMAIC – just get on and do it! Lean Six Sigma isn't suitable for everything. However, if the solution isn't clear, if you haven't got the facts and data or you aren't sure what's causing the problem, then jumping to the solution too quickly can be very costly. IT 'solutions' are notorious for promising to solve all manner of problems but failing to deliver in practice. A highly publicised example of such failure was the centralised health-care records system, which the UK government scrapped after spending billions of pounds on its development. You can probably think of smaller examples of 'jumping to the solution' without the full facts or any real root-cause analysis being carried out.

Starting a Lean Six Sigma DMAIC project will present a challenge for some managers because it will require them to *not* know all the answers and to have an open mind. The DMAIC approach is similar to good detective case-work. At the Define phase, you know you have a problem – just like the detective knows a crime has been committed – but you don't know the cause or the solution. Likewise, the detective doesn't know 'who did it'! Sure, you, and the detective, may have a few hunches but having an open mind is important – and that's a real challenge for some managers.

In assessing your candidate list of improvement ideas, think about whether the solution is clear. If it is, then you won't need to use the DMAIC method. Use a good project management approach to implement the changes needed. In the same way, some police incidents are open and shut cases. They don't require the setting up of an investigation team and there are more important cases to be working on.

At the outset, consider these three questions:

- ✔ Does a gap exist between current and required performance?
- ✔ Is the cause of the problem already understood?
- ✔ Is the solution already apparent?

If the answers are yes, no and no, the project is likely to be suitable for Lean Six Sigma DMAIC.

Prioritising projects

Your team will have only a limited amount of resources to deploy on running DMAIC improvement projects, so you need to be selective. Prioritise the candidates by considering only really serious issues where you can make the biggest difference.

Involving the senior team in a project selection workshop is a good way to engage them (see earlier in this chapter), and if you've already run an executive awareness session beforehand they'll arrive with several improvement ideas. Now you need to filter these and agree on your first set of improvement projects and who's going to lead and manage them.

If you have lots of ideas you could use a simple voting technique to reduce your long list to a more manageable number before using a more detailed criteria-based approach. A simple voting approach is effective for a first-round reduction. Don't lose the initial list, though, as these ideas can be

Criteria for Success	Rating	
Clear link to a real business need	Yes	No
Measurable cost or performance benefits	Yes	No
Customer requirements well understood or input from the customer can be obtained	Yes	No
Customer satisfaction will be positively impacted	Yes	No
Strong support/sponsorship in place	Yes	No
Scope is clear and reasonably narrow	Yes	No
Historical and current data is accessible	Yes	No
Achievable in 3-6 months	Yes	No
Not capital intensive	Yes	No
Resource is available	Yes	No
Clear ownership for delivery	Yes	No
Project is doable – the problem lies within the organisation's control	Yes	No
Now is the right time to do this project	Yes	No
Process won't be changed by another initiative during the timeframe of the project	Yes	No
Can't afford not to do this project	Yes	No

Figure 14-4:
A list of criteria for assessing project viability.

© John Morgan and Martin Brenig-Jones

added to a project 'hopper' for future consideration. Remember that this isn't a once-only task; you'll also set up a project selection process to continue after you've selected the first group of projects. After all, you want to see continuous improvement not a one-hit wonder!

Figure 14-4 is a typical list of criteria we've used in various organisations to work out which project ideas are workable. This list isn't fixed; you may have other priorities and criteria, so do adapt it to meet your own priorities and organisational needs.

Another approach is to use a weighted criteria selection matrix. First, agree the selection criteria with the senior team at the workshop. Try to keep the number down to no more than six criteria and then agree weights for each of them. Now evaluate the shortlist of candidate projects against the weighted criteria as described below.

Using a criteria selection matrix

A criteria selection matrix (see Figure 14-5) can be used in a number of ways during a Lean Six Sigma project and also help you select the projects to tackle.

Follow these steps:

1. **List the project ideas.**
2. **Identify the important criteria in the decision.**
3. **Weight these on a scale.**
4. **Look at how each option impacts the factors and score out of ten.**
5. **Multiply the score by the weighting.**
6. **Add up the weighted scores and group into high, medium or low.**
7. **Reject the low-scoring options.**
8. **Evaluate the rest and decide.**

The management team weights each criterion by its relative contribution and importance, and then evaluates potential projects and prioritises them for action.

Even where you've identified a clear winner, making sure that it's an effective option and not simply the best of a bad bunch is still worthwhile. The percentage column on the right-hand side of the diagram helps you keep a check and balance on things, and perhaps encourages you to look for ways of improving the preferred choice.

Criteria	A	B	C	Score	Rank	%
Options / Weights	1	3	5	(weighted)		
Idea one	6 / 6	5 / 15	7 / 35	56	3	62
Idea two	3 / 3	7 / 21	6 / 30	54	4	60
Idea three	1 / 1	8 / 24	8 / 40	65	1	72
Idea four	8 / 8	6 / 18	5 / 25	51	5	57
Idea five	7 / 7	7 / 21	6 / 30	58	2	64

Figure 14-5: A criteria selection matrix

© John Morgan and Martin Brenig-Jones

The criteria selection matrix provides a useful format for the selection of all sorts of things both within the workplace and outside. At home, for example, you might use it to select the next car you want to buy or the school you would like your children to attend.

If you like, you can keep things simple and use a 2 × 2 matrix, as shown in Figure 14-6, with each potential project mapped against benefit and effort, or cost. This matrix allows you to identify visually the most 'desirable' projects, as well as those that may be potential quick wins. Quick wins can be taken down a slightly different route using a Rapid Improvement approach – see Chapter 15.

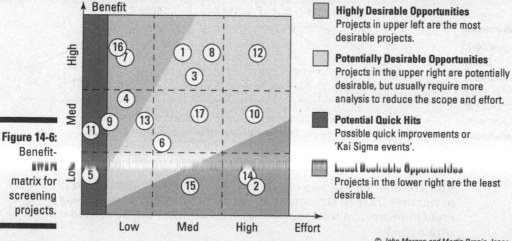

Figure 14-6: Benefit-effort matrix for screening projects.

Highly Desirable Opportunities
Projects in upper left are the most desirable projects.

Potentially Desirable Opportunities
Projects in the upper right are potentially desirable, but usually require more analysis to reduce the scope and effort.

Potential Quick Hits
Possible quick improvements or 'Kai Sigma events'.

Least Desirable Opportunities
Projects in the lower right are the least desirable.

© John Morgan and Martin Brenig-Jones

Deciding on which approach fits which project: Doing the work right

At a project level, it's important to distinguish between those problems that can be tackled using a rapid improvement approach, and those that need to be approached in a more formal way, using DMAIC over perhaps three to six months.

Start simply, securing commitment and ongoing support. As you make progress in your deployment, you can increasingly link your activities to the organisation's business plans and strategic objectives. You might look to policy deployment as the next stage, especially if you're aiming for breakthrough results. You can use cause and effect analysis to distinguish which processes need which approach. For example, Figure 14-7 uses Ys to refer to Effects and Xs to denote Causes. The organisation as a whole has to achieve its top-level business goals (the big Ys in Figure 14-7), which are 'caused' by the organisational processes performing well and delivering their outputs. The process Ys are in turn 'caused' by the in-process variables being in control. This approach will affect the way you manage the whole organisation. Significant benefits will surface at the top by focusing improvement resources on those Xs that will have the biggest positive impact all the way up the chain.

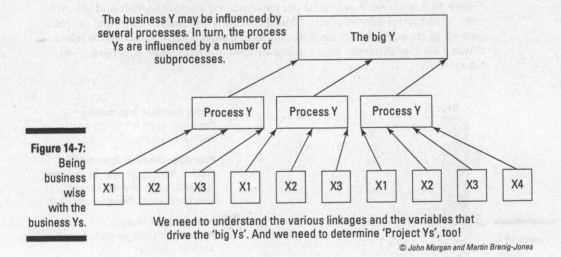

The business Y may be influenced by several processes. In turn, the process Ys are influenced by a number of subprocesses.

The big Y

Process Y   Process Y   Process Y

X1 X2 X3   X1 X2 X3   X1 X2 X3 X4

Figure 14-7:
Being business wise with the business Ys.

We need to understand the various linkages and the variables that drive the 'big Ys'. And we need to determine 'Project Ys', too!

© John Morgan and Martin Brenig-Jones

Now consider the start-up of a typical DMAIC project, which is likely to run over three to six months. In the next chapter we look at using a rapid improvement workshop-based approach that can be carried out within weeks.

Setting Up a DMAIC Project

At the senior team level, you first need to gain agreement on a number of basic details:

 ✔ **Who will take on the role of project champion?** This person will represent the voice of the organisation and ensure that the project is kept on track and steered in the right direction. (Chapter 13 covers the role of the project champion.) The project champion will need specific training, reflecting a balance between the leadership aspects of the role and a good grounding in Lean Six Sigma (to a minimum of Yellow Belt level – Chapter 2 explains the martial arts analogy).

 ✔ **Who will take the project lead?** If you're just starting up we recommend that the project leader is selected for Green Belt training and that the training is delivered in modules based on the life of the project; in this way the training exercises use and develop the real-life project. As you're unlikely at this stage to have internal experts available (Black Belts or Master Black Belts), we suggest you use a training organisation to provide project coaching to the Green Belt trainees as they work through their projects.

After these two roles have been assigned, the project champion and the Green Belt project leader can get started on the project's Define phase, focusing initially on the project charter (see Chapter 2). They also need to appoint part-time project team members. Process operators should be involved in the project as they're the people who know the process best. They'll also be much more inclined to adopt improvements if they've been involved in developing them. From here onwards, the project will move through the DMAIC phases described in Chapter 2.

Chapter 15

Running Rapid Improvement Events

In This Chapter

▶ Identifying potential improvements through managed events

▶ Checking out the role of the event facilitator

▶ Putting together a checklist of useful questions for running successful events

DMAIC provides a systematic and proven approach to improvement that can be applied to projects of all sizes. Smaller projects can benefit from an accelerated approach based on organising and running a series of workshops bringing people together to work through the DMAIC stages with a focus on rapid improvement. This approach requires a high level of facilitation skills and selection of the right tools to use at the different stages. This chapter describes this approach and how to make it work in practise.

Seeing Rapid Improvement with Kaizen or Kai Sigma Events

Kaizen means change for the better. It's often associated with short, rapid, incremental improvement and forms a natural part of an organisation's approach to continuous improvement. *Kai Sigma* is developed from the Kaizen approach and adapts the framework of the Lean Six Sigma DMAIC phases (Define, Measure, Analyse, Improve and Control) in a series of facilitated workshops. The facilitator doesn't need to use the language of Lean or Six Sigma; rather, he aims to involve the people who operate and work in a particular process in making improvements to that process. The approach makes use of team knowledge rather than detailed analysis. It allows team members to step out from the day-to-day pressure of operating a process and reflect on how the process can be improved.

The people who actually use the process may already know the solution, but maybe they haven't been listened to! The workshops typically involve the team for anything from one to five days in a series of workshops or in one continuous intensive workshop over a period of up to five days. A traditional Kaizen event takes place in less than five days. These timescales compare to perhaps three to four months, needed for a traditional DMAIC project. Refer to Figure 15-1 for an example plan that we refer to as Kai Sigma.

Kai Sigma Rapid Improvement Events

Figure 15-1:
A typical outline Rapid Improvement Event Plan.

Preparation	~1 week	
Preplanning		~2 week
Event execution		
Follow-up and implementation	~1 day · 1–3 days	5 days ~30 days

© John Morgan and Martin Brenig-Jones

Good preparation is needed, of course, especially in agreeing on the problem, which should have a narrow focus and be clearly defined. Rapid improvement workshops are biased towards action and the derived solution to the problem should be put into practice as quickly as possible. In fact, some elements of the solution may actually be actioned during the workshops.

As with a traditional DMAIC project, the Control phase is vital to ensure the improvement gain is maintained.

In our experience a traditional five-day Kaizen event is more likely to be effective in a manufacturing organisation than a service or transactional office-based environment; in the latter, the Kai Sigma multi-workshop approach works particularly well.

To ensure these workshops are a success, planning and pre-work is necessary. Where appropriate, look to see if relevant data is already available or whether you need to collect some in advance of the event.

The event involves three phases:

✔ Preparation

✔ The Workshop(s)

✔ Follow-up

In terms of tools and techniques, a set of simple but commonly used tools should handle the problems selected. They include the following:

- The improvement charter (Chapter 2)
- Critical to quality customer requirements (CTQs; Chapter 4)
- SIPOC – the high-level process map (Chapter 3)
- Process stapling (Chapter 5)
- A process and/or value stream map (Chapter 5)
- The theory of constraints (Chapter 11)
- The ten wastes (Chapter 9)
- The Five Ss (Chapter 10)
- Visual management (Chapter 9)
- Measurement and data collection (Chapter 6)
- Data displays, including checksheets and Pareto charts (Chapter 7)
- Brainstorming (Chapter 8)
- Fishbone diagram (Chapter 8)
- Interrelationship diagram (Chapter 2)
- FMEA and error proofing (Chapter 10)
- Control plan (Chapter 16)

You also need some simple selection and prioritisation techniques, including:

- The 2 × 2 matrix (Chapter 14)
- Paired comparisons (Chapter 4)
- The criteria selection matrix (Chapter 14)

DMAIC provides a systematic approach to achieving process improvements. In many ways, the key is clear problem definition followed by the successful completion of the Measure and Analyse phases. Get these phases right and the improvement solution is often very obvious. Sometimes a solution presents itself as a result of the Measure phase and you can move to a 'quick win'. Quick wins bypass the Analyse phase and go straight to Improve, but some care is needed and you should make sure you truly understand the effects of your change.

Be the detective – solve the crime – eliminate the suspects from your enquiries!

Understanding the Facilitator's Role

Good event facilitation is critical to the success of the rapid improvement workshop approach. Don't underestimate the skills needed to run effective workshops. The facilitator needs to be experienced and well versed in the Lean Six Sigma toolkit. He also needs to be a good trainer as an element of training is inevitable during the workshops.

The role of the facilitator is to:

✔ Ensure rapid improvement workshops, meetings and interactions between people are effective and productive.

✔ Make the best use of the skills and contributions from everyone involved.

✔ Ensure that all aspects of each workshop are orchestrated to ensure success.

The facilitator needs to make sure that all aspects of the event are orchestrated to ensure success, and needs to consider these three phases:

✔ Planning and preparation

✔ Running the workshops

✔ Following up and action planning

These three phases are described in the following sections.

Planning and preparation

The facilitator needs to consider the following when planning and preparing for an improvement event:

✔ **Purpose and agenda**: Does the event have a clear purpose? Is everyone attending the event clear about the purpose? Does an agenda exist that's structured to ensure the purpose is achieved? In terms of authority, is everyone clear about what they can and cannot do?

✔ **Attendees**: Based on the purpose and agenda, are you clear about who needs to attend? If critical inputs need to be made, who is going to make them? Do you need certain people at the event because they have relevant background knowledge that will add to the quality of the discussion? Everyone attending the event should be there for a reason, and they should be clear about expectations for their contribution.

✓ **Event dynamics**: With knowledge of the purpose, agenda and attendees, it's likely that before the event you can predict potential areas of difficulty. Do some attendees have very strong views that may incite conflict? Do difficult issues need to be discussed? Are people attending the event who don't get on? Either way, you can use stakeholder analysis here to identify key influencers that need some pre-positioning beforehand to make sure they attend the workshop in the right frame of mind. If you can identify these potential difficulties up front, you can structure the agenda and the event process to help address these issues and minimise any negative impact on the proceedings.

You first need to identify the stakeholders – they can help make or break your project! Your list will include anyone who controls critical resources or who shapes the thinking of other critical parties. Ask the following questions:

- Who are they?

- Where do they currently stand on the issues associated with this change initiative?

- Are they supportive? If so, how supportive?

- Are they against the change initiative? If so, how much against?

- Are they broadly neutral?

✓ **Event structure**: With an outline agenda, a knowledge of how much time you have available and awareness of the likely workshop dynamics, how are you going to allocate that time across the different agenda items? Where does the emphasis need to be placed? How much time needs to be allocated to inputs, to discussion, to decision making? In setting the event structure, you also need to take account of the need for breaks at various points (coffee, lunch, tea), and to be aware of how these breaks will impact the flow of the discussion. For long events, you also need to think about how to keep people engaged throughout the day; for example, consider giving people something interesting to do after lunch.

✓ **Event roles**: Typically, the event will have a champion or sponsor – the person who helps establish the purpose and objective of the event. He also clarifies the authority given to the team. The role of the facilitator is clearly different. As part of preparation, the champion and facilitator must agree their different roles and the overall purpose of and plan for the event. A team member should be appointed as time-keeper during the event to keep an eye on the clock and to ensure that progress is being made. Someone also needs to fulfil the role of note-taker, responsible for capturing information and recording decisions made.

✔ **Event venue:** The venue is a key part of a successful event. What sort of environment do you want to create for the outcome you want to achieve? People's behaviour during the event is likely to reflect their surroundings so consider carrying out a Five Ss exercise beforehand. You need to consider the following issues:

- Whether to host the event on-or off-site
- If on-site, how to avoid attendees being distracted by operational demands
- The layout of the room – formal or informal
- The appropriate room size
- If breakout rooms are needed
- Equipment needed and available

You need a number of things in the room and outside it. The event toolkit is likely to include some or all of the following:

✔ Flipchart and stand

✔ Paper and spare flipchart pads

✔ Pens

✔ Brown paper

✔ Sticky notes

✔ Tape measure

✔ Digital camera or camera phone and possibly a video camera (most new smartphones are excellent video cameras)

✔ Batteries (just in case)

✔ Laptop

✔ Projector

You need to think about refreshments, too. Rapid improvement events can be thirsty work!

Running the event

The role of the facilitator is to ensure the overall process is orchestrated. Good preparation means you're clear about the outline process you want to take people through. Of course, you need to be flexible and respond appropriately as the dynamics dictate, but your pre-work gives you a good framework. A successful event requires that the following issues be addressed:

- **Agenda/timekeeping**: The facilitator needs to ensure the event runs to time. If things are taking longer than planned, he must re-jig the agenda as appropriate (obviously keeping the overall purpose in mind – after all, the objectives of the event must be achieved!).

- **Expectation setting**: At the start of the event the facilitator will find it useful to ask all the attendees for their expectations. These can be logged on a flipchart and referred to throughout the session. Collecting expectations at the start allows the facilitator to make sure that every-one present understands the purpose of the event. This information also highlights different perspectives and allows the facilitator to point out how the event agenda fits with the expectations stated. In some cases it may also result in modifications to the agenda if key influencers express needs that will otherwise not be met (though with good prepa-ration that shouldn't happen very often!). The improvement charter (Chapter 2) provides an ideal framework to involve the team in shaping the event project.

- **Logging issues**: The role of the facilitator is to lead and orchestrate the discussion, focusing it on the agenda and the stated purpose of the event. If attendees stray from the issue at hand, threatening to derail the event, their points should be logged – visibly on a flipchart – and returned to later. The facilitator may be able to work in those points for discussion at suitable slots in the agenda or assign them to clear owners who will take the points away and work on them outside the event.

- **Logging next steps/actions**: It's a good idea for the facilitator to log next steps or actions as the event proceeds. Again, this should be done in a visible way (on a flipchart) so that every attendee can see what actions have been agreed and who's responsible for each. Logging in this way avoids any confusion and the facilitator can also return to the list at the end of the event and run through it item by item so that everyone leaves feeling clear about what they have to do next.

- **Noting pluses and deltas**: At the end of the event the facilitator can ask all attendees to identify the pluses of the event (what people found useful) and the deltas (what could have been improved). Not only does this activity provide good feedback for the facilitator, it also allows the attendees to reinforce the positive impact of the event or, alternatively, raise any residual concerns or issues that may not have been picked up during the event itself. The facilitator captures these pluses and deltas – getting the team to record them on sticky notes is a simple way of doing so. They can then be reviewed, and action taken, before the next event session. Remember that these rapid improvement events are likely to be scheduled as a series of one-day (or half day) sessions.

Following up and action planning

At the end of the event, or shortly afterwards, the facilitator and the champion will conduct a review. They need to consider what went well, what could've been improved, whether their objectives were met and what follow-up is required. Addressing these issues will help in preparing for the next session. Where appropriate, the facilitator needs to make sure that actions and next steps decided at the event are circulated as quickly as possible. After the improvement solution has been implemented, it will be important to ensure an effective handover has taken place and that a control plan is in place

Creating a Checklist for Running Successful Events

The facilitator may find it helpful to have a mental checklist of questions to refer to as he observes and orchestrates the event process. The following list isn't exhaustive and you may want to add to or modify it based on your own experience. The key thing is to think about it!

✔ Are the more active participants hogging the discussion?

✔ Is anyone who could make a useful contribution being excluded?

✔ Is enough being done to encourage quieter members to contribute? Often these people have the greatest insight because they've listened to all the contributions to date.

✔ Who are the influential group members? Why is this? Are they influential as a result of their subject knowledge or for other reasons? What are those other reasons?

✔ What influencing styles are used within the group? Which are accepted or rejected by other group members?

✔ Is someone updating the facts and summarising the situation to date?

✔ Is someone ensuring that all relevant data, whether facts, opinions or alternative solutions, are being collected?

✔ Is someone ensuring that the problem-solving technique being used is suitable for the task?

✔ Do people keep hopping from one subject to another, thus stopping the group from making progress down its chosen path?

✔ Are the physical surroundings having a positive, negative or neutral effect?

✔ Do group members feel able to contribute without fear of being made to look foolish or ignored?

✔ What contribution does the leader make to the atmosphere among the group?

✔ Are subgroups forming?

✔ Does an elite exist within the group?

✔ Are the subgroups helping or hindering the group as a whole?

✔ Is any obvious ganging up occurring? If so, take urgent action to rectify it.

Chapter 16

Putting It All Together

- -

In This Chapter

▶ Following the steps through a DMAIC project

▶ Answering relevant questions to ensure everything is covered

▶ Keeping a check on things

- -

This checklist chapter is a little different from the usual *For Dummies* format. It provides a map for your process improvement journey, as well as some helpful tips and reminders. The map follows the DMAIC improvement method.

As with any journey, you won't always need the map but knowing you have one is a comfort. You can use it to follow the step-by-step process that enables you to make improvements in a systematic way.

At each of the DMAIC steps you find a number of questions to consider and answer. They can help keep you on track. In answering the main questions, consider the questions and prompts in the bullets that follow. Answering every question is almost certainly unnecessary, but you may need to frame some other questions specific to your project.

Different problems may need different tools and, indeed, some problems may not need a formal approach at all.

Tailor things to suit your particular problem and experience, but make sure you take a systematic approach. Jumping to conclusions and solutions can trip you up en route. You may find opportunities to safely skip through some of the steps quite quickly, however.

Your DMAIC journey will be paused from time to time to take stock of progress. These reviews are an essential element in ensuring success. Finally, remember the need to keep people up to date with progress and what's planned.

Working Your Way through DMAIC

When you start any new improvement project, an essential ingredient for success is ensuring that you and your team have a clear understanding of why the project is being undertaken and what it's trying to achieve. With a DMAIC project, you start with a problem that needs to be solved.

Before you can solve it, you need to clearly define it, which isn't always as straightforward as it may sound. One of the key outputs from the Define phase, and one that helps you define the problem is a completed improvement charter (see Chapter 2); you need to draft this with your team and the project champion or sponsor.

Defining Where You're Going

The Define phase looks to clarify the problem that needs tackling. You need to know where you're going. You'll also need to know when you get there. You thus begin by describing the problem you're tackling and the goal you're aiming for. Make sure that you involve the improvement team members, because doing so will help gain their buy-in and sense of ownership.

You can use the *fifteen-word flipchart* to develop the problem and goal statements. Get members of the team to draft on sticky notes their own statements of the problem using a maximum of 15 words. Put them on a flipchart and, as a team, highlight key phrases or words that need to be encompassed within the eventual improvement charter statements. Naturally, the final statement can be as many words as you need.

You also need to clarify:

- ✔ Why working on this problem now is important.
- ✔ How much improvement is expected and by what date.
- ✔ Who needs to be involved.
- ✔ What roles these people fulfil.

With this information and understanding, you can start to agree a first draft improvement charter that starts you in the right direction by providing a clear description of your project and what you hope to achieve. It also helps you identify some of the additional information you need to complete your project.

At the start of the project you may not be in a position to describe the problem as well as you want, but that's okay. Provide as much description as you can and identify the information and data needed to give you a fuller picture.

The problem statement can be updated as you work through the project and it's especially likely to need revising following the Measure phase.

Ideally, your project will be bite-sized, but if it's a large and potentially complex project, the affinity diagram can help you prepare for success. Certainly it will help you develop the improvement charter. The affinity and interrelationship diagrams help provide definition (Chapter 2 describes these in detail).

In many ways, the affinity diagram can be seen as step zero in a large project, helping a team develop its thoughts on the issues involved. By the time the team has created the interrelationship diagram, the team will almost certainly have a detailed understanding of what needs to be done, the drivers of success and the many and varied interrelationships involved.

Throughout your project developing a storyboard summary of the key decisions and outputs makes sense – it helps you review progress and share your lessons. It also, of course, helps with at least some of the necessary communication.

Developing and reviewing a communication plan is an essential activity. You need to secure acceptance from those people touched by your project or the process involved (see Chapter 18 on the people issues).

Looking at the outputs from the Define phase

The Define phase needs to produce the following outputs:

A first draft improvement charter that includes the following:

- A business case
- A problem statement
- A goal statement
- The project scope
- High-level milestones
- Agreed roles and responsibilities
- The CTQs, or at least a plan to agree them (this element may need to be carried over into the Measure phase)
- A SIPOC diagram, providing a high level map of the process
- A stakeholder analysis (remember the importance of the soft stuff!)

Getting the team to develop an elevator speech may be a good idea. Whether you're in the lift, at the coffee machine or just about anywhere else, having a clear and simple project pitch up your sleeve is pretty handy. You never know whom you might bump into. If it's someone who's key to your project in some way, the prepared and rehearsed pitch can help you secure her support and commitment. Your pitch can work just as effectively in securing support for the eventual solution that you and your team select.

The pitch should describe the following:

- The project (or solution)
- The need for change
- The vision of the new desired state that you're working towards
- What you want from others

The term *elevator speech* is based on the idea that you may be in the lift and have a minute to make your pitch. The key is to keep it simple and short. But do make sure it's relevant, too. You can put it to the test with your colleagues in the team. Indeed, developing the pitch with the team is a good way of helping you all understand the project and increase your own commitment to it. Consider getting each member to write her own version and then compare notes, either choosing the best or taking elements from each. The fifteen-word flipchart can help with this process.

Finally, make sure everyone practises the delivery of the pitch. Doing so ensures that the message is delivered confidently and consistently by the whole team. After all, it's your sales opportunity and needs to be taken!

Carrying out a risk assessment for the project is also sensible, as is getting your storyboard underway. Keeping your storyboard updated will be part of the all-important communication plan.

Being prepared: Typical questions the team needs to address in Define

The following questions and prompts should help you and the team establish what you need to do and why:

- **What is the purpose of this project?**
  - What are you trying to do?
  - How do you know about it and why?

- What is the current performance level, and what should it be?

- What parameters exist (agreeing a high-level SIPOC will help here)?

- What are the customer requirements? How do you know? How well have you translated the customer's voice into CTQs?

✔ **How will customers be affected by the successful completion of this project?**

- Who are the customers?

- Will they care if this project is successful?

- Are you addressing their key requirements?

- How will they know if it's been successful?

- How will you know?

✔ **What other reasons are there for selecting this project?**

- What might happen if you don't take action?

- How does this project rank in relation to other possible projects?

- Who thinks this project is important – external customers, internal customers, your manager, your colleagues?

✔ **How will you know if things improve?**

- What measurement will you need in place and how will it relate to the customer requirements?

- What will the customer be measuring?

- What will the customer see?

✔ **What should the first draft improvement charter address?**

- What's the problem and what do you think needs to be done?

- Who needs to work on the project and will they be able to?

- Who needs to be consulted for advice or information?

- Who needs to be kept informed?

✔ **What is the scope of the project and how much improvement are you looking for?**

- What limits exist in terms of authority and resources?

- When should the project start and finish?

- How will work and progress be documented?

- Who will champion this project and provide support or clout if needed?

Considering typical questions the champion needs to ask in Define

The champion must take an active part in developing and agreeing the improvement charter. Bear in mind, though, that it changes as the team gathers more information and data. Incidentally, the champion's contribution to developing the business case is particularly important.

Key questions for the champion to ask the team include the following:

- ✔ What is the purpose of this project: What are you trying to do? What prompted it?
- ✔ How will customers be affected by the successful completion of this project?
- ✔ How will you know if things improve?
- ✔ Does everyone understand their roles and responsibilities (remember the E = Q × A formula; see Chapter 18)?
- ✔ Are all team members available?
- ✔ What data or information is missing?
- ✔ Have you started your storyboard?

At the end of the Define phase the champion needs to carry out a tollgate review (see Chapter 2 for details). When this is satisfactorily completed, you can move to the Measure phase.

DMAIC isn't necessarily a linear process, and you're likely to find yourself back in the Define phase, if only to update the problem and goal statements, for example.

Getting the Measure of Things

The Measure phase is really about understanding how the work gets done and how well. The DMAIC map provides the route ahead, but if you don't know where you are or where you've been, a map is unlikely to help. To fully understand the current situation, you need to know what's meant to happen, and why, and, of course, what does happen. Process stapling (see Chapter 5) can help you develop a more detailed picture that enables you to build on your high-level SIPOC from the Define phase.

Going to the *gemba* (the Japanese word for the workplace) can highlight what's really happening, helping you to spot non-value-adding activities and waste, and the potential for introducing Five S, for example, as we describe in Chapter 10. This approach avoids wasting time trying to find things, by helping keep things neat and tidy with a place for everything.

Obviously, knowing current performance is essential – this information becomes your baseline – but knowing what's happened in the past can also be helpful. Is the process problem something new, for example, or has it been an issue before? If it has, why is it still a problem?

Measure what's important to the customer, taking note of the CTQs but also what the customer sees. Gathering this information can help focus your improvement efforts and prevent you going off in the wrong direction. Use control charts to help you make better sense of the data.

Checking the outputs from the Measure phase

The Measure phase needs to produce these outputs:

- ✔ The confirmed CTQs, if not already agreed (ideally, these should have been completed in the Define phase)
- ✔ An updated SIPOC, where necessary
- ✔ A current state deployment flowchart and/or value stream map
- ✔ Agreed output measures (the Ys)
- ✔ Agreed input and in-process measures (the Xs; although these may not be determined until the Analyse phase)
- ✔ An agreed data collection plan
- ✔ SPC control charts
- ✔ A baseline measure of performance, possibly using Process Sigma
- ✔ An updated improvement charter
- ✔ An updated storyboard
- ✔ An updated communication plan

Noting some typical questions the team needs to address in Measure

The following questions and prompts should help you and the team to check that you're measuring the right things:

- ✔ **What has happened in the past?**
  - Is this a new problem – when did it first occur?
  - What improvements have been tried?
  - What effect did they have and why?
  - What problems or circumstances shaped the current process?
  - Do they still exist?

- ✔ **What's meant to happen now?**
  - What are the objectives of the process?
  - Are they clearly understood?
  - How does your process link to the customer?
  - What does the customer's process look like?
  - What are the requirements of the process?
  - How may a picture of the process flow help (a deployment flowchart)?
  - What are the key input, in-process, and output measures (the Xs and Ys)?

- ✔ **How do you respond when you identify problems in your process?**
  - What really happens now (use process stapling, described in Chapter 5, to clarify)?
  - Are there bottlenecks in the process?
  - Look out for high levels of inventory or Work in Progress.
  - Does the process involve unnecessary, non-value-adding (NVA) steps?
  - Could the Five Ss help?
  - Would considering the seven wastes (see Chapter 9) be useful?

- ✔ **Where and when in the process do the symptoms of the problem appear?**
  - Where and how is the problem noticed?
  - When does it occur?

- When doesn't it occur?
- Is the time of day, week or month a factor?
- Is the data appropriately segmented?

Recognising typical questions the champion needs to ask in Measure

Key questions for the champion to ask the team at this stage include the following:

✔ Are the CTQs reviewed and confirmed?

✔ How well does the process flow?

✔ What has happened in the past?

✔ What is meant to happen now?

✔ Has a process stapling exercise been carried out?

✔ What really happens now?

✔ Where in the process do the symptoms of the problem appear? And when?

✔ What do relevant staff do when they see symptoms of the problem?

✔ Have appropriate measures been put in place? In what state of your process (see Chapter 7)?

✔ Have the Y and X measures been identified?

✔ Have the seven wastes been considered and, if so, what do the results reveal?

✔ Is the data collection plan sound?

✔ Is the data appropriately segmented?

✔ Are the operational definitions free from ambiguity?

✔ Has the improvement charter been updated?

✔ With whom should the team now be communicating?

✔ What should the team be telling them?

Following the Measure phase, a tollgate review should reveal what's happening. Then it's time to find out why a process problem is occurring. Obviously, some of your activity to date may already have given you a pretty good idea!

Analysing the Data to Find the Root Cause

Identifying and removing the root causes of a problem will prevent it happening again. Possibly the cause of the problem is clear from the work you've carried out in the Measure phase, but you need to be sure. The Analyse phase is about identifying and checking the possible causes.

Don't rush off in the wrong direction! Keep asking 'why?' to get to the root cause(s).

You need to generate ideas regarding what may be causing the problem. Don't jump to conclusions but do recognise that your process-stapling exercise may have helped you home in on what's at the root of the problem. Checking the possible causes using data to verify the ideas generated and managing by fact is important; that is, you need to identify, verify and select the 'vital few Xs' for attention.

Checking the outputs from the Analyse phase

You and your team need to check that this phase has produced the following outputs:

✔ Non-value-adding steps and any bottlenecks identified, and an understanding gained of how well the process flows (your deployment flowchart or value stream map will help you here, especially if you have also captured unit and cycle time data)

✔ Waste identified (process stapling and a spaghetti diagram will help here, especially in spotting wasted movement and transport, as well as any unnecessary activities; you may also have collected data on errors in the process)

✔ Possible causes identified, probably displayed on a fishbone diagram (see Chapter 8)

✔ Key drivers (key Xs) identified using an interrelationship diagram (see Chapters 2 and 8)

✔ Agreed input and in-process measures (the Xs) in place

✔ Data analysed and displayed properly for easy understanding (this may include control charts and Pareto diagrams – see Chapters 7 and 4 respectively – and will help you verify and validate possible causes)

✔ Root cause and vital few Xs validated, probably using a scatter diagram (see Chapter 8)

✔ An updated improvement charter

✔ An updated storyboard

✔ An updated communication plan

✔ An updated stakeholder analysis (see Chapter 18), where appropriate

Examining typical questions the team needs to address in Analyse

During the Analyse phase the team must ask the following questions:

✔ **What are the possible causes of the symptoms described in the Measure phase?**

Remember the importance of getting to the root cause(s). Also note that you're not looking for solutions – not yet, at least! The fishbone diagram should help you generate and classify your ideas, and you can then link it to an interrelationship diagram to determine the key driver(s).

✔ **What are the possible deeper causes?**

Make sure you really get to the bottom of the problem by asking why five times; initial answers are often superficial.

✔ **How can these possible causes be verified? What measurement data do you need?**

Jumping to conclusions is all too easy, particularly when everyone knows the answer. They may do, but you need to prove it and manage by fact.

 • What's the data telling you, and what additional data do you now need?

 • How can you get it?

 • Does any historical data help?

✔ **What's the best way of presenting the data?**

Pictures and graphs are usually better than words and numbers. A picture paints a thousand words and all that. A Pareto chart (see Chapter 4) may help you here.

✔ **What's the data telling you?**

- Which possible causes are verified by the data?

- Are there any surprises?

- Does the data suggest some other cause?

- Would additional data help?

- Does the data need segmenting?

✔ **Who needs to be working on the project now?**

Has the data and the identification of the causes affected who needs to be on the project? Either way, remember to update the improvement charter.

Examining typical questions the champion needs to ask in Analyse

The champion needs to ask the following questions:

✔ What are the possible causes of the symptoms described in the Measure phase?

✔ What are the possible deeper causes?

✔ Have you kept asking why?

✔ How have the possible causes been verified? What measurement data do you have?

✔ What's the best way of presenting the data?

✔ What's the data telling you?

✔ Are you confident that the root cause(s) has been identified?

✔ Can all the root causes in this project be addressed?

✔ Given the importance of the benefit review (described in the next section) that follows, are you confident that you're able to quantify the opportunity?

✔ Do you feel this process can be repaired and improved?

✔ Who needs to be working on the project now?

✔ What's needed on the communications front?

✔ Is the improvement charter up to date?

✔ Has the stakeholder analysis been reviewed?

Quantifying the Opportunity

In addition to the tollgate reviews conducted with the champion at the end of each phase, your Lean Six Sigma improvement journey includes three *benefit reviews*. These reviews provide an important opportunity to step back, assess your progress and ask some key questions, such as:

- ✔ How are things going?
- ✔ Are you on course?
- ✔ What have you learnt?
- ✔ What's gone well, and why?
- ✔ What conclusions can be drawn?

In particular, though, the benefit reviews provide an opportunity to take stock of the financial details. This first review looks at *quantifying the opportunity*. Do bear in mind, however, that some quick win opportunities may exist where a less formal approach can be taken.

The primary focus of the first benefit review is to really understand the extent of non-value-adding activities and waste, and the potential for improvement. When you completed the Measure phase, you were able to understand the current situation and level of performance. Having completed Analyse, your level of understanding should have increased significantly. You'll know why performance is at the level it is, and you should understand the costs involved in the process, both overall and at the individual process steps level. You'll have identified the waste and the NVA steps, including the rework loops, and understood their impact on your ability to meet the CTQs.

To quantify the opportunity, you need to calculate the benefits and saving that would occur if all this waste and NVA work were eliminated, making sure you document your assumptions. You may feel the opportunity is too small to bother about, or so large it justifies widening the scope of the project or developing a phased approach with a number of smaller but targeted projects. Either way, this is the time to review and agree your project goals, sensibly estimating what's possible for your project and update the improvement charter, communication plan and storyboard as necessary.

Applying Solutions in the Improve Phase

The Improve phase is where most people want to start! Now you have identified the root cause of the problem, you can begin to generate improvement ideas to help solve it. This is the first of three stages in the Improve phase.

Your solution ideas need to be reviewed and prioritised, and perhaps even tested on a small scale, before selecting the most appropriate in the next stage of Improve. In the final stage, the chosen solution may need to be developed in more detail, but will almost certainly need to be properly piloted.

Sometimes the improvement solution is very straightforward – or it may seem to be. Your process stapling and value-adding analysis may have identified several steps that can be removed from the process, for example, or a spaghetti diagram may have highlighted the need to re-site people or equipment to reduce wasted travel and movement. The reduction of batch sizes or a move to a pull not push process flow may be the answer.

Some opportunities for prevention, highlighted for example using FMEA or Jidoka (see Chapter 10), may also provide readily identifiable solutions, but you'll probably need to use brainstorming in its various guises to help you. Negative brainstorming can be especially helpful. The fishbone diagram could also be used to group your improvement ideas. Here, the question in the head of the fish would be along the lines of 'how can we reduce cycle time in the order process?' or 'how can we reduce errors in order processing?', for example.

Where practical, running a small-scale pilot or test to check things out is sensible. Doing so can ensure no unexpected knock-on problems exist downstream, and can also make the selection process easier in the next phase of Improve.

If you've identified and perhaps tested out a number of solutions, you now need to evaluate the options and choose the most effective. In doing so, you need to take account of your criteria, including any known restrictions on resources. The chosen solution may need to be developed in more detail, but will almost certainly need to be properly piloted in the next stage of Improve.

A full cost–benefit analysis might be possible at this stage but may need to wait until the pilot is carried out. That said, you should be able to have at least a high-level picture of the cost–benefit situation, though do ensure the assumptions used have been documented. You can use a number of selection techniques to help you choose your preferred solution, but the priority-based matrix (see Chapter 14) is particularly useful.

You need to make sure that both your solution and the implementation plan will be effective and that, as far as possible, teething problems can be avoided. A pilot is almost certainly needed, and this may also provide the opportunity to build some prevention into your solution. As well as allowing you to try things out in relative safety, pilots also provide a selling opportunity for your approach.

Don't be so wedded to your improvement solution that you create an unreal test to make the pilot work. Avoid carrying out the test in a clean and quiet environment, for example, when in reality it should be conducted somewhere dirty and noisy. You could also ensure a falsely successful pilot by conducting the test with your best people rather than a genuine cross-section of your team with varying skills and capabilities.

You may need to face scale-up issues and, without appropriate testing, you may be going live in the mistaken belief that the pilot went smoothly. As far as possible, treat the pilot as though it's a full implementation, and develop an appropriate implementation plan to take into the Control phase when the solution will be put in place.

With the pilot complete, you can present a cost–benefit analysis as part of the next benefit review in order to justify the implementation. This review looks to confirm the effectiveness of your implementation plan and the deliverables and business case resulting from the project. A well-conceived plan can help avoid misunderstandings or mistakes.

Checking the outputs from the Improve phase

These outputs are divided into the three phases of Improve as reviews should be conducted with the champion at the end of each phase.

Generate possible solutions with the following:

- Where appropriate, a number of potential solutions that genuinely address the problem
- Where appropriate, a future state deployment flowchart or value stream map
- Where appropriate, the results from any tests or pilots you have run
- A sense of confidence that you're ready to select the most appropriate solution
- An updated improvement charter, communication plan and storyboard

Select the solution with the following:

- Evidence of a systematic selection process using a priority-based matrix, for example
- Documented rationale that the chosen solution will address the root cause

✔ At least an outline cost-benefit analysis

✔ The documented assumptions behind the assessment

✔ An updated improvement charter, communication plan and storyboard

✔ Where appropriate, an updated stakeholder analysis – not everyone may like your chosen solution!

Plan and test the solution with the following:

✔ Where appropriate, a more comprehensive pilot that helps confirm the suitability of the proposed solution and tests and shapes your full implementation plan

✔ An agreed implementation plan that takes account of the pilot results

✔ Evidence that the implementation plan has been error-proofed

✔ Evidence that prevention has been built into the solution itself, or that opportunities have been identified should their implementation fall outside the scope of the project

✔ An updated improvement charter, communication plan and storyboard

✔ Where appropriate, an updated stakeholder analysis – keep your eye on the soft stuff and the $E = Q \times A$ formula.

Eyeing typical questions the team needs to address in Improve

The team needs to consider the following issues.

✔ **What are the possible solutions?**

Take time to generate as many ideas as you can. Jumping to conclusions is easy, but, that said, the solution may be clear from your waste and value-added analysis or from activities such as process stapling. You can use a number of Lean tools and techniques to help you come up with ideas. Techniques such as the theory of constraints can help you focus on reducing bottlenecks; spaghetti diagrams or single piece flow can provide a way forward; and the 5Ss can help you avoid wasted time trying to find things. Negative brainstorming (see Chapter 10) can help you think differently about the problem and its potential solution.

✔ **How will you know the solution is going to work?**

• How can the solution(s) be tried out as a pilot?

• How can you try out some ideas in parallel?

- How will you measure their effect?

- What do you expect the result to be?

- Where would a good test site be?

- What are the barriers to a simple test or a pilot?

✔ **If you ran some tests, how did the results compare to what you expected?**

- What lessons have been gained from the pilot?

- What knock-on effects occurred?

- How does the solution need to be amended?

- Will you need a further test or pilot?

You now need to evaluate the possible solutions and choose the most effective, taking account of your criteria, including any known restrictions on resources. Implementation can then be planned and actioned, taking account of any test results as well as any potential barriers to the solution.

✔ **Have you agreed on the selection criteria?**

A priority-based matrix is an effective decision-making tool, though a simple XY grid may be all you need. Keep your focus on the problem identified in Define, and the root cause(s) identified in the Analyse phase. Make sure that you're clear on the selection criteria and their weightings – paired comparisons can help you here.

✔ **Which of the possible solutions is the most effective in meeting the selection criteria?**

- In what ways are some solutions better than others?

- What knock-on effects might occur?

- What's important for the customer?

- Have you considered issues of time and cost? Are budget issues or resources limiting the choice?

- Is the best solution good enough?

You may need to enhance it in some way. When you carry out a pilot in the next step, look to see if there are opportunities to do so.

✔ **Have you learnt anything that may be helpful in tackling other problems? Do similar problems, either in your own area or somewhere else, exist that could benefit from the solution?**

You need to make sure that your solution will be implemented properly. A well-conceived plan can help avoid misunderstandings or mistakes. Ideally, the opportunity exists for you to carry out a (further) test or pilot and iron out any teething problems before going live.

✔ **Have you prepared your pilot as though it were the full implementation and taken care not to create a false test?**

Your pilot provides a safe way to check the solution out, but make sure you don't create an unreal test. Recognise that scale-up issues will probably exist. Plan as though it's a full implementation and pull together an appropriate team. Your champion may have a key role here.

✔ **How will the results be measured?**

- What measures do you plan to have in place following implementation? (You'll need them here to provide evidence that the solution works.)

- Did the pilot identify the need to adjust the solution or help you identify prevention opportunities?

- What went well? What adjustments were needed and why? How could it have been improved? How will you share the experience?

- Are you able to build in prevention in some way? A FMEA on any new process steps may highlight the scope for prevention or error proofing.

✔ **Have you addressed communication issues?**

Recognise that you'll need to get people's buy-in on the new solution. The pilot may be part of that process. Remember $E = Q \times A$ and keep people informed, especially the stakeholders and the people in the process.

Noting typical questions the champion needs to ask in Improve

Like the outputs, these questions are divided into three phases.

✔ Generate possible solutions:

- What are the possible solutions?

- How did you generate these ideas?

- Which possible solutions seem to best address the root cause(s) identified in the Analyse phase?

✔ Select the solution:

- What are the advantages and disadvantages of each solution?

- Which of the possible solutions is the most effective in meeting your selection criteria? And is it viable in terms of likely cost benefit?

- Which tools were used in making the selection?

- How did you choose and weight the selection criteria?

- The solution may appear to be the best option, but is it good enough? Can it be improved?

✔ Plan and test the solution:

- How do the pilot results compare to what was expected?

- Are you sure you have the right team membership – do you need to involve anyone else in the implementation and in the Control phase?

- What's the implementation plan? Who needs to approve it?

- Have you given sufficient thought to the handover?

- Has everyone who needs to know about the changes been informed?

- How will the plan be communicated?

- How will the results be measured?

- Given the importance of the benefit review that follows, are you confident that you're able to confirm the cost-benefit analysis?

Confirming the Customer and Business Benefits

The second of the benefit reviews looks to confirm the deliverables from the project, and secure authority for the solution to be fully implemented. As with quantify the opportunity (covered in the first review), the review also provides an opportunity to look at the project more generally, and key questions include the following:

✔ How are things going?

✔ Are you on course?

✔ What have you learnt? And forgotten?

✔ What's gone well and why?

✔ Can the solution be applied elsewhere?

✔ What conclusions can be drawn?

The main focus, however, is to confirm the deliverables. In completing the Improve phase, you should feel confident that the chosen solution will address the root cause and ensure you meet the project goals. Given that management by fact is a key principle of Lean Six Sigma, you should have appropriate measurement data and evidence from the pilot that your solution will deliver.

A range of different benefits could result from your project, including:

- ✔ Reduced errors and waste
- ✔ Faster cycle time
- ✔ Improved customer satisfaction
- ✔ Reduced cost

In assessing how well these match the project objectives, do remember that quantifying the softer benefits of enhanced employee or customer satisfaction may be difficult. When you project when the benefits are likely to emerge, don't lose sight of the fact that a time gap will probably exist between the cause and effect, especially where customer perception data is concerned.

As well as looking at the benefits, this review also looks to confirm any costs associated with the solution and its implementation. Again, your piloting activity should have helped you pull this information together, provided you have treated it as though it were a full-scale implementation. Internal guidelines are probably available to help you assess and present the benefits and costs, but do make sure you have documented the assumptions behind your benefits assessment.

This review has some key outputs that include

- ✔ Confirmation that the project is on track
- ✔ Confidence in the solution and implementation plan
- ✔ A confirmed benefit analysis complete with documented assumptions
- ✔ An updated improvement charter

The champion needs to address the following issues:

- ✔ Are you confident that your benefit statement can be justified?
- ✔ Have you documented your assumptions?
- ✔ Do you feel that expenses associated with implementing the required changes can now be reliably forecast and controlled?
- ✔ Given the lessons learnt from the pilot, do you need to review your team membership for the final implementation?

Implementing, Standardising and Controlling the Solution

The Control phase is in two parts. The first looks to implement the solution; the second takes stock of what's been achieved. After all your hard work, you need to implement the solution in a way that ensures you make the gain you expected – and hold it! If you're to continue your efforts in reducing variation and cutting out waste, the changes being made to the process need to be consistently deployed and followed.

The handover process and a control plan are vital features of the Control phase. Getting the right measures in place is a crucial element of the control plan, and you need to be satisfied that the data collection plan has been effectively deployed.

In assessing the benefits, you have the opportunity to determine the accuracy of your earlier benefit analysis, though remember it may take a while for the change to have an effect.

Checking the outputs from the Control phase

The following outputs should result from this phase:

✔ The solution has been implemented and the revised process deployed in a standard way, confirming an effective handover.

✔ Documentation has been updated and training deployed.

✔ The ongoing data collection plan is in place and statistical data demonstrates that the process is 'in control'. Remember, however, that initially your control chart may show a special cause evidencing that the improvement has worked. So, for example, where you were looking to reduce cycle time, the evidence may be seven points in a row below the mean, enabling you to recalculate the control limits as soon as you have a little more data.

✔ Evidence of success, including actual costs and benefits or at the very least an estimate of when these will be available.

✔ Key lessons

✔ Recommendations or ideas for further improvement opportunities

✔ An updated storyboard

✔ An updated communication plan

Listing typical questions the team needs to address in Control

You're now ready to implement the solution. If you ran your pilot as though it were a full implementation, it will have laid the foundations for your full implementation plan, but you also need an appropriate control plan in place to ensure you achieve the improvement, hold it and, in the spirit of continuous improvement, prompt new opportunities!

Implement, standardise and control

The questions here are prompts to help ensure you've followed your plan and not missed anything important on the way – in particular, you need to make sure you've agreed an effective handover.

Following any adjustments from the pilot, you're ready to implement the solution and effective communication is essential. Make sure you've told everyone about the changes, including stakeholders, customers and suppliers. Draw up a communication plan and ensure any handover activity is clearly agreed and understood.

✔ **Have all the people who do this work been trained?**

- If not, when will they be trained?

- Where relevant, have you covered all the different shifts?

- How will new people be covered?

- Does the induction programme need updating?

✔ **How have the changes to the documentation been standardised? Are there any implications for internal or external audit?**

- Are the process maps up to date? Do you need to update manuals or printing records, for example?

- Are there any audit or compliance implications?

- Do you need to destroy old stock?

- What do you do if someone uses old stock?

✔ **Will the measures you've put in place help you see if the solution has worked?**

- Do you have an appropriate balance of measures?

- Are you monitoring input, in-process and output measures?

- Are you confident in your data collection plan and process?

✔ **Do you have an effective control plan?**

- Does the communication plan and the training include the importance of the measurements and the signals to look for?

- Will people recognise when the measures indicate a problem and will they know what to do?

- Is the control plan supported by good visual management and daily team meetings reviewing performance and actions?

Assess achievements and lessons

This is where the team takes stock of the journey and prepares to update the project champion and sponsor(s).

✔ **How well do the results match your expectations?**

- What objectives were agreed in Define?

- How well have they been met?

- What are the key measures telling you?

- When will the benefits come through?

- What are your customers saying?

- Do any root causes still need to be addressed?

✔ **Are you confident the new process is being followed?**

Carrying out process stapling again will enable you to see if the new process is deployed. It might highlight some misunderstandings or further opportunities for improvement.

✔ **How can the solution be improved? Is there scope for prevention? Have you carried out an FMEA?**

- What can be done to error-proof the process? Is it possible to prevent things from slipping again?

- How can the documentation be improved?

- What further training is needed?

✔ **How well did the project work?**

- What went well?

- What adjustments were needed and why?

- How could it have been improved?

- And how will you share the experience?

- What would you have done differently?

✔ **What should you do to suitably recognise the team's efforts and success?**

Recognising effort and success is an important element in creating a culture of continuous improvement. Don't lose the opportunity presented by this project. And remember that a simple thank you from the chief executive can have a significant impact on motivation and morale – not just for the team, but generally.

Noting typical questions the champion needs to ask in Control

The champion needs to ask questions related to the following two areas.

Implement, standardise and control

Consider these questions related to implantation, standardisation, and control:

✔ Following any adjustments from the pilot, what is the new standard method, process, product or service?

✔ How have the changes to the process documentation been standardised?

✔ Are there any implications for internal or external audit?

✔ Have all the people who do this work been trained?

✔ How will the measures you've put in place help you monitor ongoing results and prompt further improvement actions?

✔ Has the handover process worked so that roles and responsibilities are clear?

Assess achievements and lessons

These questions help you assess what you've achieved and learned:

✔ Has the handover proved effective?

✔ Has the process been effectively adopted and deployed?

✔ Did you solve the problem?

✔ Are any symptoms still remaining?

✔ How well did your plan work?

✔ What did you learn from this project? It's essential the team has learnt from the experience. It's also essential that you can apply this learning across the organisation.

You also need to determine the accuracy of the earlier benefit analysis, though it may take a while for the change to have an effect.

Conducting the Final Benefit Review

This is the formal post-implementation review involving the project champion and sponsor(s) or steering committee, if one exists. The questions are very similar to those posed at the end of the Control phase, but take a wider business perspective. They are as follows:

✔ **How satisfied are you that the problem has been solved?**

- How well have the objectives been met?

- What is the data telling you?

- Which root causes still need to be addressed?

- What other residual issues does the business need to resolve?

✔ **What benefits have been realised or are in the pipeline?**

- What is the data telling you?

- How do the benefits compare to what was predicted?

- Do your customers feel an improvement has occurred? How do you know?

- Are the costs in line with predictions?

- Have any other benefits resulted from the project?

✔ **Can you apply any lessons, ideas or best practices developed during this project elsewhere in the business?**

- What have you learnt?

- Where else in the business might these lessons be helpful?

- Do similar problems exist in another area and could this solution be applied there?

✔ **What should you and your improvement team do now?**

- Should you address other projects?

- What should the organisation do to suitably recognise your team's efforts and success?

Chapter 17

Ensuring Everyday Operational Excellence

In This Chapter

▶ Using the Lean Six Sigma toolkit in the day-to-day work

▶ Understanding the role of the manager

▶ Embedding continuous improvement into the organisation's DNA

Lean Six Sigma isn't just about DMAIC and DMADV projects. The principles, concepts and tools also provide a framework for operational excellence to become a reality in everyday life. Managers and team leaders need to run their processes and activities effectively and efficiently. They need to understand that their role is to work on their processes with the people involved in those processes in order to find ways of continuously improving performance.

This chapter looks at how to achieve a well-managed process and in doing so ensure the principles, concepts, tools and techniques of Lean Six Sigma become common language in an organisation.

Making Everyday Operational Excellence a Reality

Everyday Operational Excellence is achieved by ensuring managers have a clear understanding of their role and how Lean Six Sigma can help them provide a more effective and efficient way of running their area of responsibility. The details of this approach are taught and practised during a three-day training programme covering a subset of the Lean Six Sigma tools from the Foundation Green Belt level. Ideally, most operational managers would attend such training.

You apply Everyday Operational Excellence tools to daily activities rather than improvement projects.

Using Operational Excellence Tools enables processes to be owned and effectively and efficiently operated, leading to stable, predictable processes and happier staff and customers. These tools ensure that:

- ✔ Clear customer-focused objectives related to prioritised critical to quality customer requirements (CTQs) exist.

  Appropriate process maps are in place, for example a SIPOC diagram and a deployment flowchart or value stream map, perhaps both.

  A balance of input, in-process and output measures exist whereby an effective data collection process is in place. The vital few Xs and Ys are being measured and the correlation between these variables is understood and managed.

- ✔ A stable process is created that's in statistical control. Control charts are part of the visual management system helping to ensure that variation is understood. Where special causes are present improvement activity is underway and is picked up at the daily team meeting, if not before.

- ✔ The process meets the CTQs. Performance in terms of meeting the CTQs is monitored and understood and improvement activity is underway where they aren't being met. Again, this is picked up as part of the daily team meeting

- ✔ The process has been error-proofed. Failure Modes Effects Analysis (FMEA) has been carried out, prevention has been built in where possible, and the identification of new error proofing opportunities forms part of the daily team meeting.

- ✔ A control plan is in place that clearly identifies what to do if things go wrong, for example, or where the ongoing data indicates a warning.

The ongoing application of Everyday Operational Excellence also serves to begin the process of introducing a common language of Lean Six Sigma principles, concepts and tools. In turn, this approach supports the ongoing identification of improvement opportunities that can be actioned either by managers and their teams, or through more formal DMAIC or DMADV projects.

Everyday Operational Excellence training can be useful for project champions or sponsors too.

Clarifying the Role of the Manager

In many organisations, newly promoted managers are often unclear about their role. An individual may have been promoted into a management position in recognition of good performance in a 'doing' role, for example. Goes the logic: he's performed really well so make him a manager!

If he's lucky, his employer will provide training in a variety of management skills, including budget setting, interview techniques, appraisal setting and report writing. He'll be unlikely to receive training in managing a process, however. To successfully manage a process, the manager first must understand every element of it and, second, ensure that the people who work on each stage feel a sense of ownership of and responsibility for their part in that process.

Working on the process

A number of elements must be in place to ensure that a smooth, manageable process exists. It must, for example, focus on defined CTQs, be stable and understood by all. Each element is defined in the following sections.

Establishing clear customer-focused objectives

A process must focus on meeting critical to quality customer requirements (CTQs; see Chapter 4 on how to identify these). The CTQs need to be measurable and, where appropriate, have upper and lower specification limits and a target value. When the CTQs are defined, as a manager you then need to look at how a process has developed, that is, how the work gets done.

Understanding how the work gets done

A process should aim to meet specific customer requirements and add value. For that to happen, the process itself must address certain requirements, as we describe in Chapter 3. Various models and tools are available to help you work out how things get done. A SIPOC model, for example, helps you focus on suppliers, inputs, process, outputs and customers in turn to develop a full picture of everyone and everything connected to the process. Process stapling (see Chapter 5) will enable you to understand how much travel and movement is involved in the process, enabling you to then create a spaghetti diagram that illustrates the distance travelled by people and materials. Siting people and equipment together is often a simple way of reducing waste and cycle time.

Understanding how well the work gets done

Chapters 6 and 7 look at the importance of measurement and the data collection process. The CTQs enable you to determine the output measures for the process, the Ys, which show you how well you're meeting the particular customer requirements. You'll need a balance of measures that will help you understand the variables affecting that performance. The Xs look at the inputs and in-process measures needed. So, for example, you'll need to consider the performance of your internal and external suppliers: are their inputs accurate, complete and on time? You'll also need in-process measures covering time data, rework levels and work in progress, for example.

Like any process, data collection requires managing and improving. Enough variation is likely to exist in the operational process itself without the situation being compounded by variation in the measurement system.

Ensuring the process is stable and predictable

Chapter 7 covers control charts and variation. Bringing processes into statistical control so that they exhibit only natural variation is often an early challenge in the pursuit of a managed process. However, don't forget that while statistical control means that a process is stable and predictable, it may or may not be meeting the CTQs.

Checking the process meets the CTQs

If a process is in an ideal state, it's stable and predictable and meets the CTQs. If it's stable and predictable but doesn't meet the CTQs, it's in a threshold state. If it's free from special cause(s), it should be relatively straightforward to move it into an ideal state, perhaps through a DMAIC project.

Error-proofing the process

Prevention is a good way to tackle waste and delays, reducing the need for rework and avoiding other non-value-adding activities. Several tools and techniques can be used, including failure mode effects analysis and preventive maintenance, topics that are covered in Chapter 10.

Use daily team meetings around the activity board to identify error-proofing opportunities.

Establishing a control plan

Chapter 2 covers the importance of the control plan, which ideally is part of the organisation's visual management system. The control plan ensures that everyone understands the process, the process is followed consistently and improvement gains are held. It highlights the importance of monitoring performance at different stages, identifying actions required.

If working on the process in this way is a new concept to you, it's important to recognise that a control plan takes time to establish but will eventually ensure the effective and efficient delivery of products and services. Having established ownership of the process and its constituent elements, you and your team can identify and prioritise opportunities for improvement. Next, you can use the DMAIC phases to tackle that improvement, using the control plan to ensure that gains are maintained and new opportunities revealed.

Engaging the team

Owning and managing the process is part of the change in thinking and behaving that is an essential ingredient in the transformation of an organisation. The people in the process, however, also need to feel able to challenge and improve the process and the way in which they work. For that to happen, those people need to feel engaged and empowered.

In owning and working on the process, you need to ensure it really is *managed* – that you're genuinely working on the process with the people in the process. In order to make your team feel engaged, you need to actively involve those people in the daily team brief. Agreeing ownership of different activities or elements of the activity board (see Chapter 10) is one way to help increase people's sense of participation.

The people in the process need to feel empowered; they need to be an integral part of the journey the organisation is undertaking. The manager must thus work on the process with the people in the process to find ways of continuously improving the process. Konosuke Matsushita, founder of Panasonic, contrasted his organisation's approach with that of typical Western organisations:

> *'For us, the core of management is . . . [the] art of mobilising and putting together the intellectual resources of all the employees in the service of the firm. Only by drawing on the combined brainpower of all its employees can a firm face up to the turbulence and constraint of today's environment.'*

Empowerment clearly isn't a new idea; indeed, the 1620 edition of the *Oxford English Dictionary* defines it as 'to enable'. You, as the manager, must enable your team.

Our approach to empowerment centres on four vital elements from the perspective of the team member:

✔ He feels competent – he's learning from experience and gaining new skills and abilities as his potential is developed.

✔ He feels part of a team – he's contributing to the team's performance.

✔ He can see how his team's activities link to the goals of the organisation – he understands that he's an integral part of a larger effort.

✔ He enjoys his work and has fun – as everyone should!

With these ingredients in place, an individual team and the organisation as a whole significantly increase their chances of success.

Balance is the key to successful empowerment, which means adopting a whole-brain approach. Using the left brain only – focusing purely on rules and structure – means everything grinds to a halt, ossifies and crumbles. Putting the right brain to work on its own – allowing total creative and emotional freedom – means things break down and anarchy rules. Applying a whole-brain approach results in appropriate rules and structure together with creativity and freedom.

To lead and manage a strong and efficient team, you need to:

✔ Develop people

  Coach and train people during new assignments

  Help people build on their skills

✔ Build trust

  Promote an atmosphere of co-operation

  Trust people to do an effective job

✔ Promote autonomy

  Encourage people to take the initiative

  Provide appropriate coaching and support when needed

✔ Encourage openness

  Forgive mistakes made by others

  Admit to your own mistakes

✔ Recognise accomplishments

  Celebrate successes

  Reward people for innovations

✔ Shape direction

  Provide a vision of the future

  Tackle controversial activities

✔ Demonstrate objectivity

  Use facts in decision-making

  Respond to facts rather than unsubstantiated data

Autonomy isn't all it seems. Granting people autonomy with no support is like giving them a rope with which to hang themselves. People want challenging work but need development and coaching by their managers to feel assured of some success.

A direct and very strong correlation exists between employee and customer satisfaction.

Getting Better Every Day in Every Way

Everyday Operational Excellence really is about doing things well each and every day and creating a culture of continuous improvement. And it begins by understanding the customer requirements, how the work gets done and how well it gets done, as this example demonstrates.

This example puts working on a process into context and highlights how Lean Six Sigma supports everyday activities. It features a new business team in an insurance company processing new policy applications. The measurable customer requirements, the CTQs, are for the policies to be issued within five working days and the documentation to be error-free.

The organisation's executive team realises that it must differentiate itself in the eyes of its customers, that is, independent financial advisers (IFAs) who sell and, to some degree, service policies for the end customer. The company wants to establish itself as the natural choice for IFAs or, at least, a targeted segment of them. Superior service and the ability to demonstrate value are key elements of the organisation's strategy. Current performance indicates that considerable variation exists in the processing of new business applications, especially those requiring medical evidence from a GP or specialist, and as a result the organisation is not adhering to its strategy.

Time taken to issue policies ranges between two days to a couple of months, and approximately 10 per cent of all policy applications have to be reworked, either due to errors or missing information. As you can see, without significant improvement, the organisation has little prospect of being the first choice for IFAs.

The leadership team believes that the organisation could benefit from the Lean Six Sigma approach and thus arranges training for its members and the managers. The managers are tasked with reviewing their processes and determining how value is added to the work in progress at each step in the new business process, just as various elements of a car are added to it as it moves along the assembly line.

Eight Lean Six Sigma practices are applied to enable the work to flow – none involves rocket science, simply a little time and the involvement of people:

- The current state picture for the end-to-end process is developed using a SIPOC, process stapling and process mapping (see Chapter 5). The exercise involves a mix of people from the process and a Green Belt, and the team discusses outcomes with management. The exercise highlights many improvement opportunities.

- Linked processes in the chain are placed near to one another. Work was previously organised by function in separate departments and teams. This created a silo effect and delays in transferring applications to other areas that performed different functions. Delays were compounded as the work was also processed in batches. The functional silos are eliminated, product families identified and cells created, actions that also facilitate a move from batches to single piece flow.

- Processes and procedures are standardised and techniques such as the 5Ss, visual management (see Chapter 10) and daily team meetings are used to help support the overall aims. As a simple example, prior to the application of Lean Six Sigma concepts, people had been allowed to choose their own system for storing files – by policy number, date received or alphabetically – which made life difficult for new or temporary staff. The new system requires files to be stored alphabetically and in the same cabinet at each work area.

- Some processes involved returning work to a previous step for further processing, which caused confusion, disrupted flow and resulted in waiting time at some steps. A new process now avoids such toing and froing.

- The workflow is further smoothed by applying the concept of Takt time. The organisation has established a Takt time of five minutes per application or 12 applications per hour, and encourages and empowers employees to make process improvements to reduce it. Continuous improvement means the 'one best way' is regularly updated.

✔ Workloads are balanced, where possible. The previous approach whereby new applications were allocated alphabetically has been replaced by a date-received system so that every team receives the same number of applications. This reduces unnecessary delays in the system and means customers are dealt with in the appropriate time and sequence.

✔ Tasks are separated into one of two groups based on level of difficulty. One group develops applications that need to be supported by medical evidence; another handles less time-consuming cases.

✔ Visual management comes into play in the form of performance data displayed on whiteboards for everyone to see. Where practical, the information is updated by the team members. The boards are now the location for daily team meetings where work levels and improvement ideas are discussed.

✔ These actions have resulted in enhanced performance and increased employee and customer satisfaction. Policy issue turnaround times have been reduced by 65 per cent for medical cases and 80 per cent for non-medical cases; rework has fallen from 10 per cent to just more than 1 per cent.

Ongoing, the organisation has made further changes by segmenting its IFA customers into different categories and creating customer-facing teams dealing with new business through to claims. This cradle-to-grave set-up has facilitated further improvements in both employee and customer satisfaction, leading to increased market share. Although the new set-up involved a significant investment in training time, process costs have been reduced.

Importantly, people working in the process now feel engaged and involved and a culture of continuous improvement has emerged.

Using the right methodology

Everyday Operational Excellence involves creating a situation whereby 'this is the way we do things around here' and everybody knows it. The right projects are identified, prioritised and actioned using the right methodology. Not every project will need to use the DMAIC or DMADV frameworks.

In fact, a project focus may not be necessary; maybe small tweaks to a process will suffice. The elements of a managed process are in place so that the everyday activities are carried out seamlessly using the principles, concepts, tools and techniques of Lean Six Sigma. People working in the process feel they're listened to and that they're able to challenge and help improve things.

Creating a culture of continuous improvement

For Everyday Operational Excellence to be a reality, managers need to be working on the process and staff must feel engaged and empowered. These factors help get the principles and concepts of Lean Six Sigma into the organisation's DNA.

But Everyday Operational Excellence involves more than that, of course. To initiate a cultural transformation you need to consider which attitudes have to shift, and how significantly the average manager or employee needs to change his viewpoint. Maybe particular policies need to be changed, which may have implications for recruitment, appraisal, promotion or pay and reward structures.

Most significantly, leaders and managers must thoroughly understand what the organisation does, live its philosophy and teach its tenets to others. They need to support staff and the work they carry out, and take responsibility for the processes they operate. And they must demonstrate a genuine passion for Lean Six Sigma and its underlying principles and thinking.

Chapter 18

Comprehending the People Issues

In This Chapter

▶ Gaining buy-in from others

▶ Tackling resistance to change

▶ Clocking the culture of your organisation

Six Sigma and Lean originated from industrial manufacturing backgrounds, with early emphasis on tools and techniques. Now, however, most managers accept that recognising and handling the people issues is the biggest challenge in implementing Lean Six Sigma successfully.

Lean Six Sigma aims to make change happen in order to improve things. Human beings, like most creatures, are cautious and sceptical about change – it spells danger. Humans have an inbuilt resistance to change, especially when it's 'being done' to them and particularly if somebody tells them that it's going to be 'good for them'. Most people fear losing something they have as a result of change. Dealing with personal fear and loss is another big challenge in implementing Lean Six Sigma, but few enthusiasts in statistical theory cover this in their extensive training.

Understanding people is key to implementing a Lean Six Sigma project. Almost always, if Six Sigma and Lean projects fail, people issues of one form or another are the cause. In this chapter we offer guidance and tips for managing the human aspects of change in Lean Six Sigma.

Working Right, Right from the Start

Unfortunately, we don't know an easy solution to the challenge of managing people in a Lean Six Sigma project. However, in over 80 implementations of Lean Six Sigma, we have found a small number of common factors that consistently stand out as critical for success. Perhaps not surprisingly, leadership commitment is one of these critical factors. Achieving buy-in at the beginning is the real challenge. We cover leadership in more detail in Chapter 13.

Gaining acceptance

Overcoming the resistance movement in your organisation may be one of the biggest challenges you face when you introduce Lean Six Sigma. You may find lots of people are reluctant to accept this new way of working, especially with its suspiciously confusing name. You can't ignore or get away from these people: resistance exists in all organisations, no matter how big or small, and at all levels.

Making change happen successfully in an organisation is difficult. John P. Kotter, a respected expert in organisational leadership, researched 100 organisations that failed in their first business transformation attempt. In his *Harvard Business Review* article 'Why transformation efforts fail', Kotter identifies eight common failure factors:

- ✔ Not establishing a sufficient sense of urgency.
- ✔ Not creating a powerful enough leadership coalition.
- ✔ Not creating a vision.
- ✔ Under-communicating.
- ✔ Not removing obstacles to the vision.
- ✔ Not systematically planning for and creating short-term wins.
- ✔ Declaring victory too soon.
- ✔ Not anchoring changes in the culture.

In the next section, we show how you can use these factors to your advantage in your organisation.

Managing change

Turning the factors that we describe in the previous section into positives provides the basis for the model for managing change shown in Figure 18-1. You can use this model during the life of each Lean Six Sigma project and also across the entire Lean Six Sigma programme for your organisation. Work from left to right in the model, starting with establishing the need for change.

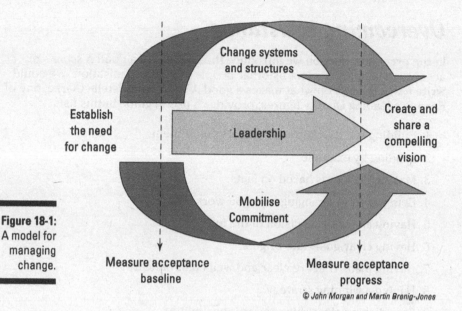

Figure 18-1: A model for managing change.

George Eckes, a well-known writer on this subject, uses a simple but eloquent expression to describe gaining acceptance for change and overcoming resistance, whether for a whole Lean Six Sigma programme or for the changes resulting from part of a Lean Six Sigma project:

$$E = Q \times A$$

E is the effectiveness of the change in practice: This represents the effectiveness of the implementation, which depends on the quality of the solution and the level of acceptance.

Q is the technical quality of the solution: The 'hard' tools of Lean and Six Sigma will have proven that the solution works when tested. An ideal solution may have been identified, but its effectiveness will depend on the degree to which it's accepted.

A is the acceptance of the change by people: Having a high 'score' for A is as important as having a good-quality solution.

Some hardened practitioners believe that the A factor is more important than the Q factor and is the real key to success in Lean Six Sigma. To understand how people perceive things and to win support, you need to score well on both factors. If you're in the early stages of deploying a Lean Six Sigma programme, the A factor is likely to start with winning support from senior managers.

Keep $Q \times A$ in mind as a simple shorthand for a highly complicated issue – dealing with the human mind.

Overcoming resistance

In the preceding section we introduce the concept of a good A *score* – or acceptance of your project by other people in your organisation. We could write a whole book on what makes a good A score, but Estelle Clarke, one of Europe's leading Quality figures, provides a useful guide in this list:

1. Building relationships on mutual commitment.
2. Leading by example.
3. Making decisions based on facts.
4. Being open to changing how you work.
5. Having an inspiring vision of the future.
6. Having clear goals and targets.
7. Having plans that are clear and well-communicated.
8. Having a winning strategy.
9. Establishing clear roles and responsibilities.
10. Dealing effectively with those resisting change.
11. Having no need to fire-fight.
12. Attracting and retaining world-class people.
13. Following world-class processes.
14. Conducting clear and open communication.
15. Learning from each other.
16. Working well together across all functions.
17. Encouraging teamwork.
18. Finding more productive ways of working.
19. Having consistency of purpose.
20. Having a high sense of urgency.
21. Making decisions quickly.
22. Continuously seeking to achieve competitive advantage.
23. Continuously building customer confidence.
24. Using measures to compare your performance with best practices.
25. Being honest and sincere.
26. Understanding your market, customers and competitors.

27. Facing up to problems quickly.

28. Rewarding the right behaviours.

29. Encouraging creativity and innovation.

30. Modifying systems and structures to support business assurance.

31. Achieving budgeted objectives.

32. Doing what you say you'll do.

33. Expecting our performance standards to increase continuously.

34. Encouraging expressions of different points of view.

35. Only reporting relevant information.

36. Wanting to learn from your mistakes so you don't repeat them.

You can map the list on to the change model in Figure 18-1 and use it as the basis for an organisational assessment involving a simple scoring mechanism. Simply adding the words 'How good are we at . . .' before each phrase can help you develop a questionnaire. For example, with number 17 on the list you can ask, 'How good are we at encouraging teamwork?'.

In practice, you can adapt the list for a specific project and add an assessment score, typically using five levels: 1 = very poor, 2 = weak, 3 = fair, 4 = very good, 5 = excellent. This technique can be useful for measuring the *acceptance baseline* in Figure 18-1. Don't feel you have to use a questionnaire for every project, though; simply interviewing and listening to people who have an interest in the project (the stakeholders) using these questions can be a really useful approach.

Creating a Vision

Clear, 20:20 vision may well be something that organisations try to develop in the next few years. Talking about 'visions' in a book about Lean Six Sigma may seem rather fanciful – but visions help you paint a picture that appeals to people's hearts and minds and can help you answer the question 'Why change?'.

Customers, business leaders and employees all view the future from different perspectives. Imagining a time machine is an ideal way to develop a vision: you can speed ahead and discover for real what it will be like when the change has been completed. What is different? What is there more or less of? Being in the future you can find out how the change has affected people's attitudes and behaviours. What does it feel like now? How does it look from the view of the customer, the leader and the employee?

A time machine is outside the scope of even the most extensive Lean Six Sigma Master Black Belt toolkit, so we use a simple technique called *backwards visioning*. This technique helps you create a picture of the future expressed in behavioural terms – that is, what the culture will be like in the future. The improvement team (the Lean Six Sigma team) imagines that their change has been completed successfully and then considers what they'd expect to see, both internally and externally, in terms of the following:

- ✔ Behaviours
- ✔ Measures
- ✔ Rewards
- ✔ Recognition

By determining the team's perceptions of these issues, you can begin to understand the actions that you may need to take as part of your progress towards the desired state – the future after the change has been made. These actions include the activities and behaviours that you need to reduce and remove and those that you need to introduce and increase.

You may want a more supportive culture, in which people help each other to a greater extent, work better in teams and operate less according to their own private agendas. For example, as a manager you see a piece of litter in the corridor. Do you walk on because you didn't drop it and cleaning this area isn't your job? Or do you pick it up and set an example? Creating a vision is about leadership, taking responsibility and working in the best interests of the business.

Writing down a backwards visioning statement provides a helpful framework for developing influencing strategies. For example, a good vision for the future for an airport operator working on reducing queues and increasing security is:

> Our goal is to transform the security experience of the travelling passenger by: (a) exceeding expectations by eliminating queues, and (b) creating a highly professional environment overseen by security staff who are rigorous, professional, helpful and proactive.

A clear vision provides clarity about the outcomes of the change effort and helps you to identify at least some of the elements that the change aims to transform. A vision secures commitment and support from anyone involved in delivering this service by helping people understand what you want to change – and why.

Understanding Organisational Culture

Defining the concept of 'culture' in organisations is difficult – yet most people have an idea of what the term means in their own organisation. They know their organisation's 'unwritten rules' and can describe 'the way things get done around here' a lot more vividly than can a written rulebook or set of documented policies.

At the core of most organisations is a set of values and beliefs that pervade everything and dictate more strongly than any management fad what people *think* should be done and *how* it should be done. These enduring beliefs create attitudes and behaviours that may undermine your Lean Six Sigma project if people consider your project to threaten them.

Alongside the formal declared change (the plan), another process is happening – often hidden in the shadows but still having a powerful impact. The best Lean Six Sigma practitioners recognise the hidden cultural, unwritten rules and manage change in the cultural process as keenly as they manage the work process being improved.

Many change initiatives fail because their proponents don't have enough awareness of the cultural factors involved. Many mergers and acquisitions fail to achieve the promised gains for this reason. Culture is complex, powerful and based on events of the past. In any organisation, rituals, stories, myths, heroes and villains play important roles. Gerry Johnson, at Cranfield University in the UK, developed the idea of a *cultural web*, shown in Figure 18-2. Essentially, the cultural web is 'the way we do things around here'.

Figure 18-2: The cultural web.

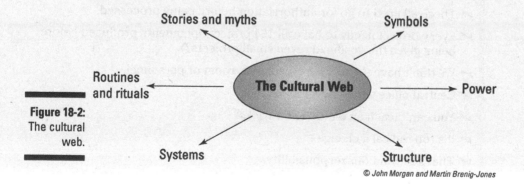

© John Morgan and Martin Brenig-Jones

Symbols in organisations may be much more significant than you think. Status symbols, language and jargon may be based on associations with power and status.

Busting Assumptions

Assumption busting is a useful tool for challenging why things are done in the way they are. Keep asking 'Why are things done this way?' to get beyond the initial, often superficial, responses.

A project to speed up land registry applications in the UK provides a good example. Registrations had always been sent to the legal department for review if the property value exceeded a particular amount. It transpired that no logic was involved in this decision as the value of the property made no difference to the complexity of the title – but it did add three months to the completion time!

Assumption busting is a quick and easy technique that works well in workshop-style sessions with groups or just as a tool to work through on your own. Question the obvious things with a fresh pair of eyes. Why have you always done it that way? Here are some common false assumptions:

- ✔ It is impossible to do that.
- ✔ The rules will not allow that approach.
- ✔ We will never get it through IT in time (okay, maybe that one is fair!).
- ✔ Department A, B, C (take your pick) will never agree.
- ✔ These all need to go for authorisation before being processed.
- ✔ Every project needs to have all 164 project documents produced before being given the go-ahead (even small projects?).
- ✔ We don't have the money, equipment, room or personnel.
- ✔ Central office would never agree to it.
- ✔ You can't teach an old dog new tricks.
- ✔ It's too radical a change.
- ✔ That's beyond our responsibility.
- ✔ The employees will reject it outright.

You need to be brave enough to see if you can bust these assumptions and challenge the status quo.

Seeing How People Cope with Change

Several models illustrate the stages that people go through when coping with change in their lives. Many people know the Kübler-Ross model, involving the following stages: shock, denial, awareness, acceptance, experimentation, search and integration.

Figure 18-3 illustrates how people typically react to change over time.

Lean Six Sigma projects are about changing things for the better. You're trying to improve processes – so change is inevitable. Blindly hoping that doing the same things in the same way will magically improve your product or service is head-in-the-sand (HITS) thinking. Unsurprisingly, although being an ostrich is a commonly encountered management practice, it's not taught in management schools or on Lean Six Sigma training courses!

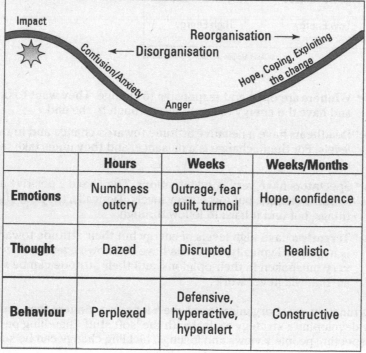

	Hours	**Weeks**	**Weeks/Months**
Emotions	Numbness outcry	Outrage, fear guilt, turmoil	Hope, confidence
Thought	Dazed	Disrupted	Realistic
Behaviour	Perplexed	Defensive, hyperactive, hyperalert	Constructive

Figure 18-3: Change reaction.

© John Morgan and Martin Brenig-Jones

Comparing energy and attitude

Not everyone reacts to the prospect of change in the same way, so looking at different responses is helpful. An 'energy and attitude scale', as shown in Figure 18-4 is a useful way to assess people's attitudes:

SPECTATOR	**WINNER**
Positive Attitude	Positive Attitude
Low Energy	High Energy
DEADBEAT	**TERRORIST**
Negative Attitude	Negative Attitude
Low Energy	High Energy

Figure 18-4: Energy and attitude model.

© John Morgan and Martin Brenig-Jones

✔ **Winners** are open and responsive to change. They want to do their best and have the energy to see things through to the end.

✔ **Deadbeats** have a negative attitude towards change and low energy levels. For them, change is a nuisance, and they undertake tasks with reluctance.

✔ **Spectators** have very good intentions. They have a positive attitude towards change, but low energy levels. Typically, they say the right things, but find it hard to follow through.

✔ **Terrorists** have high levels of energy but their attitude towards change is negative. Typically, terrorists have their own agenda. They can be very outspoken in their opinions, and their attitude can be summed up as 'that will never work'.

Fortunately, most organisations have a lot more winners than terrorists. By developing a strategy to deal with the 'soft stuff' (handling people) and respecting people's views and feelings, tackling change can be successful in even the most challenging organisations.

Using a forcefield diagram

We can take the model in Figure 18-4 further by looking at the strength of support for, or resistance to, the outcome of a specific project. We do this for different interest (stakeholder) groups using a forcefield diagram, as shown in Figure 18-5.

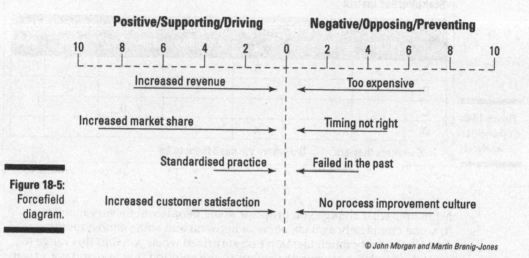

Figure 18-5:
Forcefield
diagram.

© John Morgan and Martin Brenig-Jones

A forcefield diagram is a useful graphical representation of the positive and negative 'forces' influencing a particular project. You could also use a forcefield diagram when starting to implement an entire Lean Six Sigma programme in your organisation, as this diagram indicates. The length of each line represents the strength of the force. In Figure 18-5 the programme is perceived to bring increased revenue, which is seen as a positive force, but this has to be balanced by the negative force of being too expensive. Remember that these are perceptions rather than facts; however, they'll certainly influence stakeholders' opinions, so identifying these forces, and their strength, can be very helpful in understanding why people feel the way they do.

Analysing your stakeholders

Stakeholder analysis is another useful technique for identifying the 'interest groups' (stakeholders) in your project and their levels of support.

Use the matrix in Figure 18-6 to show where the stakeholders are now on the positive/negative scale, and also where you'd like them to be in the future. This kind of stakeholder analysis needs to be regularly updated during the life of a project, and is best kept for the team's eyes only. You're dealing with sensitive stuff – how people think and whether they're for or against change.

Stakeholder matrix

Names	Strongly against	Moderately against	Neutral	Moderately supportive	Strongly supportive	Hot/Cold spots	Next steps
A	X		0				
B				X	0		
C					X 0		
D			X	0			

X = where they are   0 = where we need them to be

© John Morgan and Martin Brenig-Jones

Figure 18-6: Stakeholder analysis.

No matter what change you propose, some people will be very much for it, some completely against, some in-between and some almost indifferent. And that's pretty much life! Don't be surprised when you find this range of attitudes applying to your project, or to the solution that you and your team eventually develop. Finding out early in the project what the for/against situation looks like, both on the surface and beneath it, is a good idea.

A *key stakeholder* is anyone who controls critical resources, who can block the change initiative by direct or indirect means, must approve certain aspects of the change strategy, shapes the thinking of other critical parties or owns a key work process impacted by the change initiative. So, in your Lean Six Sigma team, ask:

✔ Who are the key stakeholders?

✔ Where do they currently stand on the issues associated with this change initiative?

✔ Are they supportive and to what degree?

✔ Are they against and to what degree?

✔ Are they broadly neutral?

Given their status or influence on your project, where do you need the stakeholders to be? Moving some stakeholders to a higher level of support may be both desirable and possible, so work out how you can do so. Consider what turns them on or off, and think about how you can present the project in a more appealing and effective way for them.

Focusing on key elements of change

To deal with the people issues we describe in this chapter and to understand the key elements involved in managing change, we use the elements of change model shown in Figure 18-7, based on work by Kotter, to help you in the deployment of the overall approach and in local and cross-company projects.

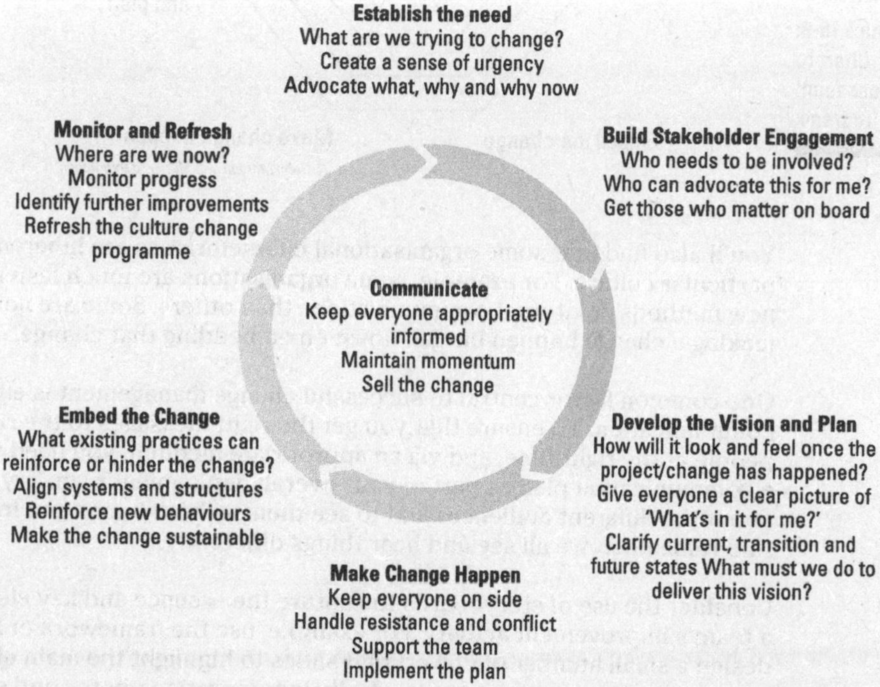

Establish the need
What are we trying to change?
Create a sense of urgency
Advocate what, why and why now

Monitor and Refresh
Where are we now?
Monitor progress
Identify further improvements
Refresh the culture change
programme

Build Stakeholder Engagement
Who needs to be involved?
Who can advocate this for me?
Get those who matter on board

Communicate
Keep everyone appropriately
informed
Maintain momentum
Sell the change

Embed the Change
What existing practices can
reinforce or hinder the change?
Align systems and structures
Reinforce new behaviours
Make the change sustainable

Develop the Vision and Plan
How will it look and feel once the
project/change has happened?
Give everyone a clear picture of
'What's in it for me?'
Clarify current, transition and
future states What must we do to
deliver this vision?

Make Change Happen
Keep everyone on side
Handle resistance and conflict
Support the team
Implement the plan

© John Morgan and Martin Brenig-Jones

Figure 18-7:
Elements
of change
model.

This model can be used as a simple but effective tool to assess how well you're doing in relation to the change management elements of individual projects and also of the overall deployment programme. You can use the radar-like chart shown in Figure 18-8 to carry out regular assessments of your team's progress.

Scoring 100 per cent means perfect, whereas scores nearer the centre indicate areas where more work needs to be done. This chart is a great tool to use in your team; everyone can carry out their own assessment initially and then share each other's to see where common themes or differences of opinion exist.

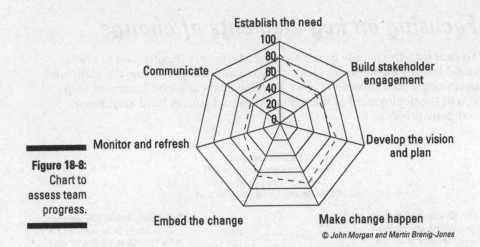

Establish the need

Communicate

Build stakeholder
engagement

Monitor and refresh

Develop the vision
and plan

Embed the change

Make change happen

© John Morgan and Martin Brenig-Jones

Figure 18-8:
Chart to
assess team
progress.

You'll also find that some organisational characteristics are inherent in a particular culture. For example, some organisations are much faster at using new methods of internal communications than others. Some are good at making a change happen but fall down on embedding that change.

One common factor central to successful change management is effective communication. To ensure that you get the right messages to the right people at the right time, and via an appropriate medium, you need to develop a communication plan as part of your overall deployment plan. Try to think about the different audiences and to see them as both teams and individuals. And remember, we all see and hear things differently.

Consider the use of storyboards to capture the essence and key elements of a team's improvement activity. For example, use the framework of DMAIC to design a small number of PowerPoint slides to highlight the main elements of a project or improvement event, ideally incorporating photos and videos.

Part VI
The Part of Tens

the
part of
tens

In this part . . .

✔ Examine ten best practices that can help you take your organisation to the next level with Lean Six Sigma.

✔ Read about ten common traps that organisations fall into when they implement Lean Six Sigma and what you can do to avoid them.

✔ Discover some of the excellent resources available that cover Lean Six Sigma and use them to help your organisation be more effective.

Chapter 19

Ten Best Practices

In This Chapter

▶ Applying Lean Six Sigma in everyday operations

▶ Using common sense and being practical

▶ Keeping things simple

You can apply the Lean Six Sigma toolkit in organisations of all sizes and in all sectors. The following sections highlight details to take care of to ensure success.

Lead and Manage the Programme

Leadership and management are needed to make Lean Six Sigma work in practice: leadership from a senior executive who takes on the sponsorship role and management through a deployment programme manager appointed by the senior team to programme manage the Lean Six Sigma deployment across the organisation. Even if you're working in a small organisation, these dual roles need to exist and, in our experience, a double act is better than a solo attempt. Even if you have the best intentions as the leader of your organisation, your Lean Six Sigma programme stands little chance of success unless you appoint a deployment manager to work with you and to make this happen. Equally, trying to start up and deploy a programme without a business sponsor to act as its leader is pointless.

If you're a senior executive, here's a quick reference list of what you'll need to do (refer to Chapter 13 for a more detailed list):

✔ Provide drive and direction.

✔ Articulate why this approach is so important.

✔ Provide the budget and resources for the team as needed.

- ✔ Regularly review progress.
- ✔ Spread the message.
- ✔ Recognise success.
- ✔ Act as a role model.
- ✔ Ensure you're not easily diverted off-track.

The Lean Six Sigma deployment programme manager's main tasks include:

- ✔ Designing the overall programme.
- ✔ Planning the initial roll-out.
- ✔ Engaging stakeholder support.
- ✔ Setting the framework and structure.
- ✔ Organising training and support.
- ✔ Reporting on progress, targets and measures.
- ✔ Dealing with internal communications.
- ✔ Sharing internal best practice.

A deployment programme manager's role is often underestimated. He should be able to focus on getting the programme off to a good start by organising the selection of initial projects that will bring early tangible benefits, engage with the wider organisation, establish a suitable training programme and achieve early results, thus increasing acceptance within the senior executive group.

As the programme develops, regularly reviewing how well the overall Lean Six Sigma programme is progressing, and comparing your approach and progress against best practice, makes sense. A small number of specialist organisations can provide this service, providing you with an independent audit report showing how your organisation matches up with others at the same stage.

Refer to Chapter 13 for more details about Lean Six Sigma leadership roles.

Appreciate that Less is More

Keeping things simple can be surprisingly challenging in a world where processes and systems can become overly complicated and not matched to changing customer expectations and requirements.

Businesses that haven't discovered Lean Six Sigma seem to have a built-in tendency to overcomplicate processes by inserting non-value-adding steps as a result of one-off failures being treated as 'common cause' events.

In one organisation we're familiar with, a high-value sales quotation was issued incorrectly. After that 'one-off mistake', a senior finance manager insisted that every new quotation be sent for additional checking and authorisation before being despatched. As time progressed and more mistakes continued to be made, even further checking and inspecting steps were added into the process in the false belief that this would reduce the defect level. Customers then complained that they didn't receive quotations in the time they expected. When we tackled this issue shortly after the organisation decided to use Lean Six Sigma, one customer stated: 'Your internal processes are like a black hole.' Applying Lean Six Sigma resulted in a simplified, faster process, a subsequent increase in customer satisfaction and a reduction in customers switching to competitors. Improving the process wasn't difficult, but no one had ever looked at the process from either the view of the customer or across the whole organisation.

Adopting the strategy of keeping it simple is a good idea for any Lean Six Sigma project. Try using deployment flowcharts (explained in Chapter 5) to illustrate the unnecessary complexity inadvertently 'designed' into processes across your organisation – you may well discover a vast number of checks and balances added into the overall process. Simply map the process across the entire organisation and count the number of different people involved in it and the number of crossover points. Then see how you can consolidate or reduce them.

One organisation we've been working with has coined a brilliant expression for the aim of their programme: 'relentless simplification'.

Build in Prevention

Prevention really is better than cure. This adage applies in business just as in health – with the added benefit in business that a prevention-based system costs a lot less than a cure.

Imagine a situation whereby an organisation ships poor-quality products to customers, or doesn't clean its hotel rooms adequately, or sends out inaccurate or late invoices to clients. The cost of putting right these failures is much higher than preventing the failure in the first place. Handling customer complaints, carrying out expensive rework and paying for additional warranty shipping are non-value-added costs that your competitor won't incur if they've fully adopted Lean Six Sigma. Losing customers adds the final insult to injury, as word spreads of your company's poor quality.

Many high-quality manufacturing plants use error detection and error prevention techniques such as Poka-yoke (Japanese slang for 'avoiding inadvertent errors' – see Chapter 10), but service and transaction-based organisations still see such techniques as a novelty. Error detection and prevention systems are inexpensive and highly effective at preventing errors occurring in everyday work.

For example, a handful of hotel chains now use Lean Six Sigma, and travellers who use several hotels can really tell the difference in quality. Think of the effect of finding a hair on the pillow just after you arrive for a stay at a premium-brand hotel. By focusing on the process of cleaning the room, a Lean Six Sigma business will almost completely eradicate the possibility of such a defect occurring, in the same way that the likelihood of an aeroplane engine failing is now miniscule.

No organisation is perfect but building quality into your processes and preventing failure before it can happen are key to the long-term success of best practice companies. And taking into account the cost of failure actually means you incur less expense overall.

Challenge Your Processes

Understanding how the work gets done, and then improving processes, is at the core of Lean Six Sigma. We don't see the word 'process' as synonymous with heavy documentation, bureaucracy or sluggishness – although we know that the word *process* sometimes conjures up an image of a constraining rather than a liberating force. According to the famous statistician, W. E. Deming, the key role of managers is to 'change the processes':

> *Eighty-five percent of the reasons for failure to meet customer expectations are related to deficiencies in systems and process . . . rather than the employee. The role of management is to change the process rather than badgering individuals to do better.*

Take the lid off any organisation, look inside and you'll find that the organisation is made up of a series of interconnecting processes. Using the Lean Six Sigma toolkit in a continuing cycle of assessing, improving and maintaining this organisational system by challenging the state of these processes will keep the organisation fit and capable of consistently meeting customer requirements.

Go to the Gemba

The Japanese expression 'Go to the Gemba' means go to the place where the work gets done. This approach is used throughout leading organisations, such as Toyota, where senior managers are almost indistinguishable from shop floor workers as they continually support and encourage everyday Kaizen (continuous improvement) activities. (Chapter 2 explains Kaizen in more detail.)

To find out how the work really gets done in your organisation, you need to go to the place where it happens. Lean Six Sigma projects get to the root of problems by actually going to the workplace and involving the people who do the work. All too often, the process map in the company quality manual is fictional – it doesn't represent reality. A real process stapling exercise – walking through the process viewed from the thing being processed – is an eye opener. (For more on process stapling, check out Chapter 5.)

Recognising and being prepared to accept that significant differences may exist between the real life 'as is' process in the Gemba when compared to the 'should be' process, let alone the ideal 'to be' process, is worthwhile.

Many organisations are now institutionalising time for senior managers to regularly 'Go to the Gemba'. After all, how can you win a round-the-world yacht race if you lose touch with what the crew are having to deal with every day?

Manage Your Processes with Lean Six Sigma

Lean Six Sigma is traditionally used as a method for improving processes but you can also use the tools to help you manage your business processes on an everyday, ongoing basis. During the control phase of a Lean Six Sigma project, all the key ingredients of process management should be put in place, including the measurement system needed to monitor the ongoing running of the process on a day-to-day basis.

In essence, the control phase leaves the process running sweetly, and with the following in place:

✔ A clear, customer-focused objective reflecting the CTQs (check out CTQs in Chapter 2).

✔ An agreed process map (plug into process mapping in Chapter 5).

✔ An agreed data collection plan with an appropriate balance of X and Y measures (we delve into data collection plans in Chapter 6).

✔ An ongoing control plan (we cover control plans in Chapter 2).

✔ A standardised process with appropriate documentation in place (see more about standardisation in Chapter 10).

✔ A visual management system to be updated and used in practice on a day to day basis using statistical control charts when needed (see our vision of visual management systems in Chapter 10).

By running a series of DMAIC projects across the processes that are at the core of running your organisation, you put in place the basis for an effective process management system. (We get down with DMAIC in Chapter 2.)

Don't spend ages putting a detailed process management system in place before you run a DMAIC project. Although such a system may seem like a sensible and logical approach, in reality your business leaders may lose patience as months or years pass by and they see little or no change. Lean Six Sigma's whole rationale is *to make a difference!*

Pick the Right Tools for the Job

A newly trained Lean Six Sigma practitioner may want to use all his newly learned tools – but in practice the Pareto principle (in this case, that 80 per cent of projects can be completed successfully by using only 20 per cent of the LSS tools) will apply in the choice of appropriate tools for different projects. Chapter 7 explains the Pareto principle in more detail. Here are a few tips for using the right tools:

✔ Consider that, used in the wrong way, even the best tools give bad results.

✔ Know what level of rigour is necessary and when.

✔ Remember that excellent influencing skills are as important as superb tools (see the $E = Q \times A$ equation in Chapter 18 for assessing the success of your project in relation to people's commitment to your ideas).

✔ Don't be tempted to disappear into your own analysis paralysis.

✔ Use the methodology and the tools together. Even the most rapid improvement event will benefit from using the Define, Measure, Analyse, Improve and Control stages. We've seen a DMAIC exercise carried out successfully in a one-day rapid improvement workshop. (See Chapter 2 for a full explanation of DMAIC.)

✔ Remember that 20 per cent of the tools will be used on 80 per cent of projects, so don't try to shoehorn every tool into a project.

✔ Keep the scope of your project simple and understandable.

✔ Don't be afraid to ask for help if you need to use a tool that you haven't used since training. Everyone needs support from time to time.

Tell the Whole Story

Most people like a good story. We learn a great deal through reading, listening to and exchanging stories. Keeping a 'storyboard' or log of a Lean Six Sigma project is an excellent way to communicate the project to the wider organisation and to pass on what you discover.

Organisations implementing Lean Six Sigma often don't bother with storyboarding. Many people miss the importance of this technique as they strive to meet project objectives. Ignoring the use of storyboarding is shortsighted, however: if you don't capture the discoveries, challenges and 'Aha!' moments of a project, the rest of the organisation is none the wiser and potentially makes the same discoveries and overcomes the same challenges over and over again.

Lean Six Sigma storyboarding is a straightforward technique to record the knowledge gained from a project. Just like the taste of strawberries in a good jam, your storyboarded knowledge lasts for many years.

Intranet sites make a good storage area, offering easy access to such 'bottled knowledge' across the organisation. They have the added advantage that, unlike jam, they're not eaten but can be used many times over! You have no excuse for losing stories from your records.

The latest storyboarding techniques use a combination of slides, words, interviews and videos to capture the essence of 'what happened' in the life of a project. Of course, a full-scale TV-style documentary isn't necessary. Simply writing up learning points and recording key events in the project 'story' on a flipchart and then taking digital photos of the various sheets can form a very useful record while the team is live and thoughts are easily captured. Lean Six Sigma projects are now featured on YouTube, where you can upload and create an 'unlisted' video that allows easy sharing across a wider group. Dropbox is also revolutionising file-sharing across groups using cloud-based systems, which use computing as a service rather than a product. Why not use Dropbox or SharePoint, a similar system, for sharing storyboards across your organisation?

Understand the Role of the Champion

Projects are more successful if they relate to key business issues and everyone realises their importance.

A *champion* is a senior sponsor who provides support, direction and financial and people resources to Lean Six Sigma, demonstrating the company's commitment to the approach and providing a direct link to company strategy.

To make Lean Six Sigma work in practice, you need to put in place two different champion roles:

- ✔ A Lean Six Sigma programme business champion.
- ✔ A champion for every Lean Six Sigma project.

Looking at the Lean Six Sigma programme executive sponsor

Visible commitment from the Lean Six Sigma executive sponsor demonstrates that senior management take the Lean Six Sigma approach seriously. In an ideal world, the most senior executive in the organisation has the role of overall programme sponsor, but in practice, a member of the senior executive management team is often a good choice.

Senior management needs to communicate its support to the whole organisation, showing that it treats the approach seriously and not as just another fad.

Perusing the role of the project champion

Every project deserves a champion who's prepared to devote the time and support needed to help the project team overcome any roadblocks on their journey.

The project champion is involved in selecting the project and the team members for it. For more details on the role of champions, see Chapter 13.

Use Strategy to Drive Lean Six Sigma

Implementing a Lean Six Sigma programme is pointless if it isn't aligned with the direction being taken at a strategic level by the business. Lean Six Sigma is about making change happen and strategy is about deciding which direction the company is heading in – so they need to work in tandem. Lean Six Sigma helps you deploy strategy within the operational business.

Many businesses now use Lean Six Sigma techniques as an essential component of their wider business transformation programme, as described in the new book in this series, *Lean Six Sigma Business Transformation For Dummies* (John Wiley & Sons, Inc.). These organisations use the essential tools of the Define, Measure, Analyse, Improve and Control phases (which we describe in Chapter 2) simultaneously across multiple processes as well as Lean Six Sigma for Innovation and Design to create a transformed business with the right set of services and products being delivered through streamlined processes.

Chapter 20

Ten Pitfalls to Avoid

- -

In This Chapter

▶ Avoiding the temptation to shoot from the lip

▶ Knowing when to stop analysing and start implementing

▶ Steering clear of project traps and doing the wrong things right

- -

*O*f course you want your Lean Six Sigma programme to be a big success. The approach has been around for a while now, so you can draw on a wealth of experience, some good and some not so good. This chapter describes things that can go wrong so you can avoid the common pitfalls. We share our experience of observing many different organisations and building up a bank of knowledge of what works and what doesn't. Unlike some doomsters who never seem to have a good word for anything, we certainly don't want to put you off. So read on and see if these pitfalls are ones that are likely to affect you.

Jumping to Solutions

Many managers seem hard-wired to jump straight to a solution when presented with a problem. In action movies, everything works out in the end and the hero makes the right decisions in a split second and lives on for another day (or film). Unfortunately, business life isn't quite the same: knee-jerk solutions can be costly and can fail to address the root cause of the problem.

Shooting from the hip – or, in business, the all too common 'shooting from the lip' – without collecting and analysing the facts and data isn't the best approach to solving complex business problems. Lean Six Sigma involves understanding what the problem is and then going through several steps to gain a better understanding of it (Define, Measure), working down to the root causes (Analyse), looking at the various solution options and then choosing the most appropriate (Improve), and implementing the solution and holding the gains (Control).

Although this approach sounds straightforward and sensible, for many business executives, who believe they know best, it's counter-intuitive.

Consider the vast number of decisions made each year about IT systems, call-centre outsourcing, business re-organisation, new products and company-wide training programmes. These decisions are often 'solutions' agreed in busy executive meetings – but companies often discover six months or a year later that such 'solutions' do anything but meet requirements or run to budget.

Unfortunately, the very organisations that might benefit most from a Lean Six Sigma-style approach are the least likely to adopt it.

Coming Down with Analysis Paralysis

Getting the balance right is important. During the Analyse phase you may be tempted to get further and further into root-cause analysis and lose sight of the primary reason for the improvement project, which is to make a difference and see positive changes in your business. Your team may get bogged down in the sheer volume of analysis options that can be carried out as they make more discoveries. Restricting the scope of the project is important to avoid going off on tangents. By all means log those potential opportunities for future projects, but for now stick to the original scope.

Knowing when to end the analysis and start the Improve phase can be difficult. Try regarding this decision as a judicial case and weigh up the balance of evidence for and against the 'defendants' – the causes of the problem in your Lean Six Sigma project.

You're probably ready to move to the Improve stage if you answer yes to the following question:

> 'Are we sure that we understand enough about the process, problem and causes to develop effective solutions?'

And no to this one:

> 'Is the value of additional data and analysis worth the extra cost in time, resources and momentum?'

The project champion has a key role in ensuring that you keep the business interests at the forefront when answering these questions and in steering the team ahead on the business track.

Achieving Six Sigma – 3.4 defects per 1 million opportunities – may be an aspiration (refer to Chapter 1 for calculating Sigma values), but you are highly unlikely to achieve it in one project. Moving from 2 Sigma to 3 Sigma and then onto 4 Sigma in your Lean Six Sigma projects is entirely normal. You'll also find that it takes a lot more effort as you climb further up the Sigma scale. Small bite-sized projects move your performance in the right direction, so be prepared to accept just a small increase in the Sigma value of your processes.

Falling into Common Project Traps

Want to know how to ensure project failure? Try a negative brainstorming technique: it's a great icebreaker at the start of a project and is certain to get your team bouncing with ideas. Instead of brainstorming ideas to make the project a success, you brainstorm the opposite: 'How can we ensure project disaster?' You'll be amazed at the number of suggestions the team comes up with! Then you can turn these negative thoughts into positive ones. You'll end up with a really positive set of suggestions based on practical experience of what really can make projects fail and how to avoid these pitfalls.

For starters, we discuss some common project traps here.

Methodology madness problems include the following:

- Not using a structured and planned approach
- Predetermining your solution
- Providing poorly managed handovers
- Allowing the Control phase to be weak, thus failing to hold the gain

Scope scandals are as follows:

- Running too many projects at the same time
- Undertaking too large a project
- Having a goal that isn't measurable or is too vague
- Ignoring 'outside-in' customer focus
- Failing to link the goal to a real business need
- Allowing the project scope to keep growing

Team turmoil to keep an eye on include

- ✔ Creating a team with the wrong mix of skills or functional representation (for example, not getting the finance or HR departments in when needed)
- ✔ Offering inadequate training
- ✔ Making a poor choice of team leader
- ✔ Failing to agree on the time requirements of the team
- ✔ Having no shared vision of success

Problems related to lack of support include

- ✔ Using unsupportive key stakeholders
- ✔ Having no active project sponsor or champion
- ✔ Running competing projects or projects with conflicting objectives
- ✔ Allowing poor leadership behaviour
- ✔ Failing to allow enough time to run the project systematically

Stifling the Programme before You've Started

Chances are, some people in your organisation don't share your vision and are all too keen to stamp on your programme before you get it off the ground. Here are a few comments we've heard people say when stifling a Lean Six Sigma programme:

- ✔ 'This is just common sense.'
- ✔ 'Our place is different.'
- ✔ 'It costs too much.'
- ✔ 'We're all too busy to do that.'
- ✔ 'Let's get back to reality.'
- ✔ 'Why change? It's still okay.'
- ✔ 'We're not ready for this yet.'
- ✔ 'It's a good thought but highly impractical.'

> ✔ 'Not that crazy idea again!'
>
> ✔ 'We've always done it this way.'
>
> ✔ 'We're no worse than our competitors!'

Chapter 18 covers dealing with the people aspects of Lean Six Sigma. Win over the doubters in your organisation and you're halfway to making your project succeed.

Ignoring the Soft Stuff

Many traditional Lean Six Sigma training courses cover the 'hard stuff', such as the statistical techniques, the DMAIC methodology and an extensive array of tools and techniques, but don't deal with the softer tools – the people issues – that you need to gain buy-in and overcome resistance.

Consequently, many novice Lean Six Sigma practitioners try to run projects that focus on statistical tools and blind people with newly learned expressions – and then they're disappointed when their managers or operational workers don't accept the idea.

$$E = Q \times A$$

The *quality* (Q) of the solution that comes from the use of the 'hard' tools and the *acceptance* (A) of the solution that comes from the 'soft' tools are equally important. You need both quality and acceptance to win support and achieve an *effective* (E) outcome. See Chapter 18 for more insight into this issue.

From our experience in countless projects, the really hard stuff is the soft stuff!

Getting Complacent

Underestimating the amount of energy you need to make your Lean Six Sigma programme a success is a major pitfall. Complacency sets in surprisingly quickly if you don't drive and lead your programme with a sense of urgency. You need an active Lean Six Sigma deployment programme manager, with support from a senior executive, to keep your programme alive, relevant and on the business agenda.

Organisational changes are frequent in many businesses. We've seen Lean Six Sigma programmes wither when a deployment programme manager is diverted to internal organisational politics. Ensuring that the senior executive team is actively involved is important. Institutionalising the whole approach is key, so that Lean Six Sigma becomes part of the 'way we do things around here'.

Thinking that You're Already Doing It

A quick skim through the Lean Six Sigma literature or rapid overview of your processes may lead you to believe that your organisation is 'already doing it'. Many managers think that they already solve problems using a systematic problem-solving process – but often they don't think about or test solution options properly before putting them into action.

You may think, 'We already use process flowcharts.' Many organisations do use this technique, but often without first understanding the true requirements of the process from the customer's perspective. Unless you adopt Lean Six Sigma in a structured way, you won't be able to fully utilise the power of process-mapping techniques to really get under the surface of how your existing processes work.

Genuine senior management buy-in for this kind of 'peripheral' process-mapping activity is also unusual. Isolated cases do exist in organisations as part of a cottage industry of enthusiasts who are doing their best but operating outside the scope of a serious senior management-led initiative. A well-designed Lean Six Sigma programme builds on existing knowledge and legitimises improvement work into a framework that involves everyone and introduces a common set of tools across the organisation.

Believing the Myths

A whole series of myths has developed around the use of Lean Six Sigma. For Lean Six Sigma to work in practice, you need to dispel the following ideas:

✔ **Lean Six Sigma is all we need.** No – Lean Six Sigma can, and should, be integrated with other approaches.

✔ **Lean Six Sigma is just for manufacturing or production improvement.** No – all processes can be improved. Lean Six Sigma has been used successfully in transaction and service processes.

✔ **Lean Six Sigma is just about statistical tools and measures.** No – Lean Six Sigma actually involves cultural change.

✔ **Lean Six Sigma is just about individuals and experts.** No – to work best, Lean Six Sigma involves everyone in a team effort, including senior executives.

Doing the Wrong Things Right

Most of us want to do the right things right. Process analysis is a great tool to show us what we're doing in practice and help us answer the questions 'Why?' and 'Are we doing this step correctly?'.

According to systems theorist, Russ Ackoff:

> *The righter you do the wrong thing, the wronger you become; if you make a mistake doing the wrong things and correct it, you become wronger; if you make a mistake doing the right thing and correct it, you become righter. Therefore it is better to do the right thing wrong than the wrong thing right.*

In fact, you have four options:

1. **Doing the right thing right – most people want to do this.**

   Serving great food and providing top-notch service in a stylish restaurant is an example.

2. **Doing the right thing wrong – apply the tools to fix the problem.**

   Imagine great service and a beautiful restaurant but really bad food. Listen to the voice of the customer, recognise that the poor quality of the food is the key driver of customer dissatisfaction and tackle the root causes of the problem. That is, you analyse the process, discover the critical factors underlying the causes of the problem and solve those. Often problems can be resolved simply; in this case, maybe by using less salt.

3. **Doing the wrong thing right – this is non-value-adding.**

   To continue the example, you concentrate on making the restaurant look even better but still serve awful food. That is, you don't find out what the real customer requirements are, jump to the wrong solution and spend unnecessary money.

4. **Doing the wrong thing wrong – working to get this right is pointless.**

   For example, spending lots of money restyling the restaurant when customers actually liked the earlier style.

The ultimate danger is kicking off a Lean Six Sigma project to fix the situation in option 4 above – and still ending up doing the wrong thing!

Overtraining

Clearly, getting trained up in Lean Six Sigma is important and a well thought out training plan needs to form part of the overall deployment programme. But training works best when it's delivered 'just in time' and at the right level.

In the early days, some organisations undertook company-wide, large-scale implementations of Six Sigma and 'forced' hundreds of people onto unnecessary 20-day Black Belt training, which resulted in putting many of them off the whole approach (refer to Chapter 2 for an explanation of the martial arts analogy in Lean Six Sigma).

An organisation just starting to use Lean Six Sigma will be full of opportunities for process improvement that can be tackled using the tools learned on a good foundation Green Belt course. Ideally, this six-day training can be split into three smaller modules of two days each, wrapped around a real project being carried out to ensure the training is delivered at the right level and at the right time to fit into the life of the project.

Avoid the pitfall of believing that Black Belt training must be 'better' than Green Belt training and sending people on a full Black Belt course, complete with advanced statistical training, before starting any projects. Start simply, develop the basic skills, provide expert coaching support to the Green Belts, run initial projects quickly to deliver tangible benefits to the organisation and then select the right candidates to be trained in the Lean Six Sigma advanced tools when needed.

Training people at an advanced level too soon is a waste of money and will probably deter people from using the approach.

Chapter 21

Ten (Plus One) Places to Go for Help

In This Chapter

▶ Tapping into a wealth of knowledge and experience

▶ Using the power of the web

▶ Considering software applications

▶ Joining a community of interest and developing a network

Sometimes Lean Six Sigma seems a bit daunting. But don't worry; plenty of help and good experience exists if you know where to look. In this chapter we show you where to find all the advice and resources you need.

Your Colleagues

A well-managed Lean Six Sigma programme relies on teamwork and support being available for everyone involved across the organisation through an internal network. Support can be offered through a spectrum of different coloured 'belts'; for example, Black Belts supporting Green Belts (see Chapter 2 for more on how the martial arts relate to Lean Six Sigma). Ideally, Black Belts will be able to call on support from Master Black Belts who are professional experts in Lean Six Sigma, but in smaller organisations this support may be outsourced to a specialist.

The 'belt' terminology isn't mandatory. Many organisations just use terms such as 'practitioner' and 'expert' instead of Green Belt and Black Belt.

Being able to access this kind of support network is important. You probably already know that a big difference exists between using a tool in a training environment and operating in the real world, where your first port of call for help is usually your own colleagues.

Your Champion

Every project deserves a good sponsor, or 'champion' (described in detail in Chapter 13). When things get tough, as most projects do from time to time, your project champion is a good source of help. Your champion supports your project team, helps unblock project barriers and assists you when you need buy-in at a more senior level in your organisation.

Other Organisations

Every year, the number of organisations deploying Lean Six Sigma increases. Over time, the combination of tools and techniques may have changed, but the essentials of using a systematic method, focusing on understanding customer requirements and improving processes are well tried and tested. Visiting some other organisations and learning from their experiences is well worthwhile. You may not be able to look deep inside your competitors' businesses, but you can discover lots by visiting similar-sized companies in different sectors. Industry and government special interest groups are a good source of help and often arrange visits for groups to observe companies at work. If you have the chance to visit a Toyota or Ricoh plant, for example, in just a few hours you'll learn a lot about the cultural approach that forms the basis for continuous improvement and Lean thinking in general.

The Internet

Lots of sites are aimed at Lean Six Sigma devotees. Just for fun, here's a snippet of trivia: if you search the web using the expression 'Six Sigma Pink Floyd', you discover that Roger Waters set up a band in 1964 called Sigma Six before forming Pink Floyd a year later. That was 20 years before Motorola came up with the idea of Six Sigma – progressive rock indeed!

Following are some of our favourite websites with extensive articles and features devoted to Lean Six Sigma:

- ✔ www.asq.org: The site for the American Society for Quality, offering very comprehensive online resources and publications.

- ✔ www.catalystconsulting.co.uk: The authors' own website, regularly updated with new articles and with access to an extensive online learning resource area.

✔ `www.efqm.org`: Full of useful material and a link into the knowledge library of the European Foundation for Quality Management – essential for anyone serious about learning more about developing quality and excellence across an entire organisation.

✔ `www.isssp.com`: Dedicated to Lean Six Sigma, with plenty of articles.

✔ `www.isixsigma.com`: The number one (US-focused) Six Sigma website, with bulletin boards, job ads and links – for addicts only.

✔ `www.qualitydigest.com`: A useful online magazine on quality.

✔ `www.qfdi.org`: The site for the Quality Function Deployment (QFD) Institute. QFD is an approach to really understanding customer requirements and linking these to processes, products and services, and is often used when Lean Six Sigma companies want to design new products and services. QFD is an additional tool used in Design for Six Sigma (Doss).

✔ `www.processexcellencenetwork.com`: The Process Excellence Network, a division of IQPC, provides access to a wide range of content for Process Excellence practitioners.

✔ `www.leanproduction.com`: A useful website providing lots of information about Lean, Kaizen and the Theory of Constraints

✔ `www.leanenterprise.org.uk`: LERC was formed in 1994, bringing together the benchmarking and lean production work of Daniel Jones (together with James Womack of MIT) and the work on supplier development and materials management of Peter Hines.

✔ `www.goldratt.com`: This website focuses on the Theory of Constraints, an approach for managing and reducing process bottlenecks.

✔ `www.shingoprize.org`: This website provides information about the Shingo Model and award.

✔ `www.nist.gov/baldrige`: This website provides information about the Baldrige Model and award.

Social Media

Here's a resource that continues to grow and provide a wealth of information. Put your keywords into a search engine, for example 'statistical process control', and you'll find all sorts of sites to look at and videos to watch.

Maybe you can follow someone on Twitter too, or perhaps you can start something yourself!

LinkedIn is an excellent source of information related to Lean Six Sigma transformations. You can access several Lean Six Sigma groups to network with practitioners and champions.

Networks and Associations

You can find all sorts of networks and associations relating to Lean Six Sigma. Some networks offer online and offline services to encourage collaboration and knowledge exchange between members, and they often hold regular members' meetings.

National and regional quality associations such as the American Society for Quality (ASQ), the European Foundation for Quality Management (EFQM) and the British Quality Foundation (BQF) provide opportunities to share good, and not so good, practice through meetings, visits to businesses, conferences, workshops and online resources, although these aren't dedicated purely to Lean Six Sigma. The EFQM provides an extensive knowledge library to members offering insights into the approaches used in different organisations.

Conferences

Lean Six Sigma conferences are a regular feature of the conference calendar these days. Conference organisers hold Lean Six Sigma 'summits' every year at different locations around the world. These summits provide a range of mainstream speakers, smaller workshops, and networking and informal discussions regarding every aspect of Lean Six Sigma. Whether you're just starting out or want to keep up with the latest thinking and new developments, these summits are a great source of information.

Books

You can find a wealth of books on the individual aspects of Lean and Six Sigma, and a few on Lean Six Sigma. Here are some of our favourites:

✔ *Practitioner's Guide to Statistics and Lean Six Sigma for Process Improvements* by Mike J. Harry, Prem S. Mann, Ofelia C. De Hodgins, Richard L. Hulbert and Christopher J. Lacke (John Wiley & Sons, Inc.): An 800-page excellent book covering all aspects of Lean Six Sigma in detail. A great reference book for the serious practitioner.

✔ *Implementing Six Sigma* by Forrest Breyfogle III (Wiley-Interscience): A comprehensive reference textbook.

✔ *Integrated Enterprise Excellence*, Vols. I, II and III by Forrest Breyfogle III (Bridgeway Books): You can't get better than this if you want to become a serious aficionado.

✔ *Making Six Sigma Last* by George Eckes (John Wiley & Sons, Inc.): Cultural aspects of making it happen and succeed.

✔ *Quantitative Approaches in Business Studies*, 8th edition, by Clare Morris (FT/Prentice Hall): An academic textbook offering a good foundation in statistical methods in business.

✔ *SPC in the Office* by Mal Owen and John Morgan (Greenfield): Full of useful case studies about using control charts in the office.

✔ *The Lean Six Sigma Improvement Journey* by John Morgan: Light-hearted coverage of each tool (of which there are many), with the aid of colour-coded illustrations, available on the UK Amazon site.

✔ *The Six Sigma Revolution* by George Eckes (John Wiley & Sons, Inc.): The principles of Six Sigma.

✔ *The Six Sigma Way*, 2nd edition, by Peter Pande, Robert Neuman and Roland Cavanagh (McGraw-Hill): Good general overview and how to.

✔ *The Six Sigma Way Team Fieldbook* by Peter Pande, Robert Neuman and Roland Cavanagh (McGraw-Hill): Practical implementation guide.

✔ *The Machine That Changed the World* by James Womack, Daniel Jones and Daniel Roos (Simon & Schuster): Latest re-issue of the classic text on Lean business.

✔ *The Toyota Way: 14 Management Principles from the World's Greatest Manufacturer*, Jeffrey Liker (McGraw-Hill): The management principles behind the Toyota approach. Very readable and helpful.

✔ *Lean Six Sigma and Minitab: The Complete Toolbox Guide for Business Improvement* (4th edition): This Minitab-based guide provides practical instructions and many screenshots.

Add in our book *Lean Six Sigma for Business Transformation For Dummies* (John Wiley & Sons, Inc.) devoted to linking transformational strategy to action through the use of Lean Six Sigma in a systematic manner.

Periodicals

Several journals are devoted to Lean and Six Sigma, including:

- *International Journal of Six Sigma and Competitive Advantage* – keeps at the forefront of Six Sigma developments.

- *iSixSigma Magazine* – for Six Sigma professionals, with specialist features on all aspects of the approach; also available online.

- *Quality World* – the magazine of the Chartered Quality Institute in the UK, with regular features on Lean Six Sigma.

- *Six Sigma Forum* – a specialist magazine of the American Society for Quality (ASQ).

- *UK Excellence* – the magazine of the British Quality Foundation, with regular features on Lean Six Sigma.

Software

You can certainly start down the Lean Six Sigma road without having to invest in specialist software, but as your journey proceeds you may want to enhance your toolkit with statistical and other software. In this section, we mention a few of our essentials.

One area of Lean Six Sigma where we recommend *not* using software, especially when starting out, is value stream mapping and process deployment flowcharting. For this, we suggest that you map the process using sticky notes, a pencil and a large piece of paper pinned to the wall.

That said, if you do decide to use software for process flowcharting, consider Visio, iGraphix or FlowMap.

Statistical analysis

Most everyday mortals use only a fraction of the full capability of their spreadsheet program such as Excel or Numbers. These programs are good at statistical analysis – but because they weren't designed specifically for this purpose, producing even the most basic Pareto chart without help from a kind soul who's produced a template for this purpose is surprisingly challenging.

Fortunately you can find several plug-ins for your spreadsheet program to help you perform Pareto analysis, and slice and dice your data quickly and easily without having to design your own template.

Microsoft provides a neat data analysis 'Toolpak' for Excel, which has been extended with the latest versions. For more complex statistical analysis, try the Excel plug-in SigmaXL, which lets you produce a variety of displays including SIPOCs, cause and effect diagrams, failure mode and effects analysis, and several types of control chart, as well as a comprehensive range of statistical tools.

Most Black Belts and Master Black Belts favour Minitab ® Statistical Software. This package has been around for many years and is also a favourite of universities and colleges teaching statistics. Minitab is a very comprehensive statistical analysis package designed for serious statistical analysis. Don't try it at home without some serious training as part of an Advanced Green Belt or full Black Belt course.

JMP ® Statistical Discovery Software is another package gaining in popularity for use in the world of Lean Six Sigma. It links statistics to a highly visual graphic representation, allowing you to visually explore the relationships between process inputs and outputs, and then to identify the key process variables.

Simulation

For more advanced statistical and predictive modelling, take a look at Crystal Ball from Oracle. This software is good for forecasting, simulation, and evaluating optimisation options. An alternative software-modelling tool is SIMUL8, which can be used for planning, design and optimisation of manufacturing or transactional service systems. These models allow testing of scenarios in a virtual environment and are often concerned with cost, time and inventory.

Deployment management

For large-scale deployments, consider forming a project library and use tracking software to help you and your colleagues across the organisation manage and report on projects. A number of software systems are designed specifically for this purpose, and are well worth investigating as your deployment grows across the organisation.

Mobile apps

The availability of mobile apps has grown exponentially since the second edition of this book was published. We suggest you simply search through your app store to check out the latest releases. We provide a free app for Apple IOS – the Catalyst Process Guide – that offers tips, hints and reminders for process improvement projects mapped against the Define, Measure, Analyse, Improve and Control phases. You can also share your responses with other improvement team members.

Training and Consultancy Companies

A wide range of specialist training and consulting companies provide services for clients in the Lean Six Sigma arena. In your quest for training, you'll find a few global players and lots of smaller specialists and one-person bands.

When you choose a supplier, try to use the quality × acceptance equation that we describe in Chapter 18. You want your trainer to have excellent technical skills, but also consider how well he'd work with your organisation. Will your organisation's culture accept the trainer? Will the trainer instil confidence and provide all the services you require?

In our experience, few organisations bother to check suppliers' references. But unlike choosing a partner or spouse, in business asking previous clients how well the partnership worked is fine! Working over a long period with a training and consulting company is a bit like a marriage – shared values are a good foundation for belief, integrity, respect, trust and honesty.

Index

• *Symbols and Numerics* •

δ (sigma), 14
1-10-100 rule, 182

• *A* •

A (acceptance)
  defined, 321
  gaining, 292
AARs (After Action Reviews), 175
abandon rate, 148
acceptance (A)
  defined, 321
  gaining, 292
acceptance baseline, 295
Accuracy CTQ grouping, 67
Ackoff, Russ (systems theorist), 323
actions
  logging, 251
  planning, facilitator and, 252
actual place, 74
affinity, 28
affinity diagrams, 29
After Action Reviews (AARs), 175
agenda, 248, 251
agreeing on rules, 102–104
'already doing it' attitude, 322
Altshuller, Genrich (engineer), 199
American Society for Quality (ASQ), 39, 326, 328, 330
Analyse phase
  about, 32–33
  analysing design, 202–204
  outputs from, 264–266
  in QFD drill-down, 218
quality function deployment and, 206–207
  in rapid improvement events, 247
analysing
  data, 264–266
  design, 202–204
  processes, 32–33
  stakeholders, 301–302
analysis paralysis, 318–319
andon, 194
ANOVA, 136–137
applying
  solutions, 267–273
  Theory of Constraints, 189–193
approach, right, 237–242
articles (website), 3
ASQ (American Society for Quality), 39, 326, 328, 330
assessing
  effectiveness, 149–153
  how work is done, 32
  opportunity, 160–161
  performance using customer-focused measures, 71–72
associations
  American Society for Quality (ASQ), 39, 326, 328, 330
  British Quality Foundation (BQF), 39, 328, 330
  European Foundation for Quality Management (EFQM), 327–328
  help from, 328
assumptions, busting, 298
attendees, 248
attitude, compared with energy, 300
attribute charts, 126

attribute data, 104
automation with human intelligence, 178
autonomation, 11
availability rate, 152–153
average, beware of the, 226
avoiding
  peaks, 184–186
  pitfalls, 317–324
  tampering, 119–120
  troughs, 184–186

• B •

backwards visioning, 296
balance, 286
balance of measures
  about, 143
  connecting CTQs, 143–145
Balanced Business Scorecard, 234
Baldrige Model (website), 327
batches, recognising problems with, 195
believing myths, 322–323
benefit reviews, 267
benefits, 36
best practices, 307–315
bias, avoiding, 64
bimodal distribution, 135
Black Belt, 38–39, 324, 325, 331
books
  help from, 328–329
  Implementing Six Sigma
    (Breyfogle III), 329
  Integrated Enterprise Excellence
    (Breyfogle III), 329
  Lean For Dummies (Sayer and
    Williams), 153
  *Lean Six Sigma Business Transformation
    For Dummies* (Burghall and Grant),
    233, 315, 329
  *The Lean Six Sigma Improvement
    Journey* (Morgan), 329
  The Machine That Changed the World
    (Womack, Jones and Roos), 329

Making Six Sigma Last (Eckes), 329
*Practitioner's Guide to Statistics
  and Lean Six Sigma for Process
  Improvements* (Harry, Mann, De
  Hodgins, Hulbert and Lacke), 328
*Quantitative Approaches in Business
  Studies*, 8th Edition (Morris), 329
Six Sigma For Dummies (Gygi, DeCarlo
  and Williams)*, 125, 148
*Six Sigma Workbook For
  Dummies* (Gygi, Williams and
  Gustafson), 125, 148
The Six Sigma Revolution (Eckes), 329
The Six Sigma Way Team Fieldbook
  (Pande, Neuman and Cavanagh), 329
SPC in the Office (Owen and
  Morgan), 329
*The Toyota Way: 14 Management
  Principles from the World's Greatest
  Manufacturer* (Liker), 329
bottlenecks
  about, 12–13, 189
  applying Theory of
    Constraints, 189–193
  layout, 195–198
  managing production cycles,
    193–195
BQF (British Quality Foundation),
  39, 328, 330
Breyfogle, Forrest, III (author)
  Implementing Six Sigma, 329
  Integrated Enterprise Excellence, 329
British Quality Foundation (BQF),
  39, 328, 330
buffers, building, 192–193
building
  buffers, 192–193
  cause–and–effect diagrams, 140–141
  causes of poor performance, 140–141
  checklists for running successful
    events, 252–253
  control charts, 122–123

culture of continuous
improvement, 290
definitions, 102
value stream maps, 84–93
visions, 295–296
Burghall, Roger (author)
Lean Six Sigma Business Transformation For Dummies, 233, 315, 329
business benefits, confirming, 273–274
busting assumptions, 298

• **C** •

candidate improvement projects,
generating a list of, 234–237
capability, of processes, 129–133
capability indices, 129–133
Capacity CTQ grouping, 67
Carlzon, Jan (chief executive), 93–94
Catalyst Process Guide, 332
cause and effect diagrams,
creating, 140–141
Cavanagh, Roland (author)
The Six Sigma Way Team Fieldbook, 329
cell, 196
cell manufacturing techniques, 196–197
chain of events
about, 73
how the work gets done, 73–77
painting pictures of the process, 78–94
challenging processes, 310
champions
about, 314
help from, 326
recognising, 231
role of the, 314
typical questions asked by, 260, 263,
266, 272–273, 278–279
change
focusing on key elements of, 303–304
how people cope with, 299–304
managing, 292–293

Changes CTQ grouping, 69
characteristics, quality function
deployment and, 210–211
Chartered Quality Institute, 330
Cheat Sheet (website), 3
checking
designs work, 204
process meets CTQs, 284
checklists, creating for running
successful events, 252–253
choosing
control charts, 126–127
between DMAIC and DMADV, 205–206
tools for the job, 312–313
clarifying role of manager, 283–287
colleagues, help from, 325
collecting data, 104–106
common cause variation, 117
comparing energy and attitude, 300
competition, looking at, 208–210
competitive benchmarking, quality
function deployment and, 212–214
complacency, 321–322
Compliance CTQ grouping, 67
concentration diagram, 106
conducting final benefit review, 279
conferences, help from, 328
confirming customer and business
benefits, 273–274
connecting CTQs, 143–145
consistency, of data, 102–104
constraints
about, 12–13, 189
applying Theory of
Constraints, 189–193
layout, 195–198
managing production cycles, 193–195
consultancy companies, 332
contact error proofing, 182–183
continuous data, 104
continuous improvement, creating
culture of, 290

control charts
  about, 121–122
  capability of processes, 129–133
  choosing, 126–127
  creating, 122–123
  histograms, 133–135
  state of processes, 127–129
  unusual features of, 123–126
control limits, 122
Control phase, 37, 246, 275–279
control plan
  about, 33–34
  establishing, 284–285
controlled convergence, 219
conventions, 78
correction, as one of the 'seven
    wastes,' 166
correlation coefficient, 146
correlation limits, 214
cost-benefit analysis, 268
C_p index, 130–133
C_{pk} index, 130–133
creating
  buffers, 192–193
  cause–and–effect diagrams, 140–141
  causes of poor performance,
    140–141
  checklists for running successful
    events, 252–253
  control charts, 122–123
  culture of continuous
    improvement, 290
  definitions, 102
  value stream maps, 84–93
  visions, 295–296
criteria selection matrix, 239–241
Critical to Quality (CTQ)
  about, 17–18
  checking process meets, 284
  connecting, 143–145
  customer requirements, 55, 65–69
  establishing real, 69–72

as improvement charter component, 28
  requirements, 53
Crystal Ball (Oracle), 331
CTQ (Critical to Quality)
  about, 17–18
  checking process meets, 284
  connecting, 143–145
  customer requirements, 55, 65–69
  establishing real, 69–72
  as improvement charter component, 28
  requirements, 53
cultural web, 297
customer benefits, confirming, 273–274
customer needs
  about, 53
  avoiding bias, 64
  critical to quality (CTQ) customer
    requirements, 65–69
  establishing real CTQs, 69–72
  Kano model, 53–55
  quality function deployment and, 208
  researching requirements, 58–63
  voice of the customer (VOC), 55–57
customer perspectives, 168
customer surveys, 62–63
customer-focused measures
  establishing clear, 283
  measuring performance using, 71–72
customers
  considerations about, 13
  external, 45–46
  focusing on, 23–24
  high-level process, 47–52
  internal, 45–46
  interviewing, 60–61
  prioritising, 57
  process of, 43–46
  segmenting, 52, 56–57
  in SIPOC model, 49
cycle time
  defined, 16
  importance of, 101

• D •

data
  analysing, 264–266
  collecting, 104–106
  consistency of, 102–104
  displaying, 120–121
  importance of good, 98
  validity of, 102–104
data collection plans,
      developing, 100–108
data presentation
  about, 117
  control charts, 121–135
  testing your theories, 136–137
  variation, 117–121
Data/Information CTQ grouping, 67
De Hodgins, Ofelia C. (author)
  *Practitioner's Guide to Statistics
      and Lean Six Sigma for Process
      Improvements,* 328
dead time, 83
deadbeats, 300
DeCarlo, Neil (author)
  Six Sigma For Dummies, 125, 148
decisions
  making, 218–220
  what to measure, 99–100
defect opportunity, 18
defective, 18
defects, 17, 18
defects per million opportunities
      (DPMO), 17–18
Define, Measure, Analyse, Improve and
      Control (DMAIC)
  about, 1, 21, 25–26, 237, 255
  Analyse phase, 32–33, 264–266
  analysing your process, 32–33
  compared with DMADV, 205–206
  conducting final benefit review, 279
  confirming customer and business
      benefits, 273–274
  Control phase, 37, 275–279
  controlling solutions, 275–279

defining projects, 26–31
defining where you're going, 256–260
implementing solutions, 275–279
Improve phase, 33, 36, 267–273
improving your process, 33
Measure phase, 32–33, 260–263
measuring how work is done, 32
phases of, 34–37
quantifying opportunities, 267
setting up projects, 242–243
standardising solutions, 275–279
working your way through, 256
Define phase, 201–206, 257–258
defining
  what needs designing, 201–206
  where you're going, 256–260
definitions, creating clear, 102
delighters, in Kano model, 54
deltas, noting, 251
Deming. W.E. (statistician), 310
deployment
  Deployment Programme
      Manager, 227–229
  Executive Sponsorship, 224–226
  key factors of successful, 223–224
  leading, 223–231
  Lean Six Sigma startup, 229–231
  recognising project champions, 231
  size, 226–227
  software for managing, 331
Deployment Programme
      Manager, 227–229
design
  analysing, 202–204
  of experiments, 148
Design for Six Sigma (DfSS)
  about, 199–200, 237
  choosing between DMAIC and
      DMADV, 205–206
  defining what needs designing, 201–206
  DMADV framework, 200–201
  making decisions, 218–220
  quality function deployment
      (QFD), 206–218

Design phase, 204, 206–207
developing
  data collection plans, 100–108
  designs, 204
  development flowcharts, 80–84
development flowcharts,
    developing, 80–84
DfSS (Design for Six Sigma)
  about, 199–200, 237
  choosing between DMAIC and
    DMADV, 205–206
  defining what needs designing,
    201–206
  DMADV framework, 200–201
  making decisions, 218–220
  quality function deployment
    (QFD), 206–218
displaying data, 120–121
dissatisfiers, 54
DMADV framework
  about, 200–201
  compared with DMAIC, 205–206
DMAIC (Define, Measure, Analyse,
    Improve and Control)
  about, 1, 21, 25–26, 237, 255
  Analyse phase, 32–33, 264–266
  analysing your process, 32–33
  compared with DMADV, 205–206
  conducting final benefit review, 279
  confirming customer and business
    benefits, 273–274
  Control phase, 37, 275–279
  controlling solutions, 275–279
  defining projects, 26–31
  defining where you're going, 256–260
  implementing solutions, 275–279
  Improve phase, 33, 36, 267–273
  improving your process, 33
  Measure phase, 32–33, 260–263
  measuring how work is done, 32
  phases of, 34–37
  quantifying opportunities, 267
  setting up projects, 242–243
  standardising solutions, 275–279
  working your way through, 256
doing the work right, 241–242
'doing the wrong things right,' 323
DPMO (defects per million
    opportunities), 17–18
drawing
  maps, 48–49
  spaghetti diagrams, 76–77
driving strategy deployment, 233–234
dynamics, event, 249

• *E* •

E (effective), 321
Eckes, George (author)
  E = Q X A, 293
  Making Six Sigma Last, 329
  The Six Sigma Revolution, 329
effective (E), 321
effectiveness, assessing, 149–153
EFQM (European Foundation for Quality
    Management), 327, 328
elevator speech, 258
energy, compared with attitude, 300
engaging teams, 285–287
ensuring process is stable and
    predictable, 284
environment
  creating the right, 224
  in PEMME mnemonic, 44
Environment CTQ grouping, 69
Equipment, in PEMME mnemonic, 43
error-proofing processes, 181–183, 284
establishing
  clear customer-focused objectives, 283
  control plan, 284–285
  real CTQs, 69–72
European Foundation for Quality
    Management (EFQM), 327, 328
evaluating
  effectiveness, 149–153
  how work is done, 32

opportunity, 160–161
performance using customer-focused
measures, 71–72
event dynamics, 249
event roles, 249
event structure, 249
event venue, 250
events, running, 250–251
everyday operational excellence
about, 281
clarifying role of manager, 283–287
getting better every day, 287–290
reality of, 281–282
Excel, 330–331
Executive Sponsorship, 224–226
expectations, setting, 251
exploit, 190
external customers, identifying, 45–46

● *F* ●

facilitator
role of in rapid improvement
events, 248–252
running events, 250–251
fact, managing by, 25, 97–100, 141–143
Failure Mode Effects Analysis (FMEA),
11, 179–181, 204
failure modes, 179
fifteen-word flipchart, 256
final benefit review, conducting, 279
finding root cause, 264–266
fishbone diagram, 140–141
Five Ss
about, 172–173, 236
red-tag exercise, 173–174
visual management, 174–177
fixed value error proofing, 183
FlowMap, 330
FMEA (Failure Mode Effects Analysis),
11, 179–181, 204
focus groups, 61–62
focusing on key elements of
change, 303–304

following up, facilitator and, 252
Follow-up phase, in Kaizan events, 246
forcefield diagram, 301
'future state' map, 78

● *G* ●

gaining acceptance, 292
Galvin, Bob (CEO), 14
gathering information
about, 97
developing data collection
plans, 100–108
managing by fact, 97–100, 141–143
sampling, 108–115
Gauge R and R, 102–103
Gemba, 24, 74, 261, 311
General Electric (GE), 14, 72, 224
goal statement, as improvement charter
component, 28
goldratt (website), 327
Goldratt, Eliyahu (physicist), 12–13,
189, 190–192
Grant, Vince (author)
*Lean Six Sigma Business Transformation
For Dummies,* 233, 315, 329
green, going, 167–168
Green Belt, 38–39, 324, 325
'green lean,' 167
Gustafson, Terry (author)
*Six Sigma Workbook For
Dummies,* 125, 148
Gygi, Craig (author)
Six Sigma For Dummies, 125, 148
*Six Sigma Workbook For
Dummies,* 125, 148

● *H* ●

Harry, Mike J. (author)
*Practitioner's Guide to Statistics
and Lean Six Sigma for Process
Improvements,* 328
head-in-the-sand (HITS) thinking, 299

Heijunka, 10, 185

help, 325–332

high-level business case, as
improvement charter component, 28

high-level process, 47–52, 48–49

histograms, 133–135

HITS (head-in-the-sand) thinking, 299

Hoshin Kanri, 234

Hulbert, Richard L. (author)
*Practitioner's Guide to Statistics
and Lean Six Sigma for Process
Improvements,* 328

human intelligence, automation with, 178

human potential, wasting, 167

hypothesis testing, 136

● **/** ●

icons, explained, 3

ideal state, for processes, 128

identifying
external customers, 45–46
internal customers, 45–46
moments of truth, 93–94
product families, 197–198
wasted movement, 195
ways to improve approaches, 106–108
weakest link, 189–190

IFAs (independent financial
advisers), 287

ignoring soft tools, 321

iGraphix, 330

Implementing Six Sigma
(Breyfogle III), 329

implementing solutions, 275–279

Improve phase, 36, 267–273

improvement charter, 27–28

improving
approaches, 106–108
process flow, 190–192
your process, 33

independent financial advisers (IFAs), 287

individuals chart, 126

information gathering
about, 97
developing data collection
plans, 100–108
managing by fact, 97–100, 141–143
sampling, 108–115

inputs
defined, 175
in SIPOC model, 49

Integrated Enterprise Excellence
(Breyfogle III), 329

internal customers, identifying, 45–46

*International Journal of Six Sigma and
Competitive Advantage,* 330

Internet, help from, 326–327

Internet resources
American Society for Quality
(ASQ), 326, 328
articles, 3
Baldrige Model, 327
British Quality Foundation (BQF), 328
Cheat Sheet, 3
European Foundation for Quality
Management (EFQM), 327, 328
goldratt, 327
isixsigma (website), 327
ISSSP, 327
Kaizen, 327
Lean, 327
LERC, 327
Morgan, John (author), 326
Process Excellence Network, 327
Quality Digest, 327
Quality Function Deployment (QFD)
Institute, 327
shingoprize, 327
Theory of Constraints, 327

interrelationship diagram, 28, 30–31, 141

interviewing customers, 60–61

inventory, as one of the 'seven
wastes,' 164

IPO, 175

Ishikawa diagrams, 140–141

isixsigma (website), 327

iSixSigma Magazine, 330

ISSSP (website), 327

issue statement, 28

issues, logging, 251

● *J* ●

Jidoka, 11, 178, 194–195

JIT (Just in Time), 11

JMP® Statistical Discovery Software, 331

Johnson, Gerry (cultural web developer), 297

Jones, Daniel (author)

  benchmarking work of, 327

  The Machine That Changed the World, 329

jumping to solutions, 317–318

Just in Time (JIT), 11, 194

● *K* ●

Kai Sigma events, 245–247

Kaizen, 245–247, 327

Kaizen blitz events, 37–38

kanban, 194

Kano model, 53–55

Key Concept icon, 3

key stakeholder, 302

Kiichiro Toyoda (entrepreneur), 7–8, 11

Konosuke Matsushita (founder of Panasonic), 285

Kotter, John P. (expert), 292

Krafcik, John (CEO), 8

● *L* ●

lack of support problems, 320

Lacke, Christopher J. (author)

  Practitioner's Guide to Statistics and Lean Six Sigma for Process Improvements, 328

lagging indicators, 145

layout, 195–198

lead time, 16

leadership best practices, 307–308

leading deployment, 223–231

leading indicators, 145

Lean

  about, 7–8

  basics of, 8–14

  website, 327

Lean For Dummies (Sayer and Williams), 153

Lean Six Sigma. *See also specific topics*

  about, 7

  DMAIC phases, 34–37

  improving existing processes, 25–26

  managing processes with, 311–312

  martial arts and, 38–39

  pragmatic approach of, 37–39

  principles of, 23–25

  startup, 229–231

  using strategy to drive, 315

Lean Six Sigma and Minitab: The Complete Toolbox Guide for Business Improvement, 4th Edition, 329

Lean Six Sigma Business Transformation For Dummies (Burghall and Grant), 233, 315, 329

The Lean Six Sigma Improvement Journey (Morgan), 329

LERC (website), 327

less is more, 308–309

levelling, 10, 185

Liker, Jeffrey (author)

  The Toyota Way: 14 Management Principles from the World's Greatest Manufacturer, 329

limits, quality function deployment and, 214

linear regression, 148

load, spreading the, 186

logging actions, facilitator and, 251

logging issues, facilitator and, 251

logical cause testing, 145

• M •

The Machine That Changed the World (Womack, Jones and Roos), 329
Making Six Sigma Last (Eckes), 329
managed, 285
management best practices, 307–308
managers, clarifying role of, 283–287
managing
  change, 292–293
  by fact, 97–100, 141–143
  processes with Lean Six Sigma, 311–312
  production cycles, 193–195
  solutions, 275–279
Mann, Prem S. (author)
  Practitioner's Guide to Statistics and Lean Six Sigma for Process Improvements, 328
mapping, 160
maps, drawing, 48–49
Mars Lander, 102
martial arts, Lean Six Sigma and, 38–39
Master Black Belt (MBB), 38–39, 325, 331
Materials, in PEMME mnemonic, 44
MBB (Master Black Belt), 38–39, 325, 331
Measure phase, 32–33, 73, 202, 247, 260–263
Measurement System Analysis (MSA), 102
measure(s)
  deciding what to, 99–100
  getting of the design, 202
  quality function deployment and, 210–211
  reviewing what you currently, 98–99
measuring
  effectiveness, 149–153
  how work is done, 32
  opportunity, 160–161
  performance using customer-focused measures, 71–72
Method, in PEMME mnemonic, 43
methodology
  problems with, 319
  using the right, 289

milestones, as improvement charter component, 28
Minitab® Statistical Software, 331
missed potential, 167
mobile apps, 332
moments of truth
  defined, 80
  identifying, 93–94
Money CTQ grouping, 68
Morgan, John (author)
  The Lean Six Sigma Improvement Journey, 329
  SPC in the Office, 329
  website, 326
Morris, Clare (author)
  Quantitative Approaches in Business Studies, 8th Edition, 329
motion, as one of the 'seven wastes,' 165–166
motion step error proofing, 183
Motorola, 14, 18
moving range, 126
MSA (Measurement System Analysis), 102
Muda, 24, 161, 186
multiple regression, 148
Mura, 186
Muri, 186
must-bes, in Kano model, 54
myths, believing, 322–323

• N •

natural variation, 117, 118
needs, customer
  about, 53
  avoiding bias, 64
  critical to quality (CTQ) customer requirements, 65–69
  establishing real CTQs, 69–72
  Kano model, 53–55
  quality function deployment and, 208
  researching requirements, 58–63
  voice of the customer (VOC), 55–57
needs, prioritising, 208–210

networks, help from, 328
Neuman, Robert (author)
   The Six Sigma Way Team Fieldbook, 329
non-conformance, price of (PONC), 166
Noriaki Kano (professor), 53–55
noting pluses and deltas,
   facilitator and, 251
null hypothesis, 136
Numbers, 330–331

• O •

observations, 63
OEE (overall equipment
   effectiveness), 152–153
on the brink state, for processes, 129
1-10-100 rule, 182
one-dimensionals, in Kano model, 54
OPE (overall process
   effectiveness), 152–153
operational definition, 102
operational excellence, everyday
   about, 281
   clarifying role of manager, 283–287
   getting better every day, 287–290
   reality of, 281–282
opportunity
   assessing, 160–161
   for prevention. *See* prevention
   quantifying, 35, 267
Oracle's Crystal Ball, 331
organisational culture, 297–298
organisations
   American Society for Quality (ASQ), 39,
      326, 328, 330
   British Quality Foundation (BQF),
      39, 328, 330
   European Foundation for Quality
      Management (EFQM), 327, 328
   help from, 326
output measures, 100–101
outputs
   defined, 175
   in SIPOC model, 49

outside-in thinking, 71
outside-in view, 55–56
overall equipment effectiveness
   (OEE), 152–153
overall process effectiveness
   (OPE), 152–153
overcoming resistance, 294–295
overproduction, 162–163
overtraining, 324
Owen, Mal (author)
   SPC in the Office, 329
Oxford English Dictionary, 285

• P •

painting pictures of the process,
   78–94
paired comparison, 70
Pande, Peter (author)
   The Six Sigma Way Team Fieldbook, 329
Pareto, Vilifredo (economist), 57
Pareto chart, 105–106, 169–170
peaks, avoiding, 184–186
PEMME mnemonic, 43–44
People, in PEMME mnemonic, 43
People CTQ grouping, 68
people issues
   about, 291
   busting assumptions, 298
   creating visions, 295–296
   how people cope with change,
      299–304
   organisational culture, 297–298
   working right, 291–295
people power, 9–10
performance
   balance of measures, 143–153
   measuring using customer-focused
      measures, 71–72
   usual suspects, 100–140
performance rate, 152–153
periodicals, help from, 330
'peripheral' process-mapping
   activity, 322

phases
  Analyse, 32–33, 202–204, 206–207, 218, 247, 264–266
  Control, 37, 246, 275–279
  Define, 201–206, 257–258
  Design, 204, 206–207
  Follow-up, 246
  Improve, 36, 267–273
  Measure, 32–33, 73, 202, 247, 260–263
  Preparation, 246
  Verify, 204
phases, Analyse
  about, 32–33
  analysing design, 202–204
  outputs from, 264–266
  in QFD drill-down, 218
  quality function deployment and, 206–207
  in rapid improvement events, 247
Piggly Wiggly, 7–8
pitfalls, avoiding, 317–324
planning, by facilitators, 248–250
plug-ins, 331
pluses, noting, 251
point
  proving your, 145–146
  seeing the, 146–149
Poka-yoke, 181–183
PONC (price of non-conformance), 166
population sampling, 110–115
practising process stapling, 74–76
Practitioner's Guide to Statistics and Lean Six Sigma for Process Improvements (Harry, Mann, De Hodgins, Hulbert and Lacke), 328
pragmatic approach, of Lean Six Sigma, 37–39
precision, 111
predictablity, of processes, 284
preparation, by facilitators, 248–250
Preparation phase, in Kaizan events, 246

presenting data
  about, 117
  control charts, 121–135
  testing your theories, 136–137
  variation, 117–121
prevention
  about, 171
  avoiding peaks and troughs, 184–186
  building in, 309–310
  Five Ss, 172–177
  preventive maintenance, 183–184
  tools and techniques for, 178–183
preventive maintenance, 183–184
price of non-conformance (PONC), 166
prioritising
  customers, 57
  needs, 208–210
  projects, 239
  requirements, 70–71
problem statement, as improvement charter component, 28
process
  about, 175
  analysing, 32–33
  basics of, 43–46
  capability of, 129–133
  challenging, 310
  checking meets CTQs, 284
  elements of a, 44–45
  ensuring stability and predictability of, 284
  error-proofing, 181–183, 284
  improving your, 33
  managing with Lean Six Sigma, 311–312
  painting pictures of the, 78–94
  in SIPOC model, 49
  state of, 127–129
  working on the, 283–285
Process Excellence Network (website), 327

process flow
  about, 24
  improving, 190–192
process mapping, 78–94
process owner, 55
process sampling, 109–110
process sigma
  calculating values of, 17–20
  practising in the workplace, 16–17
  value of, 17
process stapling
  about, 24
  practising, 74–76
process stream maps, 47
process sub-optimisation, 162, 190
processing, as one of the 'seven
    wastes,' 164
product families, identifying, 197–198
production cycles, managing, 193–195
professional associations
  American Society for Quality (ASQ), 39,
    326, 328, 330
  British Quality Foundation (BQF),
    39, 328, 330
  European Foundation for Quality
    Management (EFQM), 327, 328
  help from, 328
Professionalism CTQ grouping, 68
programme executive sponsor, 314
programmes, stifling, 320–321
project champions
  about, 314
  help from, 326
  recognising, 231
  role of the, 314
  typical questions asked by, 260, 263,
    266, 272–273, 278–279
project scope, as improvement charter
    component, 28
projects
  defining, 26–31
  falling into traps with, 319–320
  prioritising, 239

proving your point, 145–146
publications
  help from, 328–329
  Implementing Six Sigma
      (Breyfogle III), 329
  Integrated Enterprise Excellence
      (Breyfogle III), 329
  Lean For Dummies (Sayer and
      Williams), 153
  *Lean Six Sigma Business Transformation
      For Dummies* (Burghall and Grant),
      233, 315, 329
  *The Lean Six Sigma Improvement
      Journey* (Morgan), 329
  The Machine That Changed the World
      (Womack, Jones and Roos), 329
  Making Six Sigma Last (Eckes), 329
  *Practitioner's Guide to Statistics
      and Lean Six Sigma for Process
      Improvements* (Harry, Mann, De
      Hodgins, Hulbert and Lacke), 328
  *Quantitative Approaches in Business
      Studies*, 8th Edition (Morris), 329
  Six Sigma For Dummies (Gygi, DeCarlo
      and Williams), 125, 148
  *Six Sigma Workbook For
      Dummies* (Gygi, Williams and
      Gustafson), 125, 148
  The Six Sigma Revolution (Eckes), 329
  The Six Sigma Way Team Fieldbook
      (Pande, Neuman and Cavanagh), 329
  SPC in the Office (Owen and
      Morgan), 329
  *The Toyota Way: 14 Management
      Principles from the World's Greatest
      Manufacturer* (Liker), 329
Pugh, Stuart (design engineer), 219
Pugh Matrix, 218–219
pull production, 12, 193–194
pulling the work, 191
purpose, 248
push production, 193–194
push the work, 191

• Q •

Q (quality), 321
QFD (Quality Function Deployment), 46, 205, 206–218
QFD drill-down, 217–218
qualitative research, 59
quality (Q), 321
Quality Digest (website), 327
Quality Function Deployment (QFD), 46, 205, 206–218
Quality Function Deployment (QFD) Institute (website), 327
quality rate, 152–153
Quality World, 330
quantifying opportunities, 35, 267
Quantitative Approaches in Business Studies, 8th Edition (Morris), 329
quantitative research, 59

• R •

r value, 146
rapid improvement events
    about, 37–38, 245
    creating checklists for running successful events, 252–253
    facilitator's role, 248–252
    Kai Sigma events, 245–247
    Kaizen, 245–247
recognising
    importance of control charts, 121–135
    problems with batches, 195
    project champions, 231
red light state, for processes, 129
red-tag exercise, 172, 173–174
reducing risk, 179–181
relationships, quality function deployment and, 211–212
Remember icon, 3
reources, Internet
    American Society for Quality (ASQ), 326, 328
    articles, 3

Baldrige Model, 327
British Quality Foundation (BQF), 328
Cheat Sheet, 3
European Foundation for Quality Management (EFQM), 327, 328
goldratt, 327
isixsigma (website), 327
ISSSP, 327
Kaizen, 327
Lean, 327
LERC, 327
Morgan, John (author), 326
Process Excellence Network, 327
Quality Digest, 327
Quality Function Deployment (QFD) Institute, 327
shingoprize, 327
Theory of Constraints, 327
repeatability, 103, 192
reproducibility, 103
requirements
    prioritising, 70–71
    researching, 58–63
researching requirements, 58–63
resistance, overcoming, 294–295
reviewing what you currently measure, 98–99
RFT ('right first time'), 90
right, working, 291–295
right approach, 237–242
'right first time' (RFT), 90
right work
    about, 223, 233
    driving strategy deployment, 233–234
    generating a list of candidate improvement projects, 234–237
    right approach, 237–242
    setting up DMAIC projects, 242–243
risk, reducing, 179–181
risk priority number (RPN), 179
roles
    event, 249
    as improvement charter component, 28

Roos, Daniel (author)
The Machine That Changed the World, 329
root cause, finding, 264–266
RPN (risk priority number), 179
rules, agreeing on, 102–104
run chart, 121
running events, 250–251

• *S* •

Safety CTQ grouping, 67
Sakich Toyoda (founder of Toyota group), 178
sampling
  about, 108–109
  population, 110–115
  process, 109–110
SAS (Scandinavian Air Services), 93–94
satisfiers, 54
Sayer, Natalie J. (author)
  Lean For Dummies, 153
Scandinavian Air Services (SAS), 93–94
scatter diagram/plot, 145–146
scope scandals, 319
Scrub, as one of Five Ss, 172
Security CTQ grouping, 68
segmenting customers, 52, 56–57
selecting
  control charts, 126–127
  between DMAIC and DMADV, 205–206
  tools for the job, 312–313
sequencing, 10, 185
setting expectations, 251
'seven wastes'
  about, 161–162
  beyond the, 166–168
  correction, 166
  inventory, 164
  motion, 165–166
  overproduction, 162–163
  processing, 164
  transportation, 163
  waiting, 163

Shewhart, Walter (physicist), 121–122
Shigeo Shingo (consultant), 86–87
shingoprize (website), 327
sigma (δ), 14
SigmaXL plug-in, 331
simple linear regression, 148
SIMUL8, 331
simulation software, 331
single minute exchange of die (SMED), 86
single piece flow, 11–12, 194–195
SIPOC model, 48–49, 142
SIPOC (Suppliers, Inputs, Process, Outputs and Customers) model, 48–49, 142, 236
Six Sigma
  about, 14
  core of, 14–17
  points of, 20–21
Six Sigma For Dummies (Gygi, DeCarlo and Williams), 125, 148
Six Sigma Forum, 330
Six Sigma Workbook For Dummies (Gygi, Williams and Gustafson), 125, 148
The Six Sigma Revolution (Eckes), 329
The Six Sigma Way Team Fieldbook (Pande, Neuman and Cavanagh), 329
size, deployment and, 226–227
SMED (single minute exchange of die), 86
Smith, Bill (quality engineer), 14
Social Conscience CTQ grouping, 69
social media, help from, 327–328
soft tools, ignoring, 321
software, help from, 330–332
solutions
  applying, 267–273
  controlling, 275–279
  implementing, 275–279
  jumping to, 317–318
  standardising, 275–279
Sort, as one of Five Ss, 172
spaghetti diagrams
  about, 74, 195
  drawing, 76–77
SPC (statistical process control), 118

SPC in the Office (Owen and Morgan), 329
special cause variation, 118, 119
spectators, 300
Speed CTQ grouping, 67
spreading the load, 186
stability
  in Heijunka, 185
  of processes, 284
stakeholders, analysing, 301–302
standardisation
  about, 10, 187
  in Heijunka, 185
  solutions, 275–279
Standardise, as one of Five Ss, 173
startup, Lean Six Sigma, 229–231
statistical analysis, software for, 330–331
statistical control, 118
statistical process control (SPC), 118
stifling programmes, 320–321
'Stop at every abnormality'
      concept, 11, 178
Straighten, as one of Five Ss, 172
strangers, 198
strategy
  driving deployment, 233–234
  using to drive Lean Six Sigma, 315
structure, event, 249
subordinate, 191
Suppliers, in SIPOC model, 48
Suppliers, Inputs, Process, Outputs
      and Customers (SIPOC) model,
      48–49, 142, 236
Systemise, as one of Five Ss, 173

• T •

Taiich Ohno (businessman), 7–8,
      8–9, 84, 160
Takt time, 12, 149–152
tampering, avoiding, 119–120
targets, quality function
      deployment and, 214

teams
  engaging, 285–287
  turmoil with, 320
  typical questions addressed by,
      258–259, 262–263, 265–266,
      270–272, 276–278
technical evaluation, 212
techniques, for prevention, 178–183
terrorists, 300
testing theories, 136–137
theories,, testing, 136–137
Theory of Constraints, 12–13,
      189–193, 327
theory of inventive problem solving
      (TRIZ), 199
threshold state, for processes, 128–129
'Tim Wood' mnemonic, 162
timekeeping, facilitator and, 251
Tip icon, 3
tollgate review, 34
'Toolpak' for Excel, 331
tools
  picking for the job, 312–313
  for prevention, 178–183
Toyota Production System (TPS)
  about, 7, 185
  process of, 8–14
*The Toyota Way: 14 Management
      Principles from the World's Greatest
      Manufacturer* (Liker), 329
TPS (Toyota Production System), 7
  about, 7, 185
  process of, 8–14
training companies, help from, 332
transportation, as one of the 'seven
      wastes,' 163
TRIZ (theory of inventive problem
      solving), 199
troughs, avoiding, 184–186
True Stories icon, 3
T-test, 136–137

• U •

UK Excellence, 330
unit, 18
unit time, 83, 160
untapped potential, 167
upstream variables, 106–107

• V •

validity, of data, 102–104
value stream, 24
value stream maps
  about, 47, 236
  constructing, 84–93
value-added analysis, 159–160
value-adding
  about, 157
  assessing opportunity, 160–161
  beyond the 'seven wastes,' 166–168
  common definition of, 158–159
  correction, 166
  inventory, 164
  motion, 165–166
  overproduction, 162–163
  processing, 164
  'seven wastes,' 161–166
  transportation, 163
  value-added analysis, 159–160
  vital few, 169–170
  waiting, 163
variable charts, 126
variation
  about, 117–118
  avoiding tampering, 119–120
  distinguishing between types of, 119
  natural, 118
  reducing, 25
  special cause, 119
venue, event, 250

Verify phase, 204
verifying
  designs work, 204
  process meets CTQs, 284
Visio, 330
visions, creating, 295–296
visual management, 174–177, 226
vital few, 169–170
VOC. *See* voice of the customer (VOC)
voice of the customer (VOC), 20,
    53, 55–57, 64

• W •

waiting, as one of the 'seven wastes,' 163
Warning! icon, 3
wasted movement, identifying, 195
weakest link, identifying, 189–190
websites
  American Society for Quality
    (ASQ), 326, 328
  articles, 3
  Baldrige Model, 327
  British Quality Foundation (BQF), 328
  Cheat Sheet, 3
  European Foundation for Quality
    Management (EFQM), 327, 328
  goldratt, 327
  isixsigma (website), 327
  ISSSP, 327
  Kaizen, 327
  Lean, 327
  LERC, 327
  Morgan, John (author), 326
  Process Excellence Network, 327
  Quality Digest, 327
  Quality Function Deployment (QFD)
    Institute, 327
  shingoprize, 327
  Theory of Constraints, 327

Welch, Jack (CEO), 14, 72, 224
White Belt, 39
whole range, 17
whole story, telling the, 313
Williams, Bruce (author)
  Lean For Dummies, 153
  Six Sigma For Dummies, 125, 148
  *Six Sigma Workbook For
    Dummies,* 125, 148
wing-to-wing time, 72
winners, 300
Womack, James (author)
  benchmarking work of, 327
  *The Machine That Changed the
    World,* 329

work right
  about, 223
  how it gets done, 283
  how well it gets done, 284
Workshop phase, in Kaizan events, 246

X moving R chart, 126

Yellow Belt, 38–39

About the Authors

John Morgan is the author of several books, including *The Lean Six Sigma Improvement Journey, Go Lean,* and Catalyst's *Process Improvement Workbook and Guide.* He is also the co-author of *SPC in the Office* and *Lean Six Sigma Business Transformation For Dummies.* John's experience led to him being interviewed on BBC Radio about the potential of Lean Six Sigma in the UK, generally, but especially in the public sector and National Health Service.

John is a Director of the Lean Six Sigma specialists Catalyst Consulting and helped create the company in 1995. Much of their highly acclaimed material has been produced by him, including tailored work for companies such as General Electric, BAA, Saint-Gobain Glass, Paddy Power and British Telecom. In addition to training delivery and coaching, John's primary responsibilities are in the areas of marketing, product design and development. John is also Joint Managing Director of the British Quality Foundation's Lean Six Sigma Academy.

A Chartered Insurer and Fellow of the Chartered Insurance Institute, John's early career background was in aviation insurance and reinsurance. He first started to apply Lean Six Sigma techniques in his role of Customer Service Director for a North American Financial Services company before joining Catalyst where he has worked with a wide range of clients including General Electric.

A keen song writer, he is working on his first novel, Black Widow Blues, though it's taking him a lot longer to write than a For Dummies book.

Martin Brenig-Jones is Managing Director of Catalyst Consulting Ltd. Prior to joining Catalyst, Martin was Head of Quality at the global telecommunications company, BT, one of the world's leading communications services companies with responsibility for quality and business excellence across the group. Martin has also been a member of the General Committee of Lloyd's Register, on LRQA's technical committee and served on the executive board of the British Quality Foundation prior to moving into business consulting. He has been a senior assessor for the UK Excellence Award and the European Quality Award. During the last 15 years Martin has focused on the application of Lean Six Sigma to help organisations of all sizes and sectors to improve their operations. He has trained and coached more than a thousand people in Lean Six Sigma and business improvement techniques working mainly across Europe and occasionally in the United States, Asia and Africa. He has worked with organisations in a diverse range of sectors including IT, transport, computer manufacturing, local government, police, health, aerospace, rail, telecoms and financial services.

Martin studied electronic engineering at the University of Liverpool and has a postgraduate diploma in management. He is a member of the Institute of Engineering and Technology, and in his earlier career he worked in telecommunications, software, and systems development. Martin is a keen photographer and videographer, and although now living in England, he is a Welshman at heart and continues to support the Welsh Rugby team as well as being a Liverpool FC fan.

Authors' Acknowledgments

John: Writing a book, even a third edition, tends to take a fair bit of concentration, time and effort, so there's a big thank you to my wife Margaret and my family for putting up with that.

I'd also like to thank my long-time friend and colleague Jo Ballard for her help with the earlier editions.

I'm really pleased to be writing this edition as it's given me the opportunity to incorporate a series of checklists and questions that I hope will provide real help to people beginning their improvement journey and tackling those early projects.

Martin: I am delighted that *Lean Six Sigma For Dummies* has been so popular, and we've been asked to write the third edition. I particularly want to thank my best friend and wife, Di, who is the greatest wife, friend, mother, and teacher in the world. She lives with someone who spends far too much time doing what some people call 'work' and who ought to keep his office at home a lot tidier by actually practicing 5S. I also want to thank my four brilliant children, Jo, Laurence, Alex, and Oliver for being so patient with the bod who is always seeing 'process improvement opportunities' – particularly annoying when on holiday. Finally I must thank everyone at Catalyst and my clients who have given me the experience that I have tried to distil into this book.

Publisher's Acknowledgments

Acquisitions Editor: Annie Knight

Project Manager: Steve Edwards

Development Editor/Copy Editor: Kate O'Leary

Technical Editor: Jim Alloway

Art Coordinator: Alicia B. South

Production Editor: Suresh Srinivasan

Cover Photos: ©iStock.com/Oleksii Glushenkov

Take Dummies with you everywhere you go!

Whether you're excited about e-books, want more from the web, must have your mobile apps, or swept up in social media, Dummies makes everything easier.

FOR DUMMIES

A Wiley Brand

BUSINESS

978-1-118-73077-5

978-1-118-44349-1

978-1-119-97527-4

MUSIC

978-1-119-94276-4

978-0-470-97799-6

978-0-470-49644-2

DIGITAL PHOTOGRAPHY

978-1-118-09203-3

978-0-470-76878-5

978-1-118-00472-2

Algebra I For Dummies
978-0-470-55964-2

Anatomy & Physiology For Dummies, 2nd Edition
978-0-470-92326-9

Asperger's Syndrome For Dummies
978-0-470-66087-4

Basic Maths For Dummies
978-1-119-97452-9

Body Language For Dummies, 2nd Edition
978-1-119-95351-7

Bookkeeping For Dummies, 3rd Edition
978-1-118-34689-1

British Sign Language For Dummies
978-0-470-69477-0

Cricket for Dummies, 2nd Edition
978-1-118-48032-8

Currency Trading For Dummies, 2nd Edition
978-1-118-01851-4

Cycling For Dummies
978-1-118-36435-2

Diabetes For Dummies, 3rd Edition
978-0-470-97711-8

eBay For Dummies, 3rd Edition
978-1-119-94122-4

Electronics For Dummies All-in-One For Dummies
978-1-118-58973-1

English Grammar For Dummies
978-0-470-05752-0

French For Dummies, 2nd Edition
978-1-118-00464-7

Guitar For Dummies, 3rd Edition
978-1-118-11554-1

IBS For Dummies
978-0-470-51737-6

Keeping Chickens For Dummies
978-1-119-99417-6

Knitting For Dummies, 3rd Edition
978-1-118-66151-2